Sharing sounds

Musical experiences with young children

David Evans ⸝ 1940 –

Longman London and New York

Longman early childhood education

Cynthia Dawes *Early maths*
Marion Dowling *The modern nursery*
Hilda Meers *Helping our children talk*

Longman Group Limited
London and New York
*Associated companies, branches and representatives
throughout the world.*

© Longman Group Ltd 1978

First published 1978

ISBN 0 582 25006.4 cased edition
ISBN 0 582 25008.0 paper edition

Library of Congress Cataloging in Publication Data

Evans, David, 1940—
   Sharing sounds.

   (Longman early childhood education)
   Bibliography : p. 192
   1. Music—Instruction and study—Juvenile.
   I. Title.
MT740.E9   372.8'7   76-14909
ISBN 0-582-25006-4
ISBN 0-582-25008-0 (pbk.)

Printed and bound in Great Britain by
T. & A. Constable Ltd, Edinburgh.

ii

Contents

iii

Introduction

If we look at children from the height of the little
hill we have captured, they are bound to seem
unsuccessful adults.   *Leila Berg*

Musicians are very good at standing on their little hill and telling the rest
of us, adults and children, that we're unsuccessful at music.

Don't sing ! Just stand there and mouth the words.
If you can't play it properly you've no business to play it at all !

How many of you have had remarks like these made to you, I wonder ?
Or heard them made to your children ? It's not surprising that so many
people associate music with feelings of inferiority, tension, fear of
exposure and ridicule. Most of us don't feel able to make any kind of
music ourselves. And yet we love music – we want our children to be
musical.·
  Our inadequacies as musicians shouldn't matter too much in our
dealings with the under-fives. After all, only a few of us are practising
painters ; only a few of us model in clay ; yet we're happy to provide the
materials and the opportunities for young children to paint and model in
clay. We don't expect to have to teach them to paint or model. We don't
expect them to produce paintings or models to a fixed standard. We
provide them with the chance to explore and experiment in their own
ways. But we don't seem able to treat music like this.
  Why not ? I think our own musical education has crippled us. The way
Western music has developed over the last 300 years has given us all
very distorted expectations about music. During this time music has
become very complex and sophisticated. It's become something
composed and performed by specialists to a passive audience. So we
have all come to think of music as a set of difficult formal skills which
produce certain approved patterns of sound ; making music seems to us
to consist of using these skills to *perform* the patterns written and
fixed by a composer. If we haven't got these skills at a high level we feel
we can't do anything musical. Thinking this way, we assume that doing
music with young children is a matter of finding ways to teach these

formal skills to younger and younger children. The proof of success is getting a musical performance from them as early as possible. But this doesn't begin to meet the needs of the under-fives. It is a watering-down of adult music for children's consumption.

Let me nail my colours firmly to the mast.

This is **not** a book about 'music'.
This is a book about children.

It is about children in the first five or six years of their lives, about the kinds of things they do, with or without the assistance of the adults who are important to them, the kinds of things that help them to be sensitive to all kinds of sounds, to enjoy music and to have confidence in making it themselves.

You will want to know what you can do to help this, especially if you're not a musician. This book sets out to give you some ideas. In music, as in everything else with the under-fives, the vast majority of important things can be provided by adults with no special skill or qualification except their understanding and love of their children.

This book is **not** meant just for musicians and music teachers.
This book is meant for all adults who enjoy children.

It is meant to help you to look more clearly at the children you know. When you see what kinds of musical things they do you may then begin to see how and where you can help them to extend their musical experiences and to enjoy themselves. You'll find it fun too!

Many, many people have given me help with this book, but to some of them special thanks are due :

to Peter and Katherine, who composed many of the best things in it

to Paul, Daniel, Marcus, Robert, Karen, Jenson, Jenny, Gary, Mark, Sacha, Jonathan, Robert, Samantha and the thousands of other children who've made music and played games with me, never getting too cross at my obtuseness or insensitivity

to Pauline, for so much

to Wendy Bird, for sharing her songs and her enthusiasm for young children's music

to Sue Temple, for special help over pre-school movement and music

to Margaret Grubb, for her example and her kindness to us all

to Audrey, Linda, Chris and Marion, who, under severe provocation, typed and retyped uncomplainingly.

Hundreds of playgroup leaders, tutors, teachers and parents all over the country have given me opportunities, advice, encouragement, help and hospitality. Through them I've learned much of what I know about young children. This book is my acknowledgement of their kindness and, I hope, a small contribution to their work.

GETTING THE BEST OUT OF THIS BOOK

Does the mere thought of being asked to do something musical bring you out in a cold sweat? Do the musical examples in this book make you want to slam it shut as fast as you can?

You're not alone. The kind of music teaching most of us had at school has made us feel this way. We believe, deep down, that we're musical inadequates. We think that music is being able to perform skilfully – if we can't do this, we feel we can't do anything musical with young children. This is nonsense. In music, as in everything else, *you* can give to the young children you're concerned with most of the things they need, *whatever your musical knowledge or lack of it.* All you need are enormous respect for what children are, some understanding of why they do the things they do, and a little confidence in yourself.

Bear the following points in mind when you read this book.

Stop worrying about the music illustrations

They are not important to the book, and you don't have to 'read' them. They are examples, put in for the sake of anyone who wants to know what a child actually sang, or who wants to learn one of the songs. Ignore them if you like. However, they are all very simple.

Start by dipping into the book

Find the bits that interest you – don't feel you have to plough laboriously through it all. If a section makes no sense to you or seems boring, leave it out. The parts that will be useful to you will be the ones that make you think, 'Ah yes!' or 'Surely not?' or 'Well, that's complete nonsense, because . . .' The more you react like this, the more likely you are to want to go back and read it all through.

Don't expect to find here 'the truth about children's music' or 'the right answers'

To start with, this is not a book about 'music' – it's a book about children and adults playing together. It contains my observations and speculations about the musical things that young children do, and my suggestions about activities adults can encourage in order to help the process. Moreover, I don't claim that all the details are scientifically accurate. I have managed to correct some gross errors that I've discovered recently, but there are probably still lots of places where researchers may say, 'Ah, we've discovered that children don't work in the way you suggest.' To me this is regrettable but not serious. More important to me is having a valid way of looking at children and interacting with them. I am concerned to encourage you to look at young children's music in a particular way, a way that seems not to be very common. I want you to view the things they do as being powerful and intelligent and interesting, not to judge them by how far they don't meet adult musical expectations (which, more often than not, are highly distorted). I want you to see it as more important that children should develop confidence in making their own music than that they should be taught to perform arbitrary musical tasks. Above all, I want you to find *your own way* of encouraging their music. This book is to encourage you to think and experiment, not to substitute new dogma for old.

Reject anything you disagree with

There is no one right way. Think about what I say, being as open-minded as you can ; try out the activity with children, if that's feasible ; if you still don't agree, throw it out. You may well be right — certainly the activity is not likely to work for you.

Do try things with children

If you come across anything that you like and that seems suitable for the children you're concerned with, try it. If the suggested activity inspires something quite different that promises to be fun, try it. If you are not sure whether something will work, try it out. Don't be bothered if you can't do it very well, or if it doesn't seem very 'musical', or if it turns out quite differently from what the book 'says'. You'll only develop your own experience and skill by trying things ; you'll only find out whether you can do something by trying it. Remember, if you agree with everything in the book and yet do nothing with children, you've failed the children and the book has failed you.

Part one   Basic musical experiences

1
Beginnings

She's only a baby — you can't really do anything with her.

How many times have you heard that kind of remark when you've been
shopping, or while sitting on a bus ? Quite often, I expect. People still
have the feeling that because a baby is little and physically helpless,
nothing important can happen until she gets older. They feel this specially
about music, I think. If you talk with parents about their baby's music,
they nearly always say something like 'Well, we're going to get her a
good piano teacher when she's five or six.' They think, as many people
do, that musically valuable things are strange and special — different
from 'ordinary' things — and that they have to be done by special music
teachers when the child goes to school. The truth is almost exactly the
opposite. Young children's music is part of their *total* experience. The
musically valuable things we do will be those that have a special
connection with hearing and making sounds. They are very ordinary
things, but they need to be done not by music teachers but by the
child's own special adults — parents, relatives, playgroup leaders —
and they need to be done *before* the child is five.

At this stage, what are these really important 'musical' things ? No
one can be dogmatic ; individual children are so very different from each
other that they may benefit from very different things. The only way we
can find out is to look very carefully at the child in question. We may
speculate in advance about what we think may be useful for him, but
we will only *know* when we actually do things with him. And it's never
too early to start.

This may surprise you. Are there any musically valuable things you
can do with a baby ? Does a baby really hear and notice things. The
emphatic answer is 'Yes ! Even in the womb !' If a radio is switched on
very loudly near his mother the foetus reacts very clearly. Of course,
this reaction is a very crude and limited one — but it is a definite response.
Again, after birth we can all see that a newborn baby is sensitive to sound
as soon as the fluid clears from his ears. If you make a loud or sudden
noise near him, he'll start violently. But his awareness is limited because
his experience of life is limited. Indeed, it is probable that a sound he

hears he doesn't 'feel' as being different from experiences that strike his other senses. A shout, a bump, a flash of light, all startle him — but he probably has no awareness that he hears the shout, feels the bump or sees the flash. It's all 'a big, booming, buzzing confusion', as William James described it. You can make very different sounds to a newborn baby, but he will not necessarily react any differently. In an interesting experiment made many years ago scientists found that babies below the age of two months reacted in the same way to singing, whistling, clapping hands, tapping with a spoon, shouting in an angry voice, speaking in a kind voice, and making many other sounds. If the sound was loud or sudden they jumped ; if the sound was soft they ignored it. In other words, the babies couldn't tell the difference between the sounds, which did not *mean* anything to them.

There is one big exception to this. A baby is born able to do a very crucial thing. He can pick out a pattern or figure from the confusing background, whether through the sense of sight, or of smell, or of taste, or of touch, or of hearing, provided that the pattern can be made clear enough to him. At this stage his Mum is the great and obvious figure, so it is not surprising that when the first pattern emerges out of the 'big, booming, buzzing confusion' it is Mum — her look, smell, taste, feel and voice. These are not separate patterns, they are all felt as one single, total experience. You could call it the Mother Experience. Many people believe that identifying this pattern is the way the baby learns how to start making sense out of the confusion. He has something stable to relate other happenings to ; he has something on which to base his later sorting out and understanding of his experiences. You can see how important a moment this identification is.

The baby may not be able to make sense of other sounds on their own before he is about two months old, but the Mum pattern is identified very early. With some children it happens within two or three days. My nephew Paul made a significantly different response to his Mum than to anyone else when he was only two days old. Very soon this identification can work with sound only. By the age of one month even his Mum's voice when she is out of sight will calm a whimpering or restless baby, as long as he is not too upset. This shows how strongly he has made the link between the sound and the person, how aware he is of it.

Once the newborn baby can do this, then there's no reason for him not to be able to identify other patterns of sound, provided that they can be presented to him in ways that he can make sense of. This must mean using the Mother Experience as the basis. A Mum and, to a lesser extent, other familiar adults can extend this a great deal, even from the beginning. Certainly, from about two months old babies have a hunger for new experiences and we can feed this musically as well as in other areas.

What can you do ? The most important thing is to talk a great deal to your baby where he can see your face clearly, whether you are bending over his cot or sitting with him in your lap or holding him in your arms. In the same way you should make sounds, some of them rhythmic ones, where he can see and hear you. Perhaps this sounds a bit silly ? What's talking got to do with music ? We would see what if we were not so hung up with our fixed ideas that music is melody and harmony, and things like that !

First of all, the earlier the baby can get the idea of identifying certain patterns and timbres of sound as coming from you, the earlier he will be able to understand that other, different sounds come from other, different sources. To do this he must learn to attend to certain sounds out of the confusion and to ignore others ; he must learn to focus his attention ; he must practise remembering sounds. In other words, he must develop the habits and skills of listening. In the very early stages he can only get these from his Mum ; the Mother Experience is the only one he can really understand. It is worth reminding ourselves here that he will only be able to attend to something at very close range. A newborn baby finds it easiest to focus at a range of twenty centimetres – about the height of this book ! Other tests show that even older babies will not be able to attend to you at a distance more than 1.5 metres, and only then if they can see you clearly. You must get really close. This is another reason, of course why Mum is so important – she's the one who is closest. So every time you make sounds close to your baby in ways he can sense – bending over the pram, touching him, saying his name or cooing or talking – you are developing the basic skills of all kinds of communication and awareness, including music. You are also doing a great deal to encourage his own use of sounds in talking and singing – but we will come to that later.

In this connection, a baby learns a great deal from being sat on an adult's lap during a conversation with other people. This works best when he has been fed and changed so that he is warm and comfortable and can concentrate. He doesn't understand the conversation, of course ! But by the time he is three or four months old he will certainly understand that different people are making the different speech sounds.

He does this mostly by the different feeling when his 'seat' is speaking from when other people speak. He will learn other important things too : that people use a wide range of vocal sounds, patterns, intonations ; that this helps them to react to each other ; that the sounds are not just arbitrary, because patterns reappear and people understand them ; that sometimes these patterns are addressed to h.m ; and so on. By the time a baby is four months old he can localize and identify sounds by turning his head towards them. At this stage you will find he often looks intently at each person who speaks, and in between patches of play he remains quiet, concentrating on the conversation for a long time. (What's more, learning that sounds originate from different places will help his growing understanding of the sounds made by things. We will be looking at that later.) Nor is he always a passive listener in this situation. By six months many babies will engage in 'conversation' with their adults. Both Daniel and Robert would gaze intently into my face as I spoke to them ; then they would 'talk' vigorously, kicking their feet and clenching and unclenching their fists. None of the sounds were identifiable as words, of course, but there could be no doubt that they were intended as a way of communicating.

The kicking and fist clenching reminds us of something else important. Mother identification is a total experience. All the senses are involved, and for many years the child's awareness of things will depend on the links between the senses. For a long time he will not really understand things he hasn't had a chance to explore or try out or test for himself. It will be a long time before he begins to be able to listen accurately to sounds without seeing the source, or without moving at the same time. This means that musical experiences that link the senses are particularly powerful and meaningful for young children, especially for a baby. Possibly the most powerful musical experience your child will ever have comes when you hold him closely and securely, rock him gently and rhythmically, and croon in a low voice. Often this crooning is no more than a rocking between two notes :

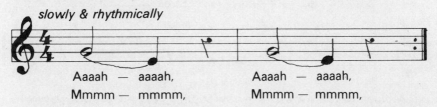

Sometimes you hum the two notes ; sometimes you sing them ; sometimes they get words fitted to them, such as the child's name :

Sometimes a little song develops, like the one my Mum used with me, and that I have used with my own children :

Pe — ter is my boy, There are lots of fat ba—bies in Strea———tham, But he's the best one of all, of all, There are lots of fat ba—bies in Strea———tham, But he's the best one of all ———.

Mothers have always known how soothing this is, but not always why. There are some simple reasons. In the womb the baby feels constant small movements and the rhythm of his mother's heartbeat. After he is born, absolute silence and stillness may make him feel deserted, cut off from the mother with whom he still feels at one. When she rocks him, reunited in the familiar security, it obviously calms this fear, and hearing her heartbeats again is also settling. Several interesting facts confirm this. A recording of a heartbeat in regular and soothing rhythm will often soothe restless babies. Professor Hajime Murooka (a Japanese doctor) in an experiment with crying babies, played a recording of sounds made inside the womb. It stopped the crying of every one of the 403 babies in the experiment and put 161 of them to sleep ! (The recording is now marketed by the Toshiba Music Company under the title *Lullaby Inside Mum*). Again, a large majority of mothers (over 80 per cent) hold their baby on the left side, nearer to the heart – and this is unaffected by whether they are left or right handed. Finally, if you rock a baby, humming to yourself gently and rhythmically, and let your mind go blank you will find that your rocking settles to the speed of your own heartbeat. Try it sometime.

So it is important for you to do lots of rocking and singing. Easy and obvious extensions are all the tickling, rocking, patting, finger counting and toe counting games and rhymes to do with the baby. I have already pointed out how the importance of the rocking lies in the way that the senses are involved *together*. Traditional games extend this by linking movements with rhythmic patterns of words and sounds. In fact, you are doing basic rhythmic training when you hold the baby on your knee and pat in turn the sole of each foot in time to the traditional rhyme :

Pitty Patty Polt

Pitty, patty polt !
Shoe the wild colt !
  Here a nail,
  There a nail,
Pitty, patty, polt !

Another example of rhythmic training is when you sit the baby on your lap facing you, hold his wrists and rock him forwards and backwards in time to :

See-Saw, Margery Daw

See-saw, Margery Daw,
Johnny shall have a new master.
He shall have but a penny a day
Because he can't work any faster.

See-saw, Jack in the hedge,
Which is the way to London Bridge ?
Put on your shoes and away you trudge,
This is the way to London Bridge.

Of course, it doesn't feel like rhythmic training ! It is just the sort of fun parents and babies share without thought of anything further. All the same, it is very important, as will be seen in Chapter 6 on 'Patterns of rhythm'.

There are many sources for such rhymes and games. One of the best is *This Little Puffin*, an excellent collection which is very cheap ; *This Little Pig went to Market*, though more expensive, is particularly good on rhymes and games for babies (see Bibliography). But you must use books like these as a way of learning rhymes, *not* as books to read to your baby. You can't do these rhymes and games clutching a book. To start with, you would need a much bigger lap and three hands ! But more importantly, the whole of your attention and personality needs to be focused on the baby. If it is not, the child will sense it and some of the particular quality of the experience will be lost. So pick out some rhymes you like, and learn them before you try them with the baby.

There are other kinds of musically valuable games which are less formal than some of these finger-play or rocking games. An example is the way you frequently nuzzle against your baby's skin and make sounds : you hum or blow or speak. The baby not only hears the sound but has his attention focused on it by the movement of your head and by feeling the vibration of the sound against his skin, the warmth of your breath. This is an intensely powerful learning experience, intimate, physical, simplified, with all inessentials stripped away. Your baby can become aware of the key elements in the sound-making : person, vibration, breath. It is the kind of experience that only the baby's meaningful adults can provide for him. Any variations you can devise will be good. One that always worked with my two children as babies was to lift my head slowly, saying 'Aaaaaaaaaah -b-b-b-b-b-b- *bubble*'. On the 'b-b-b' I would bring my head down towards the baby's tummy or forehead or ear, and *'bubble'* would be said with my lips against the skin. And the game would be repeated many times, so that the baby had lots of chance to understand, to be aware of what was happening, to anticipate and to relish it.

Another good game is to blow out air noisily, holding the baby's hand in front of your mouth and moving your head from side to side. It makes the baby laugh, of course, but it also helps him to become aware of the mouth, the air and the sound that comes from it. Most babies soon try to poke their finger or hand into your mouth, as if to see where the stuff is coming from. A nice variation of the game, to play perhaps when the baby is lying in his pram or on his blanket, is to puff out your cheeks with air, then pat them with your hands, or with the baby's own hands. This makes the air pop out with a most enjoyable and satisfying sound. Later, when he is a bit older, he will pat your cheek himself.

My next suggestion may sound even sillier ! A very valuable thing you can do for a baby's musical development is to take him securely in your arms and dance around the room, either singing or chanting yourself, or singing or la-la-ing to a favourite piece of music on radio or record. Gormless ? Going barmy ? Not at all. You are doing at least two very important things.

First you are showing the child that this kind of spontaneous physical response to sound is natural and enjoyable. In Britain we tend to be very tense and inhibited about this kind of thing — it isn't proper ! (Perhaps a generation of young parents who have grown up with pop music will not have quite the same difficulty.) A child who sees and hears and feels his adults doing this kind of thing will not be inhibited himself when it comes to moving and dancing to music. And it's particularly good if Dads and Uncles do this, especially with boys. Second, as in the rocking games mentioned earlier, you are making children aware of rhythmic patterns of movement linked with patterns of sound. The baby *feels* them throughout his whole body, and in dancing to music you can often make him aware of more subtle and complex rhythmic patterns than will be possible just through saying rhymes, singing songs or clapping.

You can see the importance of these two things if we look for a moment at the widespread myth of the *innate* rhythmic ability of Africans and West Indians. A myth ? Yes, yes, yes ! No one denies the physical suppleness or the great rhythmic ability and confidence of most West Indians and Africans, but it has nothing to do with the colour of their skin. It comes from being brought up from birth with adults who love and value rhythmic activity – dancing, clapping, singing – and who do these things spontaneously, frequently and without embarassment. A five-year-old Ghanaian has probably had twenty times as much rhythmic experience and practice as a five-year-old Cockney, so it is not surprising that he is much better at it. Significantly, West Indians and Africans brought up on the British pattern show no more rhythmic ability than any other children. This should alert us to the need to encourage a lot of spontaneous rhythmic activity with all young children, and to do such things ourselves. An interest in music and a fear of music are equally easily communicated.

What makes the dancing experience so significant is, of course, the combination of movement with sounds *made by a person*. This is why you have to sing to the record ! Neither the movement nor the sound is nearly as significant on its own as the combination, the connection between the two. This sense of the connection between things, often a relationship of cause and effect, is one of the most important things for young children to learn. Even very young children can realize this, if the connection is simple and obvious enough, and done within the security of a game with a familiar adult. John Holt describes the game of 'Bump !', played with a child of seven or eight months old :

I was carrying her around, and for some reason, I forget what, we bumped heads gently. I said, 'Bump !' She seemed to enjoy the incident, so I said, 'Bump !' again, and again bumped my forehead lightly against hers. After a few times she understood the game, and when I said, 'Bump !', would bump her forehead against mine – and then give me a huge smile.   (*How Children Learn*)

The episode with Marcus and the beads, described in Chapter 4 on 'Understanding sounds' is also very interesting in this connection.

The cause/effect link is important in all areas of a young child's learning, including music. It becomes especially important when he begins to experiment with making sounds from objects, but it is also crucial when he finds out where voices are coming from. Here lies one significance of all the different kinds of peek-a-boo games played with babies. As you know, an object ceases to exist for a very young baby when it disappears from his sight ; so does a person. Even the sound of the person's voice will not always reassure the baby. All the occasions when something 'returns from the dead' help greatly to develop his understanding of the world. Peek-a-boo games are especially valuable here. The adult appears and disappears rapidly and repeatedly, so that the child sees him return again and again. Nearly always, while the person's face is hidden, he goes on making a sound — 'Aa-aa-aa-aa . . .', so that the baby may know that the person is still there, even when he cannot be seen. From experiences like these the baby begins to be aware that something familiar can make a sound even when you can't see it. He begins to identify such things by the sounds they make, rather than needing the object to be in front of him. This is an enormous help in his growing understanding of the way sounds are made by so many of the things around him. Especially in a town, where it is often impossible to see the source of many of the sounds surrounding us this is important.

As well as all the simple and spontaneous forms of peek-a-boo that you can play with a baby, there are fixed versions of the game that are great fun — like the following little song. It is played by holding up your two hands in front of your face and peeking round each side; on '*Boo*' you part your hands and poke your face through:

Peek-a-boo!

When older children are used to the game, they hold up their hands too, and it can even be sung as a question and answer between the adult and the child — but that's jumping ahead!

10

One more very important activity with a baby. It is vital that the baby should be sung to from the very earliest days of his life, especially by his mother, even if she has an appalling voice! (Another widespread myth is that you can somehow spoil a child's voice by singing to him out of tune – rather as if you were scratching a polished piece of furniture! You can't, and I explain why when I talk about how children learn to sing.)

What sort of songs should you sing? It doesn't matter in the slightest – any songs. But one thing is worth remembering. We have already talked about improvising rocking songs and chants. The sort of song that emerges from things you are doing with your baby is special and valuable in every sense. For instance, when my son Peter was a baby he had a lot of trouble with wind, and so the burping process tended to be fairly lengthy and accompanied by lots of talk. Pauline would say things like 'Come on, Peter, let's have a burp ... just a little burp for your Mum ... burp, burp, a burpington ... burpington, burpington ... urpington burpington ...' This playing with words got a bit of tune put to it, repeated many times with back-patting.

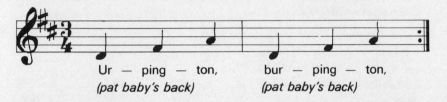

From this start other bits got added (though the original was a splendid baby song on its own) and we finished up with:

You don't have to make up your own tune, of course. Many of the best baby songs come from putting your own words to a tune you know. Pauline learned the Laurel and Hardy theme tune as a little girl from hearing her Dad whistle it when bathing her. When she had babies of her own a version of the tune became attached to the mixing of the baby's bath-water – at first just hummed, and then sung to nonsense syllables:

11

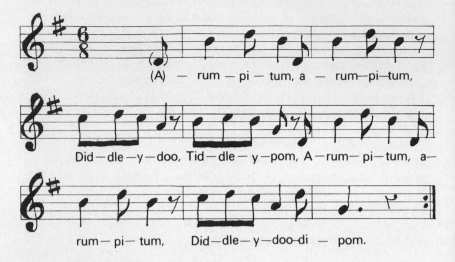

Later it got words, like :

Swish the water round and round,
   Diddley-doo, tiddley-pom,
Swish the water round and round,
   Diddley-doo-di-pom !

Here's a bath for Katherine,
   Diddley-doo, tiddley-pom,
Here's a bath for Katherine,
   Diddley-doo-di-pom !

or any other words that came to mind. Later still Peter and Katherine sang it themselves in the bath as they mixed the water – and they still do sometimes !

This sort of song, that 'grows' out of doing things with your baby, is very important, but just as significant are *any* songs sung by a mother, within the child's hearing but perhaps without thinking about the child at all. It doesn't matter what kind of songs they are – pop songs, grand opera, folk songs, hymns, bits of musicals – any or all of these that you might sing naturally.

Why is doing this so very important ? Well, as we will see in a later chapter, they are vital for a child's vocal development, both in speech and singing. But there is an even more basic reason. A mother is a baby's first and most important music teacher. I don't mean, of course, that she teaches him to read music or to play an instrument. But if he hears his mother singing, feels her rhythmic movement, associates these with pleasure, comfort and security, he begins to build up a concept of what it means to be 'a musical person', to use music naturally, enjoyably. If this concept is strongly established early on he will be able to draw on it later, to give himself musical confidence, to govern and influence his own musical behaviour. All this will stem from the kinds of very basic experience I have been talking about.

A baby who has had such experiences will become increasingly aware of sound. By about two months old he will have begun to respond selectively to the sounds he hears, paying more attention to voices, smiling more at the voices of people he knows well. He will have begun to realize that voices come from people's mouths, and may try to 'take' his mother's mouth when she speaks. When a sound is made out of his line of sight he will cock his head slightly in an attempt to find the sound, and by about the age of four months he will turn his head towards the sound. By six months he will usually show pleasure at his mother's voice, even though he cannot see her ; he will know the difference between scolding or threatening noises and loving comfort noises ; he may well show pleasure at music or fear at a dog's bark. Most important, he will show great interest in unusual sounds and delight in things that make new sounds. Even by six months old he will have learnt that listening to sounds, making them and sharing them, is a highly enjoyable part of living, and that is the basis of all musical development.

2

Sounds from things

Once a baby has begun to hear and identify sounds made by familiar people he can extend this understanding to the sounds that *things* make. Part of this process is becoming familiar with certain repeated sounds through association – the splashing noises when his bath is being prepared, the clatter of his cot-side being raised or lowered – and this is helped by the way his Mum talks to him about what's happening. However, this association will not take him very far. He may well not *identify* the sounds as coming from the water or from the cot. For instance, if his Mum always baths him while 'The Archers' is on, he may well associate the sounds of the programme with bathing, but of course they are not made by the bathing process. The only way for him to make a firm identification is to experiment himself, to do things to objects and find out what kinds of sounds he can make them make.

As a small baby there are not many ways he can do this. Apart from anything else, his physical control and awareness are very limited. Because of this, his understanding of sounds from things probably begins with the way meaningful adults respond to his movements or actions. He realizes (at some level) that *he* can make his people react and make sounds, by pulling their hair, by knocking their glasses off, by smacking their flesh, by poking them in the eye or nostril, and all the other painful things that babies do to their loving relatives. Instinctively the adults respond. 'Oh you saucy girl, let go', they cry ; or 'Go on, son, bash him !' ; and they exaggerate their reactions, pulling away their heads with great cries, taking hold of the exploring fingers and shaking or kissing or tickling them, and so on. Without this kind of exaggeration the cause and effect is much less clear to the baby, and his understanding less likely.

We have already talked about the significance of the child realizing this kind of cause/effect relationship. This can happen surprisingly early. When Peter was four or five months old and having his breast feed, he would sometimes do a very striking thing. About two-thirds of the way through, when the worst of his hunger had passed, he would take his mouth from the nipple and look his Mum straight in the eye. Then – grr ! he'd bite the nipple as hard as he could. Pauline would jump and yelp (naturally) ; then she would say something : 'You little horror, that hurts !' or 'Hey, you're not old enough for solids yet !' or something else, depending on her mood. Peter would look at her, then he would go back to his sucking for a bit. In a minute, off would come his mouth once more, he'd look Pauline in the eye, and — grr ! The striking thing, of course, was that he always looked before biting. He obviously understood that *he* was doing something.

As I have said, this kind of understanding depends crucially on the *response* of the adults. Peter could only have got his understanding about his biting as a result of a reasonably consistent response by Pauline to his experimenting. If on one occasion she had paid no attention, on another had walloped him, on another had stuck him back in his cot without a word, on another had screamed with rage, on another had giggled indulgently, it would have been more difficult for him to reach any clear conclusion about what he was doing. And, even more importantly, too much violent or frightening disapproval would have discouraged him from further exploration, both with her and later with things. Bruno Bettelheim, the famous American psychiatrist, has frequently pointed out that if a young child's efforts to get a response are thwarted or attacked more than a few times, he is likely to give up trying, with a disastrous effect on his curiosity, his exploration, and so on all his learning. Even at a few months old a baby can get the sense that his exploration is valued, that it produces results, and this is the basis of so much of his later development.

The way an adult helps a very young child to develop a sense of cause and effect by responding consistently is very important. It helps him in exploring the world of objects and the sounds they make. It is much easier for a baby to make sense of a response by an adult he knows than to disentangle the sound caused by one of his actions from the 'big, booming, buzzing confusion'. An adult's response tends to be meaningful and simplified and the child's attention is focused by the personal relationship at close range, as we saw in the first chapter. With objects, however, he needs all the clues he can possibly get from seeing, hearing and touching suitable things. It is in the area of providing and organizing such opportunities that the adult can be particularly useful. But where ? and how ?

Cots and prams
It may surprise you to hear that lying in the cot or pram is one of the most productive situations for a baby to learn about the sounds that things make (that is, of course, if there are things in or above or around the cot or pram for him to learn from.) The reason is that in the pram the baby can only do or see a limited range of things, so it is easier for him to make sense of what he sees and hears. The situation is simplified. For instance, if the baby is in his pram where he can see leaves moving or washing

flapping in the wind, he is in a position to notice that when the leaves move rapidly or the washing flaps violently there are rustling or banging sounds that are not there when the leaves or washing are still. This is a matter of association ; I am not suggesting that the baby analyses what is happening in the way I have ! But at some level (and we just don't know whether it is conscious or not) he is absorbing the connection between movement and sound. You know from your experience, I expect, how carefully and intently babies watch such things. So one simple thing you can do at this stage is to check what a baby can see and *hear* from his position in the pram and try to make sure there is something to interest him.

Exactly the same applies to the baby's view from the cot. Most Mums have pictures up on the walls, or interesting wallpaper ; sometimes there is a mobile hanging above the cot ; but there is rarely anything to hear. One of the best things for this is a set of hanging chimes because the baby can see them moving in a draught or breeze and hear them sounding. You can buy (especially from shops specializing in oriental goods) chimes made of glass or metal or bamboo, but you can also make them very easily from scraps of wood or rustling strips of stiff crepe paper or tinfoil, or from old pieces of costume jewellery like bangles or strings of beads, or from the tops of small tin cans opened with a rotary tin-opener.

Even if you get your baby a set of chimes, there is a tendency just to stick to the one set, which limits what he can learn. Why not get or make several different sets of chimes ? Try hanging them in various rooms, so the baby can associate certain sounds with certain places. You can also use the variety to change the set above the baby's cot — but you need to be careful here. It is very confusing, and may be distressing, if something familiar suddenly disappears. The best way to make the change is to hang the new set near the old for a few days, so the baby gets used to the new one, and then to remove the old one. This avoids any sudden shock or confusion.

Don't forget when you first provide something like this to point the chimes out to the baby, to tell him what they are, to tap them with your finger, making the sound, and to use his hand to tap them. You may think this is silly, especially the talking. 'A baby can't possibly understand what I'm saying !' At an intellectual level there is some truth in this view, though of course babies understand much more than they can convey to us.

Nevertheless, this process helps to focus his attention and awareness on the chimes ; it reassures him that they are safe and enjoyable, and lays the foundation of his understanding of the role of language in describing and making sense of sound. It is specially effective if looking at the chimes becomes a regular routine. You may be astonished how clearly babies do understand and remember. From a very early stage Marcus got used to being carried by his Grandmother to see and play and listen to her hanging metal chimes, to which he listened with great attention. Well before a year old, before he could talk, he would, when arriving at her house, set up a cry to be taken to the chimes, and at the room doorway he would peer round the corner towards the place where he knew they were.

Either the pram or the cot is often the place of one of a baby's major discoveries about sounds from things — that he can make them himself. Both cot and pram are places where a baby is left free to move, and move he does ! As Peter said, watching his baby cousin threshing, arm-waving, bumping and bouncing in the pram : 'If he were a ball he'd bounce over the wall.' The baby waves his arms and legs like a demented octopus. They bang against the plastic padding inside the pram, the wooden slats of the cot-side, the mattress or the blanket, and this makes sounds. The baby makes these noises in a completely random way, day after day after day. The repetition is accidental, not deliberate, but gradually two things start to happen. He begins to become aware from the physical sensations in his fists or feet or elbows that it is his own body banging things ; he begins to become aware that the same types of sounds happen when he does this. At some point in this process comes the great mental leap. The baby recognizes that a certain sound is made *by him*.

At this moment there ought to be a fanfare of trumpets ! It is a very significant moment in a baby's development — but of course we don't know when it happens, so we can't celebrate. Nevertheless, happen it does. For a few children the moment may come very early. Most babies probably confirm the understanding only when they get enough physical control and awareness to repeat a movement deliberately, for their own pleasure. But at this moment, whenever it comes, we can say that the baby has mastered the connection between actions and sounds, and the sounds he makes are his first piece of instrumental music. The earlier and more securely the baby can make this connection, the more rapidly his understanding of sounds will develop. The more frequently he can make such connections between things and the different sounds each makes, the more powerful and useful will be his generalization about the nature of sound.

You can help this by putting into the pram or cot things that make this piece of understanding easier. One of the most common but most valuable is the set of beads or rattling balls strung on elastic across the pram or cot. They are quite safe in this position, but the baby's involuntary movements can easily strike them and make sounds. Then, because they are so easy to see and hear, it's simpler for the baby to make the deduction that he is causing the sounds by his own movements. Once again, it is not enough just to buy a string of pram beads and forget about them. There is much scope for buying different strings, or for making your own strings ; indeed, home-made strings with only a couple of different-sounding objects (a small bell and a bunch of plastic strips or discs perhaps) may make the discovery even easier. Another possibility in summer is to stretch a transparent plastic cover across the lower half of the pram, above the baby's legs, and put several lightweight rattles on top, where he can make them sound by kicking them : this technique was used in one of the classic experiments of Piaget, the Swiss psychologist.

Rattling and dropping things

Obviously a baby cannot get very far in his exploration unless he develops skill with his hands, and during the early months he is working very hard at this. It is no coincidence that a baby in pram or cot 'plays' a great deal with his hands and watches them so intently. If you sometimes tie a coloured bow round each wrist this helps him. As he looks at his hands and by chance they touch, he sees and feels them touch and this links nerve cell pathways in his brain. This touching experience is repeated and enjoyed, practised and observed by the baby, so that gradually he brings his hand movements under control. As he gains this physical control he watches what he does, and so teaches his eyes to follow his hand. This leads to his being able to reach out and grasp a desired object that he has seen. A lot of babies can do this by the time they are four months old, and so from this age holding and shaking objects becomes an important part of their investigation of things. Later, deliberate dropping will become important too.

At the shaking stage rattles become an essential plaything. It is easy for us to overlook the musical significance of rattles. They are probably the baby's first full set or family of musical instruments, and by comparing his rattles he learns a vast amount about making similar and different sounds. For example, let's think just about the very common pair of dumb-bell rattles, so easy to grasp and shake. The rattles are usually the same shape but different colours. With one in each hand the baby waves his arms and gets a loud rattling sound. But when he waves only one arm he gets a somewhat different sound, and he gets yet another sound when he waves the other arm alone. It takes a vast amount of shaking, including a lot of shaking other things that make a rattling sound, before the baby sorts out that it is the rattles making the sound ; that they each make a separate and different sound ; that this behaviour is consistent ; and that the sound is related to the kinds of noises that other rattles make when shaken. It is not a sign of stupidity or lack of imagination when a baby shakes rattles for hours and days. He is doing a lot of important discovering. You can help him by making sure that there are plenty of interesting rattles of varied types and shapes and colours for him to play with. Later, when he begins to put things in pots for himself, you can shake the pot of beads or box of bricks or posting toy and so help him to realize that this sound too is related to rattles and their behaviour.

Incidentally, when the baby gets to the dropping stage, you will find that rattles get dropped or thrown more often than shaken. It is very easy and very natural to get cross with a baby who keeps dropping his rattles out of the pram. I once heard a mother say, 'He just does it to annoy me ; he wants me to keep picking them up. He's got me on a string !' Of course the baby wanted his Mum to keep picking them up, both to keep her near him and to be able to go on with his experimenting ! But he was not doing it to annoy. Once again, when a baby does this he is finding out some important things : dropping objects is a major technique in his exploration of all kinds of things.

As we discussed in Chapter 1, a very young baby cannot understand that when an object disappears from his view it is still there but out of sight. To him the object has ceased to exist. But by about one year old he has come to the realization that though the rattle has gone from his view it still exists ; he may shout for it back, or peer over the side of the pram looking for it. Clearly, the adult returning something he has dropped greatly helps in developing this understanding, just as do the peek-a-boo games.

More important from a purely musical point of view is the way that the baby who drops an object out of the pram on to the floor or a concrete path *hears* a consequence of his dropping, even though he can no longer *see* the object. This is similar in importance to hearing his mother's voice when she is in another room and he can no longer see her. The separation of sight and sound that experiences like this give him is crucial for a child's later ability to hear sounds (say, in the street) and to identify or make sense of them without necessarily being able to see the source of the sound. You will see in Chapter 4 how the hiding of sound-making objects is a significant part of listening training for the young child.

Invaluable in this whole process is the indulgent uncle or grandmother who will sit with a baby while he drops things and who will talk about what is happening. 'Are you dropping your rattles ? Bump ! Didn't it make a loud noise when it hit the floor ? I'll pick it up again – there you are. You villain ! You're going to drop it again. Bump ! I'll pick it up again. . . . There it is . . .' And so on. The talk is not complicated ; there is no special 'musical' language – but such talk is so important in helping a child to make sense of things and to feel that experimenting and finding out is an enjoyable and approved activity.

I cannot stress this enough. It is terribly easy for adults to discourage experiment, especially with things that make a noise ! And yet they are often very keen that their children should be confident, skilful, full of initiative. In this respect I shall never forget the mother of Michelle, a very inhibited and withdrawn girl I once taught. The mother came to talk to me about Michelle's difficulties in school, and brought her three-year-old as well. While we were talking the toddler became fascinated with some plastic bricks on a table. 'I keep telling Michelle to have a go at things, Mr Evans, to have a try, but she doesn't seem . . .'

She broke off sharply to grab the toddler. 'Don't touch!' she snapped, ramming home her words with a sharp slap.

I know — it's an extreme example. But lots of adults discourage more subtly, by their tone of voice, by removing things suddenly from a child without explanation, by talking about a child's play as 'messing about', by a lack of interest and encouragement. It is easily done. We should always think hard about what the child is getting out of the irritating thing he is doing before we stop him, and this is particularly true about his sound-making.

Once a baby begins to sit up securely and to pick up and drop things, his experimenting with sound extends enormously. But he still needs a lot of adult help and encouragement. One very good way of doing this is by letting the baby play with things on your lap. We have already mentioned the lessons about people's speech that can be learned on someone's lap; well, a lap gives a very comfortable, interesting and secure platform for a child to experiment with making sounds. The play usually starts naturally with the adult handing the baby something like a rattle. The baby shakes it a bit, then loses interest. The rattle slides down, the adult retrieves it and hands it back for some more shaking. Often the adult holds the rattle in front of the baby's eyes and gives a good shake before handing it over, and often the baby will then watch the adult while shaking it himself. It is amazing how early the baby will enter into this kind of game; certainly by a year old he will make up patterns of his own for it. Deborah, aged fifteen months, made up a version. After the rattle had been passed backwards and forwards two or three times, with a shake each time, she would hurl it to the floor with great glee. The rattle had then to be retrieved and handed back to her to start the game again. At a simpler level Daniel threw his toy car to the floor with a noise; I picked it up and dropped it with a cry of 'Crash!' He was delighted and we played the game for several minutes. He was ten months old at the time.

Another marvellous source of materials for lap play is what the adults are wearing. I often think that one of the reasons babies are so fond of their grandmothers (as well as their willingness to play this sort of game) is that they often wear interesting bits of jewellery — earrings that wiggle and tinkle, strings of beads that sway and clatter, bracelets that shake and rattle — and they are often happy to have them bonked, prodded and pulled. My mother's beads and bracelets have been an unfailing source of delight to all her grandchildren. But for lap play you don't have to restrict yourself to objects the baby is holding or you are wearing. You can bring things, and you should. There is no point in my suggesting a list. The best things are very often those you have around you, like money in a purse or pocket, or those you find around the house, like a couple of yoghurt pots to tap together. Anything that is safe and that makes a sound will be suitable (it has to be safe because the baby will almost certainly want a go !). The crucial thing about music at this age is not *what* you provide but *how* you make it possible for your child to use it. You can buy £30 worth of equipment and use it to destroy your child's confidence and enjoyment of music, and you can give enormous delight and musical understanding with everyday bits and pieces from around the house. A baby's greatest need is to feel that you enjoy and approve of what he is doing. This he will get best from the reassurance of your playing with him and talking about what you are both doing.

Prodding and banging

Prodding and banging become important techniques in exploration as the baby begins to sit up securely. Because both movements usually require hitting or poking downwards, they are practised later than the kicking, waving and rattling; they also depend sometimes on the baby being able to grasp something to hit with. Often this hitting grows out of the earlier rattling. Matthew, aged eight months, was shaking a rattle when it hit against the chair seat, making a noise. He was delighted, and went on from there, hitting the rattle against the seat – when he didn't miss ! Most prodding and banging starts with lap play, for obvious reasons. Funnily enough, 'playing' the piano is something a baby can do quite early, if he is sitting on an adult's lap. He sees the adult striking the keys with his hands, and so flails away. To his surprise he can make a sound himself ! Often this becomes a favourite game. Usually babies hit out more or less at random, but some children will learn very early the technique of playing notes with single fingers by watching the adult's way of doing things : I know two who learned this before they were nine months old, and lots who could do it before fifteen months.

Many things can be profitably prodded or banged by the baby, but at the stage of sitting up and reaching for things (before crawling begins) you have to be largely responsible for providing materials on the blanket or in the playpen where he is playing. I have already discussed the importance of a wide range of rattles and rattling things. Other useful musical objects at this stage are : an old saucepan lid, frying pan or biscuit tin with a couple of spoons, preferably wooden ones, for the banging ; various wooden, metal and plastic containers for dropping small objects into, and a supply of small, *safe* objects ; a postbox toy (or some other box with a hole in its removable lid) ; an old Tupperware container, Lyons coffee tin or other plastic-lidded box or tin, also for drumming. You can provide a chime bar, if you want, but it is not necessary. (See Chapter 8 on 'Musical instruments – what and when', pp. 138–160.) You will probably need to introduce these objects to your baby by sitting on the floor and having a go with him (and, of course, talking about what you are doing) but he will soon find lots of things to do with them.

These activities may seem unimportant, even unmusical, but you only have to observe children closely to see how important such games can be to them. At about the age of twelve months, when Katherine could crawl but not walk, she would often choose a particular old biscuit tin and wooden spoon and crawl to a corner. There she would bang and shout for long periods. This seemed to be at random, but if you listened and watched carefully you began to notice patterns. She would stop very deliberately; then start banging; stop and sing; sing and bang together; stop deliberately. You could also hear certain patterns in the banging and singing. She would bang a pattern, then sing it – not an exact repeat, but almost the same. This play with the biscuit tin was obviously very important to her. She did it for long periods over three or four months. Interestingly, after this time she did nothing like it for nearly two years. She was then given some proper chime bars and immediately was able to use them correctly and with great delicacy and skill.

This is significant in view of the parents and teachers who ask anxiously, 'Providing things like these is all very well, but how do you develop it? After all, it's not really music, is it?' Katherine's play, and many other instances, show that a child senses its own needs very clearly and has a strong urge to improve and extend its understanding and skills. 'Musical' development will come naturally, provided that the child's curiosity and urge to explore are not inhibited.

Something more needs to be said about this play. Katherine received very important support from her Mum during this time. To start with, she was allowed to go on making what was to adult ears a racket! She was not interfered with, even after a couple of months, when some adults would be tempted to try to push her on to what they might call 'something more productive'. At the same time, what she was doing was constantly acknowledged ('Oh, you've got your tin again. Are you going to play your music?') and her Mum was always willing to talk about it. This sort of support, in particular the talking, is crucial for the child's experiment – it makes the exploration truly productive. It is easy to see just how crucial by comparing the development of human babies with that of baby chimpanzees. Young chimpanzees closely resemble young children in their play, except that they tend to do better earlier because of their more rapidly developing muscle system. They explore percussive sound in very much the way that babies do. Yet their early advantage rapidly disappears. This is partly because their brains are less complex, but largely because they lack the verbal contact with their adults that enables them to develop their powers of concentration and to reinforce and extend their discoveries.

What is particularly fascinating about this is that the patterns young chimpanzees show are very similar to the patterns we find in children who have received very little meaningful adult conversation or response; for instance, those looked after extensively by a poor child-minder. Both groups have very poorly developed powers of concentration; both show interest in new objects for a short time but cannot extend or develop this ; the approach of both to materials tends to be destructive, not constructive. This suggests very clearly that it is the contact with adults that is significant in developing understanding – and in particular the talking about the child's exploration.

Are there no limits to tolerance ?

What I have said may well have raised a big question in your mind. How much does the adult have to put up with in the cause of children's understanding of sound ? Are bitten nipples, biscuit tins bashed for hours, smashed ornaments, all essential ? How many hundred times do you *have* to pick up that bloody rattle ?

Perhaps the clearest example is the baby who hits his dinner with a spoon. Sitting in a high chair with implements to hand gives an excellent opportunity for the baby to bang, and he learns a great deal from the different sounds he gets when hitting the tray, the plate, the mashed potato or the gravy ! Should this be stopped ?

I think the answers are fairly straightforward to arrive at, if we think of the way a child grows up. First of all, he grows up as part of a family of personalities, and these personalities shape the family patterns. One group will tend to be free and easy ; another will be tightly organized. Like all his other learning and growing, the child's musical exploration will have to fit into the family pattern, and that pattern will tend to suit him. Again, adults in a family don't have to give up all their rights to the child. Something that discomforts the adult doesn't *have* to be endured. Indeed, if you do endure something, feeling resentful towards your child, you can be sure that he will sense it. This is likely to make him anxious, and actually to discourage his experimenting. So there's nothing intrinsically wrong in stopping a child's activity that is disruptive. On the other hand, looking as we have done at some of the annoying and seemingly pointless things that young children do should have made us realize how important some of them may be. A child needs a wide range of opportunities and a lot of encouragement to fulfil his potential, and we ought to be very careful not to clamp down on things just because they annoy us.

What should we do, then ? I think there are two key principles. The first is that any one particular object is rarely essential to the child, and it is almost always possible to replace it by something less noisy or less messy or less dangerous. Often it gives us the chance to substitute something better suited for the child's discovering, such as giving him a transparent pot containing beads in exchange for the tin of drawing pins he's shaking. The second is that the fact of some things being unsuitable for experiment with sound, or dangerous, or unpleasantly noisy for other people, is an important quality of those things. Provided that the child is told this clearly, removing the object or forbidding the activity is part of his learning. We are back once again (and not for the last time) with the crucial business of adults talking about things, explaining, making sense of them. If you always explain, even a very young child will realize quickly that you always do things for a reason, though he may not understand the explanation.

So my simple answers are : tolerate as much as you can ; when you cannot tolerate something, distract the child from it, or substitute something for it, or forbid it ; explain why, even when you don't think the explanation will get home. The resulting blend of actions is likely to suit your children pretty well.

Talking with your child is important at this stage of his exploration ; it becomes crucial in his later experiment, discussed in Chapter 4, 'Understanding sounds'.

3
Early vocalizing

In Chapters I, 'Beginnings' and 2, 'Sounds from things' we looked at the kinds of things you can do to help a baby identify sounds and enjoy them. But we didn't talk about a major part of his world of sounds – the ones he makes himself. I didn't leave these out because they are unimportant; quite the opposite. I left them until now because the way in which a baby comes to make sounds deliberately is a key area of his musical development, even though it happens so early. It therefore needs to be looked at in greater detail.

You may know that much research has been done on the way a child learns to speak. You probably won't be surprised that many of the scientists disagree about how precisely it happens. Perhaps I am reckless in taking my own look, but I am convinced that speaking and singing have the same roots and arise from the same kinds of very ordinary experiences with adults. Even if my theories about *how* it happens do not agree with yours, or with a particular scientist's, I think we should be able to agree about *what* we see happening with a baby.

Reflex sounds and deliberate sounds

I am sure we will all agree that a baby makes vocal sounds from the start, beginning with his bawl on entering the world. He cries, gulps, vomits, burps, hiccups and sneezes, as well as making his own individual combinations of these (Jonathan, for instance, had a distinctive burp-sneeze). By the age of two months a baby gurgles and begins to babble sounds; soon after he chuckles and whimpers. A wide range, you will agree. But it is important to realize that at first he is not making these sounds deliberately; that is to say, he is not conscious of making them. Some scientists call them 'reflex sounds' because they are jerked out of the child by the state of his body or his feelings, just as your leg jerks when the doctor taps your knee with his rubber hammer. If the baby has a tickle in his nose he sneezes; if you stick the nappy pin in him he cries. He doesn't think, 'Oh dear, my bottom hurts, I'd better cry.' Babies of all races make such reflex sounds and so do many species of animals. If any sounds are universal these are, because they are a physical response to universal situations.

At somewhere round about two months a baby begins to babble – that is, he begins to make vocal sounds that seem less a result of something impinging on him, more an exploration. He makes sounds like 'aaa', 'mmm', and 'oo' which seem to be close to speech sounds. But these are still reflexive sounds. They arise directly from typical mouth actions and movements. When he opens his mouth and vocalizes he tends to go 'aaa' ; when he closes it again he goes 'mmm' ; closing and opening produces 'ma-ma-ma'. Try it for yourself. The sound 'oo' is closely linked to the lip movements of sucking ; the famous 'raspberry' sound is produced by blowing out air through closed lips. They are not in the first stage deliberately produced sounds, however much doting aunts may like to pretend so ! Proof of this lies in the fact that totally deaf babies will gurgle, babble and make reflex sounds, but by the time they are about six months old they will have stopped completely. Because they are deaf they cannot become aware of the sounds they make, and so cannot go on to the stage of making them deliberately.

A normal baby learns to make sounds on purpose – how ? We have just mentioned the key element – becoming aware of what is happening when sounds are made. By making sense of the Mother Experience, by learning to separate her from himself, he can start to identify sounds she makes. This means that he can understand that his people make sounds – and that other sounds he hears are made by himself. He *feels* himself doing things with his mouth at the same times as he *hears* sounds. Just as with the sounds from things there comes a moment when he makes the connection, and it is this connection that makes it possible for him to repeat sounds deliberately, to practise them and to use them. All the previous reflex sound-making will have built up muscular skills and vocal patterns that are now at his service.

To some extent this process is natural and inevitable, but, even more than with sounds from things, the role of the adult is crucial if the baby is to develop at a normal speed. *You* are the most important element in making possible speech and singing development. If you feel that a baby will learn to speak and sing without any special adult intervention, take warning from the fact that babies in institutions, or in homes where they hear little speech, babble much less and make fewer speech sounds than babies who are listened to and spoken to often by adults. Why is this ?

The role of the adult
A child needs to be physically ready to speak and to sing, to have developed through sucking and making reflex sounds the musculature and the control required. But that's only a part of it ; other things are necessary. He must want to communicate with people, and at this age the only people he will want to talk to are those with whom he feels secure ; if he doesn't love you he won't want to talk to you or sing to you. He also needs to become aware that he can make a very wide range of vocal

sounds, and to practise making them himself. He needs to learn which of these sounds mean something to those people speaking his language, and how to use these sounds to communicate with them. In all these areas the adult's contribution is very important, and particularly in the first. Your major contribution to speech and singing development is to love and value your child. In a poor orphanage, where care is largely limited to the physical needs of the children and there is no consistent pattern of a loving, caring adult, babies don't wish to communicate in the way your child will.

Given this, he will achieve some of the other things for himself. As he grows he will naturally make an increasingly wide range of vocal sounds. It was thought at one time (and some scientists still hold this view) that a baby makes at this stage all possible language sounds of all the languages in the world. This has been challenged and it seems likely that most babies have to be taught a number of the characteristic sounds of their own native languages, since they will not necessarily make them spontaneously. Nevertheless, a baby has the potential to make all possible language sounds, and you know well that at the age of three or four months he makes a lot of sounds that do not appear in your language. At this age also it is impossible to distinguish a Chinese baby's babbling from that of an American baby. Three months later you will probably be able to tell, even from a recording, not only that the two babies are from different countries but even which is which.

How has this happened ? As the people around him talk and sing, the baby becomes conscious of certain repeated, satisfying patterns of sound and intonation. Some of these are spoken – words ? Some of these are interesting sounds – music ? They 'reach' him because they are made by people meaningful to him, at close range or within his attention, and are repeated again and again. He is able to hear them clearly and respond to them. He also comes to realize that the making of sounds is a natural, safe and approved activity ; this encourages him to make sounds himself. Now, all this response to adult speech is happening at the same stage as he is becoming increasingly aware of the patterns of sound he makes himself. When he hears in the adult's speech a pattern that he can make himself this is of tremendous significance to him. He recognizes it clearly ; he gets a strong reward and feedback from this recognition ; he can imitate and practise it himself. In every way it is strongly reinforced. But many patterns he can make are never reinforced in this way. An English child probably never hears at this stage the French 'tu' sound or the Welsh 'llan' sound, and so, even though potentially able to make them, they atrophy, they become redundant. Some scientists believe that this redundancy mechanism accounts for a child's early speech development ; others see a more positive part played by the adult's teaching and the child's imitation. It doesn't really matter which theory you find more satisfying. In either case the adult's role is a central one in reinforcing the patterns characteristic of his native language and dialect (and of the style in which he sings). The more often adults speak and sing to the baby at close range rather than just letting him struggle to hear the ordinary flow of family conversation, the more rapid is likely to be his speech development.

Adults make one further major contribution at this stage. They tend to seize on those of the baby's sounds that are close to important words in their own situation and to imitate these sounds. Often they attach meaning to them. Leila Berg vividly describes the baby in this situation :

Mmmm and *nnnn* he says, like a sexy woman, snuggling and desiring. And *p p p* and *d d d* he says, delighting in play. All over the world mamans, mums, nanas and nannies, dads, papas, pas and babushkas, we cry 'That's me !' and turn his expressive sounds into the role we choose to play, answering him. The baby is amazed and delighted. He makes his magic sounds again and again, and again we exclaim with joy and admiration, identifying ourselves as his family, and he crows in shared delight.   (*Look at Kids*)

(Perhaps my earlier remark about doting aunts falsely attributing meaning to a baby's reflex sounds is less justified than we might think !) Such adult imitation of the baby's own sound is very helpful. It separates the significant sounds from the stream of sounds the baby produces, and so focuses the baby's attention on them. This makes it easier for him to imitate them in his turn. It must also be, as Leila Berg suggests, a very reassuring and encouraging experience for the baby to find that a particular sound is so powerful, so meaningful, so effective at communicating with his adults. No wonder he is motivated to practise sounds so hard.

Speaking and singing
You may be wondering how all this business about learning to talk is relevant to a child's musical development. It is relevant because singing *must* develop from the same roots and experiences as talking. Indeed, you can see the connections very clearly. When a baby is babbling he repeats vocal patterns like 'da-da' or 'ba-ba' or 'mum-mum', often with a rhythmic sing-song quality, and he experiments with inflection and differences in pitch. At about seven months Peter would lie for long periods in his pram, singing to himself. One of his favourite patterns was :

Oooh!   Oooh!   Oooh!

At the same age Daniel would sometimes 'sing' a long meandering tune that went up and down, over and over again. Matthew would also sing short patterns to himself. Most babies do the same, but we often don't recognize it as singing. It is only when we get something like Peter's song which has a 'tune', that we notice it – indeed, many adults would dismiss even that as 'noise-making'. We have such narrow ideas about what constitutes 'music' and these often blind us to what is happening with very small children. It also limits our expectations. For instance, from the time when a baby begins to babble he is already beginning to sing in tune, and by the time he can speak he should be able to sing.

Are you astonished? Many adults are. After all, they say, at the age of seven many children can't sing in tune – 25% is a normally quoted figure. But it never ceases to astonish me that this is accepted as normal and natural. What is so special and difficult about singing? By eighteen months old many babies are talking, and it is common to hear a baby, well before he is able to speak words, speaking what Leila Berg calls 'an English tune' – a pattern of rhythm, intonations, expressions that sound exactly like an English person talking, except that there are no identifiable words. To do this requires most of the skills that are needed to sing in tune. Why then can't a baby sing?

The answer is, of course, 'No reason why not!' All the babies I've known who have had plentiful experience of being talked to, played with and sung to have been able to join in accurately with snatches of the tunes of familiar songs or nursery rhymes at the age when they are starting to talk. In a number of cases this happens during their first year of life, before they have spoken any words. What has made this possible is not an exceptional musical ability – only one of them has turned out to be really musical – but that they have heard lots of singing by people of significance to them, without the distraction of accompaniments. It is the *familiarity* of the kind of sound we call singing, the *meaningfulness* and *closeness* of the experience, that makes all the difference.

Most children who are good talkers are quite good singers too, for obvious reasons, but there are certain things you can do to help encourage their singing. The most important thing at this stage is to do lots of singing to the baby, at close range, where he can see the shape and movement of your lips as they produce the sounds. It is important to do this because the baby needs to understand clearly where the singing sound is coming from if he is to understand that he can make such sounds with his own mouth. Moreover, as I have already pointed out, sounds the baby can make which he hears others make also are strongly reinforced. They obviously seem worth making and practising. Now, your baby makes many singing sounds amongst all his other sounds. If he rarely or never hears you make sounds like them, he doesn't consider them any more valuable than, say, French sounds or Chinese sounds. Consequently he doesn't practise them at this stage of his development. It is a particularly important stage too. As you know, the developing child has periods when he is especially receptive to a certain kind of experience or is particularly able to develop a certain kind of skill. The period between twelve and twenty-four months is when a child's ability to imitate and his instinct to do so are at their greatest; moreover, the period between ten months and eighteen months is the crucial time in the development of confidence and competence in performing tasks. Clearly a child who is not encouraged to imitate and practise singing skills between six and twenty-four months is going to be seriously handicapped.

It is therefore particularly helpful for you to do activities that encourage the baby to imitate and play with sounds. However, it is not easy for me to suggest specific ones. Each individual situation is so different, and the kinds of games you do with a baby must be spontaneous. But one kind of thing you can try with your baby is to respond to some of the sounds he makes. This may crop up, perhaps, when you are holding him on your lap after changing him. He is comfortable and cheerful and making noises. When he makes a distinctive noise, especially a singing sound, make it back to him. He will probably look intensely surprised and stop. Don't be put off by this — it's a sign that he has realized something striking has happened. Make the same sound once or twice more, looking straight at him. Usually he will respond with a burst of sounds, often waving his arms and legs violently; you can then wait for another of his sounds to pick out and imitate. Sometimes he will listen very carefully each time you make his sound, and then smile; sometimes, with quite a lot of babies, he will repeat his own sound. This may seem a rather dull, monotonous activity to you, but do you remember the rattle-dropping in the last chapter? A child learns much about consistency from the same experience repeated again and again, when he is in his pram, when he is lying on a blanket, when on a lap. Sometimes, of course, the baby pays no attention at all when you imitate his sound. Try imitating one or two more sounds, and if there is still no reaction drop it (the game, not the baby!) You won't have done any harm. Occasionally, *very* occasionally, the baby may show distress or anger at the game — I am sure I don't need to tell you to stop immediately! But this does stress again how individual are children's reactions and how the things you do must arise from your sense of what is appropriate with your child at any particular moment.

Similar to this game, and also very illuminating to the child, is for you to imitate distinctive sounds heard around the house, especially if you also talk about the sound and what it's caused by:

'Listen! There's the kettle whistling. Whooooeeeeeeeee. I can make that noise — whoooeeeeeeee.'
'The door chimes are ringing — ding-dong. Someone must be at the door. There it is again — ding-dong. Let's go and answer it — come on, Georgina.'

Lots of sounds in a house can be imitated — the vacuum cleaner or mixer or washing machine, the running taps, the swish of drawing curtains, the click of a light switch and so on — and this leads us directly into games we play with things that make sounds (see Chapter 4 on 'Understanding sounds, pp. 49–72). Because many of the sounds are also strongly rhythmic, such imitations are also important for a child's rhythmic development (see Chapter 6 on 'Patterns of rhythm', pp. 103–126). Don't get me wrong, though. When I talk about 'imitating the sounds' I am not expecting from you a professional mimic's skill. A rough approximation is all that is necessary to focus the child's attention on the sound and help his understanding.

From a pure singing point of view it is valuable at this stage to play spontaneous games with sounds, to make patterns with words, and so on, all at close range within the baby's vision and hearing. These games often sound very silly to adult ears. Sometimes I listen to myself saying to a baby, 'Boogle-oogle-boo!' or 'Weedle-eedle-ah! Weedle-eedle-eedle-ah!' and I think, 'You steaming nit!' Yet I think you will bear me out if I say that such games are very natural ones to play with a baby — just think of the 'Boo' games we talked about in the first chapter. They also lead very naturally into many of the traditional fingerplays and toe-counting games you can play with your baby on your lap. Try this one, starting with the little toe:

Wee Wiggle

Wee wiggle,	(*wiggle the little toe*)
Poke piggle,	(*wiggle the next toe*)
John whizzle,	(*wiggle the next toe*)
Tom grizzle,	(*wiggle the next toe*)
And old.... big.... GOBBLE, GOBBLE!	(*give a sudden wiggle to the big toe*)

Here's another fun rhyme (which much older children enjoy too):

Jelly on a Plate

Jelly on a plate,	(*take the baby under the arms and*
Jelly on a plate,	*wobble him gently in time to the*
Wibble wobble	*words*)
Wibble wobble	
Jelly on a plate.	
Porridge in the pot,	(*'stir' him round and round on your*
Porridge in the pot,	*lap — or trace a circle on his tummy*
Piping hot,	*with your finger*)
Piping hot,	
Porridge in the pot.	

All such rhymes have a very important function in making the young child aware of the games we can play and the patterns we can make with sounds. The strongly rhythmic ones are particularly important from a musical point of view. And don't forget to do them over and over and over if the baby's enjoying them – you will get bored before he does!

When talking about these kinds of patterns with sounds I don't think we should ignore baby-talk. I mean here the 'Oosa mammy babbykins, den ?' style of conversation. Such baby-talk has rightly received a hammering from teachers and educational researchers, especially those concerned with language development. They have pointed out that babies pick up language by hearing people speaking it. If you only use 'coochie-woochie-igglie-diddums' language to the baby while speaking normally to other people within his hearing you confuse him and seriously limit his ability to make sense of language as a means of communicating. Consequently parents tend to feel guilty about using it.

I adopted this very serious attitude myself as a teacher, but it took a big knock when I had a baby son of my own. I talked to Peter a great deal in a very adult way – my wife remembers me rocking him (aged two months) at 1.30 a.m., saying 'You must realize that you can't expect your mother and me to be especially pleased when you wish to be awake at this time so kindly behave like a reasonable baby and go to sleep.' But, nonetheless, at certain times I felt a very strong urge to use baby-talk with him, and did. I know many intelligent parents, well aware of the need to talk to young children in an adult way, who have done the same. Why should this be ? I think the key element is that these feelings usually occur in intimate play situations, like cuddling or tickling games. I now believe that baby-talk is an instinctive adult response which helps to develop the baby's awareness of sound as something to be played with, experimented with, modified, controlled. As such, it is an important element in both talking and singing . We shall see in Chapter 5, 'Singing and making up songs', how it has particular significance in the way children make up songs. But it must be *in addition to* the ordinary talking to your baby, not instead of it.

All such activities help your baby to get some very important kinds of awareness and confidence. Above all, he realizes that he can make vocal sounds for fun or to communicate with other people, *and that these can be separate from his mood or need.* This is a vital step. The very young baby who has learned that his parents will come to him when he cries in rage or pain or need almost certainly does not know that it is the *sound* of crying that brings them. He probably thinks/senses that it is his emotional state, his anger or his pain, that draws them – after all, he still feels his mother as part of himself. Realizing the particular role of sound in this comes from putting together a range of experiences ; for instance, times when he cries experimentally (not in anger or pain) and his Mum still comes ; the talking and calling to him that his parents do when they are out of sight ; the way they say things like 'Why are you crying ? I heard you – what do you want ?' ; the way they take up and imitate patterns of sound that he makes. All this gradually makes him aware of vocal sound as a tool of communication, play and rhythmic patterning.

Given this awareness, and the confidence that comes from lots of enjoyable sound experiences with his adults, a baby will experiment widely with sounds he likes. John Holt quotes the year-old baby in the supermarket :

. . . he was absorbed in his own affairs, playing with his stroller, looking at cans of fruit and juice. I watched him. Suddenly he said to himself, 'Beng-goo'. After a few seconds he said it again, then again, and so perhaps ten times. Was he trying to say, 'Thank you' ? More probably he had hit on this sound by accident and was saying it over and over because he liked the way it sounded and felt in his mouth. (*How Children Learn*)

Peter similarly used the word 'Bidoon' for a long time, revelling in its sound. We saw earlier how many of the baby's sound patterns in babbling arise from physical actions – like sucking, or blowing out air – and this continues to be true of the older and more aware baby. However, during the second six months of life it becomes a much more deliberate and frequent process. Try creeping up on a happy baby in a pram, and listen. The sounds are also used expressively. I heard Daniel, aged eight months, making very loving raspberries to a large, orange plastic spoon.

We mustn't be deluded by such observations into thinking that this kind of behaviour has to be gone through *before* the baby begins to join in with talking and singing. From a very early stage, certainly by the age of three months, the baby listens carefully and intently to adult conversations that are not necessarily directed to him, and we are coming to realize that many of his sounds and actions in such situations are not random, but real contributions to the social situation, even though they may not seem to be. Similarly, many of his sounds during singing by the adult or the playing of music may be real musical contributions. Often, I think, our preconceptions get in the way. We need to remember constantly that a child's ability to make sense, to decode, to remember, to understand is far in advance of his ability to perform. Thus he can understand something said to him long before he can say it back ; he knows a word or tune and can 'speak' or 'sing' it well before what actually comes out of his mouth is the correct word or tune by adult standards. I have already mentioned how babies 'converse' with people well before they can actually speak. Katherine used to do this a great deal, especially between ten and fourteen months. The best example was at her first birthday party. She was clearly conscious of this as a special occasion and from her high chair at the head of the table she 'talked' almost non-stop, turning from one guest to the other. From the next room it sounded exactly like speech – only when you got up close to her could you tell that they were not proper sentences.

Or were they ? I suspect that they had a very clear meaning. We should be warned about this by the way that older children, or adults who know the child very well, will frequently be able to interpret seemingly incomprehensible sounds. Leila Berg quotes a perfect example of a Mum interpreting :

A small, sandalled girl, still a baby, aged about one and a half, stood outside a shop, pointing very excitedly down the street. 'ello ! ello ! ello ! ello !' Her mother came out of the shop and the child with tremendous excitement shouted again, still frenziedly gesturing. 'ello ! ello ! ello !' I thought she was greeting someone. But the mother looked the way the child was looking and said instantly, with identical pleasure and excitement, 'Oh yes ! that little girl has yellow flip-flops just like yours, hasn't she !' (*Look at Kids*)

I am sure it is not necessary to stress that a Mum whose response was 'Shut that horrible row !' or even 'Fiona, my darling, you are really making too much of a silly fuss' would have a limiting, even damaging, effect on the child's confidence and speech development.

As I have said, interpreting a child's early singing is even more tricky than interpreting speech. I think our best line is to assume that most of a child's vocalizing is significant and important, and be very careful not to discourage it. In particular, we must not fall into the trap of assuming that because it doesn't sound 'musical' it can't be musically important. Very young children can have a clear idea about specifically musical behaviour. Daniel, for instance, is very used to people singing and talking about singing. If you say to him, 'You can sing, can't you, Daniel ?' he will produce, a high-pitched, squeaky sound that is quite unlike his other vocal responses, and he will produce the same kind of sound each time you talk to him about singing. He is clearly singing in his own way. Similarly a baby will often join in with your singing by chanting or groaning or shouting in his own way, without any ability to carry the tune or the words. He is 'playing' at singing. This corresponds exactly to his play speech, or to the way in which children play at digging the garden or making jam tarts or driving a bus. It is a way of finding out what it is like to do the activity before having the skill to do it properly ; it is a trying-on of a role. As such it is a crucially important stage. If you make fun of the child, or try to pressure him to do it more accurately, you run the great danger of putting him off completely. We will return to this when we talk about singing songs and about rhythmic development.

Sentences and tunes
You may know that your baby is talking or singing to you, but he is not making patterns that are recognizable as sentences or tunes. He has learned to make *sounds* that are characteristic of the speaking or singing in his family ; he has taken in a good deal about the structure and the

nature of speaking and singing ; but there is still a big step to take. Even the few words we have heard him utter, like 'mama', are not labels he can consciously apply to his experience. They are closer to the noises made by many species of animals – the snarl of an interrupted lion, the purr of a cat being stroked, and so on. His early 'words' are known as 'holophrases'. They are very important, but it is only when he begins to string them together to convey meaning that he takes the final step into speech. In the same way, it is only when he begins to link sounds together into recognizable and repeatable patterns that he takes the final step into singing.

He can take such steps because his innate abi.ity to pick out patterns from a background give him a special skill. We call the speech pattern a language acquisition system : this is just a label to describe the way that children in all societies and cultures can *pick out* from the complex adult speech around them the important underlying patterns and rul es of speech. There is much learned argument about *how* this happens, but no questioning that what children do is much more than simply imitating what they hear. Imitating adults cannot begin to explain the things young children say. For instance, no adult taught Samantha to say, '*He* done'd it, Mummy', or Timmy to say 'You oughted not it', nor did Robert hear an adult refer to 'deers'. But at the same time we must be clear that the things the three children said are not just stupid mistakes or misunderstandings. They have listened to adults talking and picked out certain rules – about past tenses, or the way you form the negative, or plurals of words – then they have applied these rules to new situations. In our three cases English doesn't happen to behave according to the rules the children have deduced, but this doesn't affect the intelligence of the children's behaviour. It is very clear from many exampes of this kind that young children don't just learn *what* people say ; they learn *how* people speak. They don't just copy what people say ; they copy the ways people say things. They manage this because their language acquisition system enables them to recognize the patterns even in the seeming confusion of complex adult speech. This, as we shall see, is highly significant for their singing too.

As they identify these patterns they practise them in all sorts of ways, not just by talking with other people but in various kinds of play situations. One is the spiel, the kind of monologue that often accompanies play with cars or dolls or make-belief play – I am sure you have heard examples from your child. It often has a highly rhythmic quality and sometimes contains snatches of nursery rhymes or songs. Another practice situation is the pre-sleep monologue. When a small child is in bed, relaxed before going to sleep, he frequently talks to himself about subjects that concern him. This talk is very free ; much of it seems to be stimulated by the associations of words or their sounds and it usually includes much that can only be described as practice of vocabulary and syntax. Perhaps a couple of examples from Peter, aged two and a half, will remind you of the kind of things children do :

Banana . . .	(*which he'd had for supper*)
Big banana . . .	
Banana time . . .	
Banana in bed,	
In bed . . .	
In bed at bed-time . . .	
Banana go to bed at banana bed-time,	
Peter go to bed at Peter bed-time.	

'Sing a Song of Sixpence'	(*which he'd heard just before being*
Mummy sing that song . . .	*put to bed*)
Daddy sing that song . . .	
Peter sing that song . . .	
Gammer sing that song . . .	(*Grandmother*)
Everybody sing that song . . .	
Not Amber	(*our dog*)
No . . .	
Not Amber,	
Not Amber *not* sing that song.	

Andrew Wilkinson comments about pre-sleep monologues :
   The sentences have some resemblance to foreign language learning drills ; but they also resemble nursery rhymes and jingles. The poems which young children themselves produce . . . have . . . very similar characteristics. (*The Foundations of Language*)

   I find the links he makes with other kinds of language activity very revealing, especially since the third way of practising is in play situations with the adult, where there is a great stress on nursery rhymes and jingles, on making and repeating patterns of sound, on baby-talk and on throwing words backwards and forwards. It leads inevitably to very valuable nonsense play, which has already been mentioned.

   Through his language acquisition system and these various ways of practising, a child will pick up a certain amount of language even in a situation where he gets little adult help. However, the kind of language background he has at home, and the ways his adults speak with him, make his learning easier or more difficult, quicker or slower. Andrew Wilkinson claims that 'the fundamental fact in language development seems to be the nature of the child-adult dialogue.' Adults instinctively *teach* young children. At times they shorten what they say ; a mother will often say 'Bath time, Peter, bath time', rather than 'Come along Peter, it's time for you to have your bath'. They repeat key phrases, as in the previous example. They stress key words – 'Shoes, Katherine, shoes, let's put your shoes on' – and they often emphasize their meaning by waving the shoes or holding the child's foot. They comment on things that the child is doing or that they are doing – 'You *have* got a smelly bottom, haven't you. Let's wipe it clean. Let's make it nice and clean.' They show the child the actions or movements that go with a particular phrase or sentence – for instance they wave the child's hand, saying 'Say "bye-bye" to Daddy'. (Once again, isn't it interesting that all these patterns can be seen in the kinds of fingerplays and games with babies we talked about earlier?)

In turn the child selects the simpler patterns to imitate or use. This is made easier by the adults' clarification and simplification, but the child simplifies the speech patterns even further. His main technique in doing this is called 'stripping'. He tends to seize on the words that carry most information (usually nouns, verbs and adjectives) and to use those, leaving out prepositions, conjunctions and so on. For instance, instead of 'My Daddy is singing a song' he will probably say 'Daddy sing song'. This is also helped by the fact that 'content words' tend to be the ones that receive the stresses in adult speech; because of this they are the ones that his limited memory span can hold on to. This limited memory span also accounts for another of the child's stripping processes, that of repeating key words or phrases from the *end* of an adult's longer utterance. If you say to a young child, 'Go to the table and get the big tin', he will often say 'Get big tin'. It is significant though that his sense of the underlying structure enables him to repeat the words in the right order. He doesn't say 'Tin big get', nor does he say 'Big tin table'. He has perceived the pattern and the meaning of what was said, even if he cannot repeat all of it.

Another way in which adults teach is by expanding what the child himself says. Research has shown that they do this as much as 30% of the time. The yellow flip-flops incident is one example. Even clearer is to think of the ways a mother might expand, at different times and in different situations, her small daughter's remark, 'Dink, dink!':

'Oh, do you want a drink? You must be thirsty. Come on then, I'll get you one.'
'Yes, we must give Rover some water to drink — his bowl is empty. He's drunk it all.'
'Yes, that's Daddy's drink. It's beer. We bought it at the Off Licence, didn't we?'
'You've spilled your drink *again*! You silly girl, now your trousers are all wet. Be more careful!'

Through these expansions the little girl hears how her meaning can be communicated more precisely by using further words. At the same time she is given confidence that her speech can be understood. She is loved and encouraged and taught all at once.

We see identical development patterns in young children's singing, though because much of the child's vocalising is wordless it's more difficult for us to recognize or record it. Just as with speech, your baby makes lots of singing sounds during his babble and vocal play ; just as with speech it is the example and response of the adult that influences which of these sounds (if any !) the baby selects to use. Hence babies in the Appalachian Mountains of America learn to sing with the characteristic high nasal tone of the region ; babies in southern India learn to sing the quarter-tones and ornamentation characteristic of certain *ragas* ; babies of opera singers learn the vocal tone and vibrato of *bel canto*. But this will only happen if the child hears a great deal of unaccompanied, close-range singing by people with whom he feels secure. This is what makes it possible for him to 'strip', to imitate, to abstract usable patterns. It also makes it possible for him to learn the ways in which people sing – the 'how' of singing as well as the 'what'. As with speech, he has the ability to do this ; but, as with speech, he has to hear a very large range of singing patterns and hear them repeated frequently before this ability can come into play. Again, as with speech, it is very much more difficult for him to do this with complex models. Think how complicated the musical sounds heard on radio or record or TV are when compared with an adult's close-range, unaccompanied singing. It is no wonder that children who only hear such complex singing should be much less competent singers than those children whose adults sing to them.

At the very young age about which we are talking 'stripping' in singing shows itself in a number of ways. Sometimes the child's response is so slight as to be almost unnoticeable unless you know what you're looking for. For instance, I was playing the 'Aa-aa-aa-aa-bubble !' game (p. 8) with George, aged fourteen months. He watched my mouth intently. When I said 'Aa . . .' he would open his mouth slightly ; on 'bubble !' he would bring his lips together, making a very soft 'b' sound. This kind of 'soundless' joining-in is very common with babies. Another early way of 'stripping' is for the baby to do only the action to the song – for instance, to do the hand-patting in 'Pat-a-cake, pat-a-cake' but not to sing. Another is that he may sing 'strong' notes only, such as the final note of a phrase or verse ; in *Ding dong bell* he may only sing 'bell', and in *Baa baa black sheep* he may join in with the last word 'lane', having sung nothing before. These notes or words may not be sung in the 'right' place. Frequently the baby comes in with them a little after the adult, as if it takes a moment or two for him to realize the appropriate way of joining in. Sometimes it seems as though coping with words and tune together is too much, so the child either speaks the words or hums the tune, and sometimes he combines humming with speaking loudly the final word. These ways of joining in are the basis of his singing refrains and choruses, as we shall see in the next chapter.

Children also practise their singing in the same kinds of situations as they practise their speech, though, as I have explained, we frequently only realize that they are practising singing when they happen to repeat a snatch from a song we recognize. But if we listen carefully to their play we can often identify examples of singing practice – remember Daniel's high-pitched squeak or Katherine's singing with her biscuit tin ? During the spiel which often accompanies play you hear lots of vocalization which is closely related to singing if not actual song performance. Peter had a range of ululations – high-pitched yodels, wails, squeaks and slides, delivered with shattering volume and precision – which he used in his play. One of the most mind-bending went :

Another was :

Brrrrrrrrr_____

He also had a huge array of car, fire-engine, gunfire, laser, X-ray and other noises which he used, as well as snatches of nursery rhymes, songs and TV theme tunes with which he accompanied his play. Other children have a similar repertoire, though not all are quite as noisy as Peter ! Bedtime is another singing time for young children, especially if you sing a song or two as part of the bedtime ritual. You will often hear a child who is sung to in bed going on humming or singing, often one little fragment over and over again, as part of going to sleep. And, of course, play with adults often involves singing practice, though this will overlap very much with the joining in with actual songs that is a main subject of Chapter 5, 'Singing and making up songs'. The spontaneous play-singing is therefore probably the most important way a child builds up singing confidence, so you should be careful not to stamp on it as mere 'noise'.

Teaching singing by direct adult expansion of a child's singing doesn't happen very much, largely because singing is not the same kind of communication as speech. If your child makes a vocal sound or sings a note it is rare for you to be able to guess what the child is trying to sing and so to expand it for him. It happens most often when the child sings or says a snatch of a familiar song or rhyme as an encouragement to you to sing the whole of it, or when you are doing with him some of the improvised singing described later in this chapter. On the other hand, the nursery rhymes and songs you sing to him are very simply patterned forms which show him how to expand the fragments he invents in his play.

I must stress again the crucial importance of this singing *to* children, however young ; it is at least as important in their musical development as talking to them is in their speech development. You may be inhibited from doing so because you don't know the 'proper' songs for particular ages. Don't be ! There's no restriction on what you sing, except that it must be something you enjoy singing. Many people have the strange idea that a child who hears Maria Callas will somehow become more musical than one who hears Perry Como ; that *Your tiny hand is frozen* is somehow 'better' for children than *I wanna hold your hand*. This is rubbish. None of this music is of any use to a baby on record ; any of it will be musically meaningful if sung by an important adult, and so will be almost anything else. Many professional singers, in all sorts of styles, talk of their early and highly significant memories of hearing adults singing, like Doc Watson, the great American folk singer and instrumentalist :

My first introduction to music came from my memory of being held in my mother's arms very comfortably. I remember the feeling was very warm and the sound was like that of 'The Lone Pilgrim' being harmonized by the congregation. From my early childhood on, I can remember my mother singing. She'd sing around the house while churning butter, or while patching some of Dad's overalls that he'd worn the life out of. (*The Songs of Doc Watson*)

The quality of such singing is not terribly important either, as you will realize if you have ever heard Mrs General D. Watson sing. She has an ordinary, not very good voice, like most of ours, yet her singing was immensely significant to her child. You can sing what you like, for your own pleasure, and your child will get a tremendous amount out of it. He will have the pleasure of a simple ritual, a shared activity – 'the feeling was very warm'. He will be taking in a sense of musical shape and style – how tunes go and finish, and the way the patterns are repeated accurately from phrase to phrase and verse to verse. He will be storing away a range of musical patterns that will make his musical 'stripping' easier. He will be absorbing something of the power of songs to arouse and express emotion, to deal with serious subjects beyond his present understanding. Above all, he will be identifying with you as someone who makes and enjoys music, and thus he will be reassured that it is safe and proper for him to do the same.

Sing any songs that you know or learn ; but don't ignore the
importance of less formal singing, not using fixed songs at all. One of the
greatest problems of many children in learning to sing is that we make
much too rigid a division between singing (very formal and difficult) and
speaking (very ordinary and easy). Thus children are in danger of not
carrying over their speaking skill and confidence into their singing, even
though we have seen that in their early babbling and speech experiment
they make no distinction between sounds which are words and sounds
which are just vocalized tones. If, as frequently happens, the separation
is stressed by the adults speaking a lot but singing a little or not at all
(except in very formal situations like a hymn at a wedding), the child
may be very self-conscious and inhibited when, as at school, he is asked
to sing. You need to show your children from the beginning that there is
no separation, that speaking and singing are part of a continuum of vocal
sounds and that adults switch naturally from one to another.

A very helpful thing in the process is to chant or sing a remark to your
baby instead of speaking it. This sounds terribly unnatural again,
doesn't it ? But it really isn't. I am sure you have often listened to a Mum
calling in her child from the street or the garden. Quite naturally she calls
things that sound like this :

These are only approximate notations of course. The music makes it look
very formal, and obviously I'm not suggesting that Mums call their
children like soloists in *The Messiah* or the prima donna in an opera.
Nevertheless, their calling has a definite tune, largely because they are
pitching their voices across a distance. So there is nothing odd about
doing such calling (in the house, if you're embarrassed about the
neighbours hearing). No complicated tune is needed – you can do it on
one note :

41

Of course, it makes it more interesting if you can use more than one note, perhaps like this:

Dan—iel and Paul ———, wash your hands now.

You notice that the two notes used here – the cuckoo sound – also happened naturally in 'Johnny' and 'Samantha'. It is a very common interval in spontaneous singing and one that children themselves in many cultures use for making up chants and songs. I was passing through some flats at Victoria on a drizzly winter afternoon a couple of years ago. Coming towards me, head down, no coat, thoroughly damp and miserable, was a six-year-old boy. As I got closer I could hear him singing slowly under his breath:

I am a mon — ster,   I am a mon — ster,

I am pow er — ful,   I am the great — est

(and so on)

It is a particularly easy interval to sing, and so if you use it in play you may encourage your child to use it freely.

Another very good situation for spontaneous singing is when a child is doing some kind of rhythmic play, like rocking in a rocking-boat or swinging on a swing. There are lots of composed rocking and swinging songs, but why bother about trying to remember them? Why not just let your voice play in time to the swing?

Oo—wa, oo—wa;   oo — wa, oo—wa;   oo — wa, oo—wa; .....

There is no need for anything more than that – it's a splendid improvised song in itself, but if you get into the rhythm of it you may well find things like this coming out:

Swing swing, swing swing, swing swing,
swing swing, Swing a girl up and down,
back—wards & for—wards up and down, Jen—ny's swing—ing
up and down, back—wards & for—wards, up and down

(and so on)

It is very simple, you see, using only our two notes, but Jenny's delight will show how satisfying it is to her. Just as when you dance with your baby in your arms, the very simple pattern of pitch, repeated over and over in time to the movement of the swing, sinks deeply into a child's musical consciousness. Above all, the child becomes aware of such play songs as enjoyable and satisfying, and this encourages him to make up more of his own play songs.

Our two note pattern is not the only one you can use. All kinds of simple tunes can be used. You might try 'Hi-ho, hi-ho, it's off to dig we go' during a sandpit or gardening session. And don't think that you necessarily have to sing a song all the way through every time. Snatches of tune and words are usually enough :

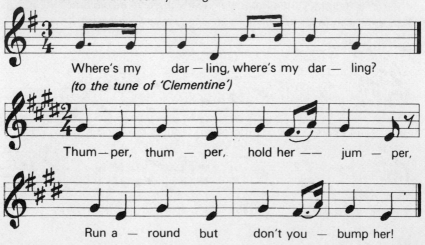

Where's my dar — ling, where's my dar — ling?
(to the tune of 'Clementine')

Thum—per, thum—per, hold her —— jum—per,

Run a — round but don't you — bump her!

43

You can use some snatch of a well-known tune, anything from a nursery rhyme to a Gary Glitter hit, to put some words to. Perhaps it might be *Come to the cookhouse door, boys* that you use:

John, come and put your coat on, Time to go to the swings.

or perhaps something like this, to the *Yellow Submarine* tune:

Put your boots on and but — ton up your coat.

But you don't have to be particularly bothered about the shape of the tune. You don't have to fit in to an existing tune. All you have to do is to show your child that singing can be spontaneous and informal. Don't be surprised or depressed if you don't find this easy to do at first, or if when you try it out it seems to your musical ear to go wrong. After all, how many times do you go to *say* something to your child and get mixed-up or tongue-tied? Quite often, if you are anything like me. The same will happen sometimes when you improvise snatches of tune; like all skills, it improves with practice.

It is very nice too if you can make up lines or verses to go into the simple songs you already sing with your children. They greet this with enormous delight. When Peter was nearly three years old and Katherine only just born we used to sing *Old Joe Clark* a lot:

Old Joe Clark

Chorus: Round and round, old Joe Clark, round & round I — say,

Round and round, old Joe Clark, now I'm going a — way.

Verse: I went down to old Joe's house, He in—vi—ted me for sup—per, I

stuck my head in the bread & cheese & I stuck my feet in the but—ter.

There are literally hundreds of traditional verses to this song, some of which we used to sing, but the favourite verses were two we made up during Peter's tea-time and Katherine's breast feed :

Peter Robert has for tea
A lovely piece of cheese,
But when he goes to eat it up
The crumbs fall on his knees.   *Chorus*

Katherine Mary drinks her milk
Out of Mummy's nipples.
She can't drink out of a cup
Because she is too little.   *Chorus*

Peter loved these above all others, and joined in vigorously with bits of them.

In connection with this there is a particular value in singing to all ages of young children the kind of songs that are intended to be made to fit the child or children you are singing with — songs about what you do outside, about the clothes they are wearing, about the daily routine. For instance, one of the most successful songs I have used has been this one :

The Clothes Song

Da—vid wears a blue shirt —, blue shirt —, blue shirt —,

Da—vid wears a blue shirt — All day long.

45

I usually sing a couple of verses about what I'm wearing, then say to the child, 'Would you like me to sing about what you're wearing ?' So we sing things like :

Michelle wears a stripey shirt,
   Stripey shirt, stripey shirt,
Michelle wears a stripey shirt
   All day long.

Michelle wears a blue ribbon. . . .

Michelle wears brown sandals. . . .   and so on.

It is very unusual to be allowed to stop before every single item of clothing has been sung about ; children sometimes partially undress in order to make sure you appreciate and sing about their pink knickers, or the plaster on their foot ! With very small children you will probably name each garment and then sing about it ; the child will participate by nodding, smiling, maybe humming, maybe touching or holding the piece of clothing being sung about. At a slightly later stage the child will want to tell you what to sing about. This can lead to minor complications. Michelle may say, 'Sing about my new special jeans with the rabbit on' – and it doesn't quite fit the tune as written ! You can, of course, exercise your adult editorial prerogative, and sing :

Michelle wears her new jeans . . . .

but I think it is much more valuable to say, 'Oh, that's a lot of words to squeeze in, isn't it ? Let's try', and then to sing something like :

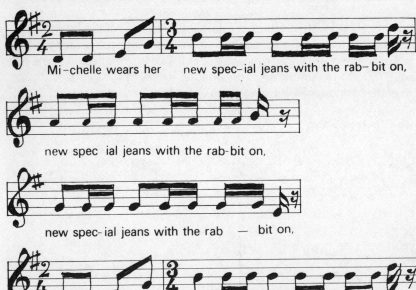

46

All   day   long.

It may look very complicated written down, as music usually does, but all you have done is to sing the words in the rhythm you'd say them, using the pattern of the tune. And because you are singing without written music, without accompaniment, you are completely free. If you want to leave out a note, or add a couple of beats, you can.

Singing about things a child does is another sure-fire activity. Any simple, repetitive tune will do to base your song on. Ones like *Skip to my Lou* are obviously convenient; another is *Here we go round the mulberry bush*, with verses like:

This is the way we yawn and stretch,
   Yawn and stretch, yawn and stretch,
This is the way we yawn and stretch
   When we get up in the morning.

This is the way we run downstairs . . .

This is the way we eat our food . . .

This is the way we clean our teeth . . .

But there are lots of other tunes and patterns. Here is an American folksong which I use a lot:

What shall we do when we all go out?

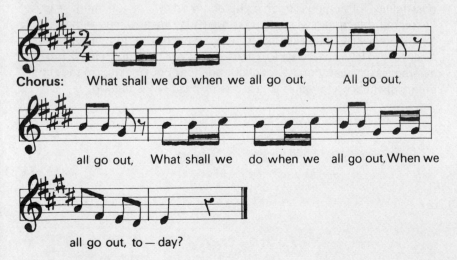

Chorus: What shall we do when we all go out,   All go out,

all go out,   What shall we   do when we   all go out, When we

all go out, to — day?

We will go to the High Road shops,
   High Road shops, High Road
      shops,
We will go to the High Road shops
   When we all go out today.   *Chorus*

We will buy some tins of beans. . . .   *Chorus*

We will look at all the cars. . . .   *Chorus*

We will change our library
   books. . . .   *Chorus*

We will go to the Common
   swings. . . .   *Chorus*

And so on, and so on. You can sing about almost anything you do, and the child's suggestions are likely to be the particularly interesting ones, of course.

Songs of this type can be found in a lot of books ; the two I have found most useful are *American Folk Songs for Children* by Ruth Seeger and *Music Activities for Retarded Children* by D. R. Ginglend and W. Stiles (see Bibliography for details). As well as being great fun, such songs have a wider significance. As the child joins in with you in making up verses he gets a great stimulus to his own invention, and we shall see in Chapter 5 how significant this is. Secondly, there is a particular involvement and closeness of relationship created by this kind of song — it is personal in the very deepest sense of the word. For a child to find that music is something he can create with and which can speak directly about himself is to learn a very important lesson.

By the time your child is beginning to talk fluently, the range of possibilities for singing is opening up enormously. For one thing, he is becoming able to sing whole songs and to play vocal games with you ; for another he can increasingly talk about what he is doing. (These are discussed in later chapters.) But already you will have given him a great awareness of vocal sound, a lot of confidence about making sounds and plenty of chance to practise : these are the basis of his singing.

4

Understanding sounds

A child's development from the kinds of activities described in Chapter 2, 'Sounds from things', is very natural and simple. It comes from his increased mobility and his increased ability to talk about what he is doing. In the first place he moves further afield, and so he finds more and more sound-making objects to explore. This is often a source of difficulty, as all parents know, and I have already made it clear that there is no necessity for the child to disembowel the kitchen cupboard. But even eliminating the things that he cannot be allowed to have, there is a lot left; and this enlarged range inevitably extends the child's musical possibilities. In the second place, talking becomes increasingly important as a tool for extending his musical experiment, especially as the child's own powers of speech and understanding enlarge, and true discussion at a simple level becomes more common.

You may be wondering why I lay such a stress on the importance of talk in this process. Perhaps you can see for yourself how significant it is by trying a simple experiment. Take a transparent plastic pot or jar with a lid and put into it some dried peas or rice or paper clips or drawing pins. Give it a single hard up-and-down shake and listen carefully to the sound. Do it again. How would you describe the sound? Put it into words.

Most people tend to say something like 'a dry rattling sound', which is a fair enough description. Now shake again several times and answer for yourself the following questions:

Does the pot make only one single sound when you shake?
Are there different sounds when the filling hits the lid? When it falls back to the bottom?

Which sound is crisper, more together?

Is the sound of the filling hitting the lid the first sound you hear?

Are there any sounds from the filling hitting the sides on the way up?

Any other little sounds you notice as a result of the shake?

When you have answered these questions for yourself, shake the pot again, listening very carefully.

After answering the questions I expect you found yourself aware of a greater complexity in the sound. That complexity of sound was present the first time, and you *heard* it the first time – but you didn't become aware of it because you were not thinking in those terms. Increasing your awareness of the sounds that are there is very largely the effect of language on listening and understanding. Because you could understand the questions and apply them to the sound, you were able both to focus your listening and to define and analyse what you were hearing. This would have been just as true even if you had not used my questions directly but had just determined to listen very carefully. Either you would have asked yourself mentally some focusing questions, like 'Is there some sequence of the sounds in time ?' ; or you would have isolated certain aspects of the sound and used language to put your impressions into precise thoughts or words.

The words don't do the listening for you, of course. They help you to organize your experimenting, to define what you are doing, to make precise observations, to generalize by relating the sound you hear to other categories of sounds or similar ways of making sounds. In short, they help you to understand. They don't do the emotional responding to the sound either, but they do make it possible for you to understand and organize your emotional response.

You may not be convinced about this effect of language. Catherine Landreth quotes a famous example from the training of aeroplane spotters during the Second World War. When they began they could identify only four different kinds of planes ; after certain aspects of wing flow had been pointed out to them and labelled, they could identify seventeen different kinds of planes. As she says :

A child who has many labels for identifying an object — big or little, round or square, red or blue, half or whole, hard or soft, etc. — has many ways of looking at, thinking about and remembering an object. (*Pre-School Learning and Teaching*)

This is particularly valuable with sound, which can't be seen, can't be examined repeatedly at length (as can a picture), but has to be remembered and examined mentally.

You can see from this the key role that language must play in the development of a child's response to sound and his understanding of it. Indeed, many people believe that 'deprived' children are not children lacking experience (which everybody has all the time) but children who have an inadequate symbolic system to organize and become aware of their experiences. Language is the main system of this kind. With limited language skill a child only *perceives* a small part of what he *hears*. With limited language skill his musical progress will be immensely hindered, whatever his musical potential. So a major part of his musical education will be helping him to acquire the language to talk and think about sound.

Talking about sounds

Where does the ability to talk and think about sounds start? As with many other things it starts with your child becoming aware of you doing it. He sees that you think it is important, and he realizes that there are some special words that can be used about the sounds he hears.

He also begins to realize that other people hear and see things from a different point of view, and this is something that can be learned through a *sharing* of experiences. Remember, all that is necessary in this process is for the adult to comment on sounds that the child is making, or that they can both hear. No special 'musical' comments – just the sort of thing that a Mum does naturally at home or when pushing the pram:

'You *are* doing some big bangs on the saucepan, aren't you! Bang! bang! bang!'

'Can you see the peas in the pot? Do you see them wiggle when I shake it? They bang against the sides and make a rattling noise. That's right, you shake.'

'Did that dog make you jump when he barked? Yes, there he is. He's not cross, he's wagging his tail. He's barking because he's excited – he opens his mouth and barks loudly . . .

'There's a big red bus coming along the road. Can you see it? Its engine makes a loud noise – brrm, brrm! There it goes.'

Do these quotes sound unnatural? not like you? I expect they do. Take any remarks like these out of context and they sound odd, but they are very much the kind of things one says to young children.

Do you feel that it is a bit ridiculous to be saying things like this to a youngster in a pram? Can't it wait until the child is four or five and able to understand properly? The answer is, 'No, it can't.' The advantages to the child of an environment where he hears and is involved in a lot of talking are at their greatest at around two years old, and fall off very sharply after five. The nursery class or playgroup is already too late to start this. So carry on with your talking.

Do you notice something very important about the remarks I quote? They are not concerned directly with the sounds themselves but with the things making them, the mood or situation in which the sounds are made – in other words, with putting the sounds in their context. This is a very significant part of young children's growing understanding of sound, and we shall return to it later. This kind of talking also encourages the child to make his own observations or comments, to ask questions, to show the adult what he knows or doesn't know, to become involved in the process of discussion. The significance of this cannot be overstressed. As James Britton comments:

Obviously there are a great many things for a child to talk about when his parents can listen. What they can do then is probably something that can never be done at any other time by anybody else. The Russian psychologists we have quoted [Luria and Yudovitch ; Vinogradov] believe that the higher forms of human mental activity begin their development as a process shared between two people – a child and an adult : that qualitative changes take place in a child's mental process as a result of speech and co-operation with his parents in infancy. (*Language and Learning*)

Think again of the Bruno Bettelheim theory that a lack of adult response to a child's questions and explorations greatly inhibits his curiosity. Your talking and sharing of your child's experience is fundamental to his learning.

The most staggering aspect of this is that the talking and sharing does not necessarily have to be with an intelligent or educated adult. Two pieces of research done in America are fascinating. In the first, researchers were looking at the abilities of pre-school Negro children in New York, and they found a few who were distinctly more able than the rest. When they investigated they found that the only big difference between these and the rest was that the more able children each had a grandmother living with the family – so they got much more talk with an adult. Even more striking was an experiment with orphanage children below the age of two. Twenty-four children of low ability were divided into two roughly matched groups. One group of twelve was left at the orphanage ; each of the other twelve was sent to be looked after by a weak-minded adolescent girl living in a mental home. The idea was to see whether the close contact with one person, rather than the more impersonal care at the orphanage, would make a difference. After two years the researchers found that the children looked after by the girls showed great increases in measured intelligence when compared with the orphanage group. Even more staggering – when the children were contacted twenty-one years later it was found that the group looked after by the girls had reached an average twelfth grade level in school (that of normal seventeen-year-olds), whereas the orphanage children averaged fourth grade level (ten-year-olds), a difference of seven to eight years ! The fact that the adolescent girls and the grandmothers had this effect in all the cases is striking, but not particularly surprising if you consider that they were in the particularly intimate relationship with the children that we have seen to be the crucial element in early learning. I expect, like most parents, you have been worried at times about your ability to help your children learn. You can see there is no need for your worry !

Making sense of the sounds around us
All this talking about sounds is useless if your child cannot listen carefully to the sounds around him. Many children in a town or city can't

— and I am not thinking about those who are deaf. Lots of ordinary children can't. The reason is that listening doesn't just involve hearing a sound. It also involves being *ready* to hear the sound. You have to be able to pay attention, to concentrate, to focus your listening on the sound you want to hear and to cut out other sounds you don't want to hear. These skills have to be learned by the child, and the urban child often finds learning them more difficult than one who lives in the country.

The 'landscape' of a modern town or city is often ugly and confusing — so is its 'soundscape'. The jumble of buildings, lampposts, graffiti, signs and notices make it very hard for a child to pick out important visual details ; the jumble of raucous, intrusive and sometimes ugly sounds makes it very hard for a child to pick out a particular sound, let alone identify what is making it. It is much easier in the country. For a start, the country is quiet. Loud sounds are immediately obvious to the listener. Many delicate sounds can be heard, and the identification of sounds like a wagtail's cry, the bleat of a lamb in pain, the squeal of a rabbit taken by a hawk, is an integral part of country life. Even mechanical sounds become part of this careful and significant listening. I remember my eighty-year-old Grandad in Breconshire cocking his head and saying 'Listen, Dai-bach, Gwyn Jeffries is hay-making in his bottom field'. The field was three-quarters of a mile away, and out of sight. Another time we were standing at the back of the cottage and Grandad said 'The postman's coming.' It was three minutes later when the van came up the hill — Grandad had heard its characteristic sound from across the valley, when it was heading towards us. In the country you need to know about such sounds, so children pick up from the adults around them the importance of listening, the background information and the physical disciplines involved. They also have plenty of chance to practise.

This can happen with city children. Billy is the six-year-old son of a motor mechanic, and can identify a wide variety of cars by their engine note alone. As a rule, though, city noise is so intensely overpowering and complex that we all have to blot out much of it. We do identify some sounds, but many we don't bother with. Mechanically produced music frequently surrounds us. It is rarely quiet. There is little motivation or opportunity for children to listen carefully unless their adults can encourage it.

In this situation many young children don't develop the attention and focusing skills. They don't understand clearly that sounds are always produced by a sound-making object of some kind. They aren't clear about the basic ways of producing sound. As a result you need to help them to listen ; you need to relate sounds very closely to the world of everyday objects and happenings. We've already seen how this is based on the kind of talking that adults do spontaneously with young children, whether about the domestic objects they are playing with, or about the sounds they hear when they are out.

Several activities will help a lot with this.

Firstly, one way of helping and preparing a young child to make sense of the jumble of sounds he hears outside and inside the home is to take every opportunity to talk about and imitate the sounds that things make, to name the things, to place them in their context. One simple opportunity often arises with pictures of things – in newspapers or magazines, in story books, or in special books about things that make sounds, a number of which are now available. A book like *I Hear – sounds in a child's world* contains simple pictures of things that make distinctive and familiar sounds (clocks, ambulances, lions, etc) and of actions associated with particular sounds (clapping, whistling, sneezing, etc). Looking at the pictures with a child, you can ask him to name anything he recognizes. Ask too what sort of sound the object or the action makes. If he can't tell you, you say things like : 'When you sneeze, you go *A-tchoo*' and you encourage him to make the sound with you. When he is used to this, and is familiar with a lot of the pictures, pick a page and make the sound of one of the things illustrated. 'Can you show me the thing that makes this sound ?' Lots of other games can be played with the pictures and sounds from this book – a number are outlined in the introduction.

A child will naturally link up such games with the sounds he hears and the things he sees making them when he is out of the house, going shopping with his Mum, for instance. This is a great help to his identification of them.

When you talk about the things you and your child see, either in a book or in the house or street, the discussion can lead naturally into telling stories that include sounds. Another kind of book useful here is the sort that tells a story with indications of the sounds that go with the story. A good example is *The Listening Walk*, which describes the sounds a boy hears on a walk with his Dad and their dog Major :

My dad walks along very slowly, puffing his pipe. His shoes go *dup, dop, dup, dop, dup, dop*.

Of course, as well as reading the story you can both imitate the sounds – and this links up with some of the games described in Chapter 3.

Even better than using a book, and far more meaningful and enjoyable to the child, is for you to *tell* a story including some simple sounds, whether made with the voice or with improvised instruments – this links up naturally with the use of a book like *I Hear*, since familiarity with a lot of vocal sounds gives both you and your child a wide range to draw on. Any kind of story is usable, but particularly good are those that relate to things he is familiar with, especially if the story can be made to include things that are currently interesting him.

Let's have an example. This story was stimulated by seeing a building site, and was told to a young child used to going to fetch an older brother from school.

The Building Site
Paul and his Mum were going to fetch Paul's big brother David from school, but they were very early, because they'd finished the shopping very quickly.

'Let's walk down to school slowly' said Paul's Mum. 'Perhaps we'll see something interesting.' They walked down the road, and Mum's heels made footstep sounds on the pavement.
>(*Tap the rhythm of the footsteps with fingers on the palm of the hand, or with two bricks, or sticks.*)

By the road there was a building site, and as they got nearer they could hear some very interesting sounds. They went close and looked.
'I can hear a big banging sound,' said Paul. 'Who's making that sound?'
>(*Bang on thighs or cardboard box, slowly*)

'It sounds like something very heavy,' said his Mum. 'Look over there.'
>(*Repeat the sound*)

They both looked, and they could see a workman with a heavy sledgehammer. He was knocking a big wooden post into the ground with slow, heavy blows.
>(*Repeat the sound*)

'That's it,' said Paul, 'and I can hear someone else hammering too. But he hasn't got a big sledgehammer.'
>(*Tap something metallic that doesn't ring: tap quickly and lightly*)

'I can't see anyone with a small hammer,' said his Mum. 'Can you?'
'Yes,' said Paul, 'over there, mending the fence.'
>(*Repeat the sound*)

Paul was right. The man mending the fence was knocking in small nails with an ordinary hammer. He hammered quite quickly.
>(*Repeat the sound*)

Paul and his Mum were looking and listening for some more sounds on the building site, when suddenly they heard a sound they weren't expecting. It was the church clock striking four o'clock.
>(*Tap something metallic that does ring, a metal eggcup, for instance. Count the four strikes out loud*)

'Goodness gracious, it's four o'clock,' said Paul's Mum. 'David will be coming out of school, and we're not there! Come on, Paul, let's run!'
>(*Make running footsteps as above*)

When they got to the school gate David was just coming out, looking for them. Paul told David all about the sounds they'd heard, and on the way back home they stopped by the building site and listened to them again.

Perhaps I ought to stress that the very ordinary nature of this story is one of its greatest strengths. It is exactly the kind of thing that most people (including a lot of young children) can make up, stimulated by the ordinary sights and sounds around them. If such things don't provide any stimulus for you, many of the stories for children of this age, like the Topsy and Tim stories, contain incidents or ideas that you can use as the basis for similar stories of your own. But you will need to adapt them to your own situation.

The immediate value of a story like this is that it interests the child, and the inclusion of sounds itself encourages and focuses his careful listening. But with most children their interest rapidly becomes a wish to be more directly involved ; by making the vocal sounds with you ; by suggesting or joining in with a related song or rhyme ('Paul hammers with one hammer', or 'This is my little house', for instance) ; by taking over the making of the instrumental sounds themselves ; by suggesting other sounds that might be included (building site sounds, for instance) and by finding or suggesting ways that these sounds may be made. This has immense value, of course. It helps the child to realize the potential of using the combining sounds for dramatic and musical effect, and to become confident in his own ability to do this. This confidence and experience will be invaluable later at school, when he is likely to be encouraged to create his own dramatic or musical structures by experiment with a group of other children. Also, the experience of making sounds within a simple structure and having to meet the demands of the story (for example, the running footsteps have to be faster than the walking steps) is one basis of performance skill, which will be an invaluable asset in his later music making.

Listening games
These ways of talking about sounds, looking at pictures, storytelling, imitating sounds, are all tremendously valuable in focusing the child's attention on the sounds he may hear and the contexts in which they may occur. But in the sound jumble of the city it is hard for the child to pick out the sounds around him, to hear them clearly, to develop his powers of attention and discrimination. In any case, research findings suggest that a child's ability to pick out sounds from a confused background may develop more slowly than we think, and may need a good deal of assistance. So there is a real place for the adult to help by playing some simple games in ways and at times when the child can really concentrate. (I should not need to tell you that the radio and TV should be off, and noisy older, or younger, children should be out of the room.)

One game is to use an everyday object to make different sounds ; for example, a sheet of scrap paper. I often say to a child something like : 'Do you know that you can make lots of different sounds with a piece of paper ? Watch and listen very carefully and see if you can tell me how

I'm making this sound.' Then I tear the paper . . . 'Yes, you're right, I tore the paper ; it made a tearing sound. Listen to the tearing sound again. . . . Do you know any other ways of making a sound with the paper ?' The child has a go, tapping or shaking or stroking or crumpling up the paper. We talk about his way of making the paper sound, and then he repeats it, so we can both listen carefully to the characteristic quality. So we go on, making sounds and talking about them and listening to them for as long as the child is interested, or until the game changes into something else, which often happens. For instance, I was once doing this with a small group of children, and a little girl called Danielle said that the shaken paper sounded like thunder to her. We started singing *I Hear Thunder*, to the tune of *Frere Jacques* :

I hear thunder, I hear thunder ;
Hark, don't you ? Hark, don't you ?
Pitter-patter raindrops, pitter-patter raindrops,
I'm wet through ; so are you.

Danielle shook her paper vigorously every time we came to the thunder line, and this was so satisfying to her that when I suggested that we should go on to something else she refused. The other children were getting a bit fed up with this – not because they disliked the activity but because they didn't have anything special to *do*. So I asked, 'Can you think of a part of this rhyme where you could do something as well ?' Obviously, the raindrops ! so they 'pattered' with their fingers or their voices or both, and everyone was delighted. This is the kind of unexpected development that will often come from an initial activity. There is no way to prepare for it ; you just have to be flexible and use any ideas – yours or the children's – to keep things going.

This is particularly important when you are dealing with very young children. Indeed, with such children it is quite likely that you should not think of organizing a fixed game, but simply of playing with the child. What he may want to do is often more interesting than you would plan. I remember an episode with Marcus, then just two, which contained lots of interesting things. Marcus came into the room with a box of small glass beads (Galts !) that he had got from Katherine. 'Katherine given me sweets,' he said, and shook the box very violently. 'Nice sweets . . . my sweets,' he said, and he tapped the lid with his left hand. Unexpectedly this too made a rattling sound. He was delighted. He tapped with his left hand and listened several times. Then he stopped, and was obviously thinking. He changed the box into his left hand and tapped with his right. It worked ! He gave a great beaming smile. He put the box down on the floor, opened it and took out a small handful of beads. One by one he named the colours – then he dropped the handful on to the hardboard floor. They skittered and rolled ; and Marcus, after a moment riveted by the sound and sight, hissed and shook his hands horizontally very fast, fingers outstretched. Then he got out another handful and repeated the process, complete with sounds and movement. The beads were very small, the box was very big, and after two more handfuls I could bear it no longer ! I had visions of hours on hands and knees under the furniture. 'Let's pick some up !', I said and I dropped one back into the box, saying 'Ping !' This, thank goodness, was fine, and Marcus and I alternated our dropping and pinging. (When I inadvertently omitted to say 'ping', he reminded me forcibly.)

When all the beads were back and he had put the lid back on, a gleam came into his eye. Before he could start over again, I hastily substituted a transparent plastic pot with a snap-on lid, containing some larger wooden beads. Marcus shook this a couple of times and then demanded, 'Open it !' He tipped out the beads, then picked up one and dropped it into the pot, saying 'Ping !' – but the sound was much heavier than that made by the glass beads, and he was obviously worried. He picked up another wooden bead, dropped it into the pot and looked at me anxiously. There was a pause, but he wouldn't look away – so I said, 'Bonk !' A great smile came across his face. 'Bonk !' he said happily and popped in the rest of the beads to the accompaniment of his new word.

When he had finished he went straight to the box of glass beads again. He took out glass beads and the wooden beads, then started dropping them alternately into the appropriate pot with the appropriate word – 'Ping ! Bonk ! Ping ! Bonk ! . . .' At this moment his Mum, late for her appointment, arrived and carried him off – to his intense annoyance ! I can only speculate on what he might have gone on to do. One thing is clear however. I could never have planned that particular game – but what a lot went on ! Many of the best games with young children will be quite unpredictable. This is good. Nevertheless, provided that you are prepared to be flexible and to let the child show you how *he* wants the game played, there is no harm in setting up some simple activities.

Another good one is the Sounds Game. Ask the child to find two things that make sounds and to show you how the sounds are made. He may bring you a box of beads and a stick to bang. Talk for a bit about the things and the sounds they make. Then ask him if he thinks he can tell you, just by listening, which one is making a sound. If he likes the idea, hide the two things away. (A cardboard box on its side, as in the illustration, is a good way of doing it, since you can have it on a table-top or on your knees, and it discourages the very natural instinct of the child to peek round a screen !) Play one of the sounds *very gently* and see if he can distinguish it ; then the other ; and so on. Don't hesitate to play the same sound two or three times running – that's all part of the fun.

You can play this game, in my experience, with any child you know well, as long as his speech is sufficiently developed to understand the questions and to give the answers. Certainly at the age of two plus the majority of children can play this with their mothers. Once you have

introduced the game with objects that the child finds himself, you can go on to play it with things *you* find, provided that you take care to talk about the things with the child and give him a chance to play the sounds himself before you hide the objects. For instance, you might play it with a bunch of keys and a metal eggcup to make the different sounds, or you might play it with some of the paper sounds from the game described above, provided the child has already got used to making and naming the sounds that the paper makes.

You may well find that as the child gets used to this game, he may suggest having more than two objects at a time. This is fine, provided that it is *his* suggestion, but I am a bit doubtful about pressing under-fives to tackle more than three objects at a time. It is better to make the task more demanding gradually by chosing pairs of things that make very similar sounds (two metallic ringing sounds, perhaps) and so encourage more and more subtle discrimination between the two, rather than making the game more and more complex by adding extra things.

All such games with sounds are bound to involve and provide practice in listening skills — attention focusing, concentrating, discriminating. You will probably have noticed some other features of them. The objects used are always things the children are familiar with, and they are always talked about to make sure that they are related clearly to the child's experience. This is important because of the way we perceive and understand sounds. We always have to fit what we hear into our previous experience – to make sense of it – or we don't hear it properly. The main tool in doing this is, of course, language. Hence the stress on the *talking* about familiar objects. Another important feature of the games is that the child usually sees the object as well as hearing the sound it makes. I think this is necessary in the early stages, because disembodied sound is very tricky to concentrate upon and understand. Have you ever had the experience of listening to something on the radio that you want to hear, but finding in the middle that you have not actually been listening for the last bit? Even as a teenager I used to listen to Test Match commentaries or Promenade Concerts with my eyes fixed on the loudspeaker grill of the set! Young children don't naturally or easily separate one area of sensory awareness from the others, and they need the help of every clue in making sense of things. Thus starting with a situation which enables them to see, move *and* hear is very useful. For instance, here is a game I play with the pot of peas we listened to earlier.

I start by talking with the child about the pot. 'What can you see in the pot? It's got a lid on so that the peas can't fall out. You can't eat these peas like this because they're dry and hard. Mum would have to cook them in some water to make them soft.' (This isn't my script for the conversation, of course! You can't lay down how you talk with a child. For one thing the child will intersperse his own comments and questions; for another he may well want to handle the pot, to take out the peas and so on. However, this is a fairly common sort of pattern to such a conversation.) When I feel that the pot is fully understood, I go on to introduce the element of sound. 'Are the peas making any sound now? No, that's right, they're quite still.' Then I shake the pot. 'Did you hear the sound when I shook the pot? The peas wiggled and rattled – did you see them? I'll do it again. Can you wiggle your fingers like the wiggling peas? . . . Very good! Can you stop wiggling as soon as I stop the sound? . . . That's very clever!' I shake the pot in irregular patterns, with lots of pauses and false starts, which always make the child laugh. You can see how the chance to see the process of the sound-making and to respond by movement helps a child both to listen and to understand. I go on with the game (whether at the same time or on a later occasion) by introducing a different sound from the pot, probably by making the peas 'jump' sharply, and I get the child to 'jump' with his hands. In the middle I do things like keeping the pot still but making my left shoulder jump. This too causes a lot of giggling! Then we sometimes play a game where I say, 'If I make the peas rattle, you wiggle your fingers; if I make them jump, you make your fingers jump. But I'm not going to tell you which I'm going to do first, so you look and listen very hard.' This is quite demanding for a young child, but he greatly enjoys it, especially if we vary it so that he can wriggle or jump with his whole body. He also enjoys making the sounds himself for me to move to!

You can make the game even more demanding, and focus even more on the specific listening skill. When the child is confident with the game, I often play with the pot hidden away in the cardboard box on my lap. He then has to get his clues purely from listening, though his response is still the easy one of movement. This gradual process towards more 'abstract' listening is particularly valuable for urban children, as we have already seen. But you notice that it *follows* a great deal of confidence-giving and experience-giving activity and talking. To me it is precisely the lack of such confidence and experience that makes listening problems for many urban children.

The significance of such listening games

It is easy to underestimate the importance of very simple games in children's growing understanding of music. We see better why they are important if we think what a game does. It structures some area of experience, making it simple enough for the child to control and be secure with. The structure of the experience makes specific demands on the child, but the enjoyable nature of the game encourages him to meet them. Meeting the demands is intensely satisfying, so you find that a child setting up a game usually adds refinements or complexities as he becomes more confident about the basic structure. We saw this happening with Marcus and the beads.

The famous American educationalist John Holt, who is fascinated by the games children play with adults, has summed up the value of games in a passage from his book *How Children Learn* :

The spirit behind such games should be a spirit of joy, foolishness, exuberance, like the spirit behind all good games, including the game of trying to find out how the world works, which we call education. But in an even more narrow sense games like these are educational. They give a child a stronger feeling of cause and effect, of one thing leading to another. Also, they help a child to feel that he makes a difference, that he can have some effect on the world around him.

Understanding cause and effect ; developing confidence ; enjoying himself ; once again these basic ingredients in a child's learning are being stressed.

It is not surprising that when you play games with children you very often find that they want to take the dominant role. Thus a child playing the Sounds Game will frequently want to use the cardboard box himself to make sounds for you to identify. This is immensely valuable and should be encouraged, but don't be surprised or cross if you find that the game has suddenly become something rather different from the way you began it – a boo game or a piece of dramatic play, for instance ! It is also easy to dismiss such games as being rather trivial, not really concerned with major matters, whether musical or educational (if you can separate the two). But interesting and important issues do emerge from them.

For instance, the Sounds Game frequently reveals the overwhelming concern of some children to get right answers, and the strategies they use to do so. I can give a simple example of this. When playing (with a group of children) the game using the two sound sources in the cardboard box, I often start by playing the same sound twice running. The first time all the children say correctly 'It's the box of beads', but when I play the same sound again at least one child often says confidently 'It's the stick!' It is important to realize that this is not a stupid answer – quite the reverse. What the child is doing is *predicting* what the sound is going to be instead of listening and identifying the sound as I want him to do. He wants to give the right answer. What you mustn't do in this situation is to say firmly, 'Wrong', showing the child up as a fool and probably convincing him (and the others) that your game is unpleasant and risky. In any case, you don't need to do this. If you are playing with a single child, just make the same sound again and ask what it is. If the child originally identified the sound correctly, he is in a position to put himself right. He will usually say 'Oh – that's the beads,' and when you play the other sound, 'And that's the stick.' If you are playing with a group, you usually find that when you play the sound the second time you get contradictory answers from the group – some say 'beads', some say 'stick'. In that situation you only have to say 'We don't seem to agree. I know – I'll play the same sound again ; we'll all listen *especially* carefully and see if we can be sure.' And they all are, because their listening is focused and not complicated by other strategies or ways of guessing.

Sometimes a child, particularly an older one, will deliberately make a ridiculous answer. This may be teasing, if he knows you well – or it may be a strategy of deliberate failure. As John Holt says :

If you can't play a game the way it is supposed to be played, turn it into a game that you can play. If you can't do it right, do it wrong, but so obviously wrong that everyone will see that you are not trying to do it right, and that you don't think it is worth trying to do right.

Children whose confidence has been sapped by bad experiences early are particularly liable to do this, but any child may on a day when he doesn't feel like the game. It reflects how individual children's responses are ; how complex it is doing demanding things with a large group of children ; and how essential it is that most of such activities with young children should be done by adults who know them well. In particular it stresses how careful you must be not to press a game like this when the child is not keen.

Clearly the kinds of games I have described are not basically concerned with getting right answers. So what are they concerned with ? One thing is that they give children confidence and skill in the separation of sight from sound – something we have already talked about over the child dropping the rattle from the pram. At the same time, the use of ordinary familiar objects to make the sounds (and talking about them) roots the sounds, even when they are made by something out of sight, in the child's everyday experience. Another thing is the development of listening skills and of habits of concentration. Children are already encouraged by many aspects of the modern world to react only to those things that make a great impact on their hearing, whereas we want them to use listening as a tool, a sensitive tool to explore and find out things that might not otherwise come to their attention. As with any other tool, you need to develop the skills to use it. Basically you do this by presenting children with situations which are interesting enough to make them want to listen and simple enough to make listening possible, but demanding enough to develop their concentration and discrimination. Listening should be something very positive and dynamic, not passive, and games like these make children *use* their listening skill.

Connected with this is another aspect of the Sounds Games: playing the sounds *very quietly*. It is easy to involve and excite people by playing sounds very loudly. Musicians as diverse as Tchaikovsky and the Rolling Stones have done this with great effect. There are dangers, however, quite apart from the growing one of deafness! What do you do when once you have caught up people by loudness? The tendency is to escalate — more brass, drums and cannon in a performance of the *1812 Overture*, more instruments and amplifiers for *Satisfaction*. This has created an artistic problem for thousands of years. 'This time we'll have 500 Christians eaten by lions *and* fifty pairs of gladiators'; 'This time we'll have 100 chorus girls with ten changes of costume *and* a real waterfall on stage.' Once you start on this route there is only one way onward — bigger and bigger, but rarely better and better. The trouble is that in art size and importance are largely subjective. Once you are used to 100 chorus girls and a waterfall, they do not seem particularly important.

But there is an escape route. Instead of compelling attention by size, you can offer a person something small-scale, intimate, inviting, something that becomes increasingly significant and important to them as they explore it. It is fascinating that there is a rapidly growing interest in Early Music, which is domestic in scale, and in instruments like the lute, which draws your attention to it, rather than attacking you with its sound. Meaningful experiences are those in which you become personally involved, and an adult can make most things important to the young child with whom he uses them. Of course, something small-scale and quiet can easily be overlooked by the insensitive, particularyl if they are used to the loud, the large-scale. All this suggests that it is important to get children used to the small-scale, to the seemingly unimportant object which with attention and involvement yields its riches. Much of what I do with young children is of this kind, attracting them by a game situation which can reveal the potential of small ordinary things that they can later explore and fully experience.

You can see from all this that much is involved in such simple games as the ones I described earlier. But I must stress again that there is a danger in such games. Though they are flexible and easily adaptable to the particular responses of children, they perhaps imply that adults should always structure 'educational games' and impose them on children. This is misleading, as John Holt again makes clear:

The best games with little children flow easily and naturally from the situation of the moment. We are not likely to get good games by planning them far in advance, but we probably will get them if we play with children just for the fun of it. And whatever the game is, we must be ready to give it up, instantly and without regret, if the child is not enjoying it. It's tempting to think, 'If I can just get him to do this for a while, he will enjoy it.' But he won't — and we won't. (*How Children Learn*)

A book like mine can describe things that children do, and can outline activities which are likely to help children to develop in certain ways, but only if they are ready and are interested. Being aware of a child's interest and readiness is one of the most important qualities for someone using these kinds of activities.

Scientific experiment
Games help understanding, help attention and focusing, help the development of the language necessary for a full awareness of sound. They are immensely valuable. But talking about games must not distract us from the need for children to experiment themselves with materials if they are to come to a real understanding of their properties. We have seen this process in operation throughout the book, and nothing I have said about organizing games is meant to detract from it.

However, when stressing the need for experiment it is easy to fall into another trap — that of assuming that an adult's proper role is to divorce himself completely from a child's experiment, to provide materials and get out of the way. This is a misunderstanding at two levels. It is true that some children will be inspired by imaginative and attractive materials, but most children at some time will need adult help and interest if they are to become aware of the possibilities of the materials. They will certainly need adult guidance in safe and appropriate behaviour with the materials, especially those which are more complex. This is at the practical level: at a more fundamental level, the fear of interfering in a child's experimenting is often a misunderstanding of the nature of a child's play. To me a child's play is always an interaction between himself, the materials of his play and the social expectation (whether in the shape of adult contact or of the accepted rules of conduct). In many cases the child dictates the pattern, but often the adult shapes and structures what goes on and sometimes the materials themselves are clearly the shaping factor. But whichever influence is the most powerful in dictating the shape of the play, all three are always present to some degree. Thus the question should always be 'How does the adult best influence the child's play ?', not 'How can the adult avoid influencing the child's play ?'

In any case, in the kinds of flexible situation I have described young children have plentiful opportunities to alter the adult's games or to experiment with the materials in their own ways. You will frequently find that the child takes great delight in the objects you use for musical games and may well want to commandeer them to play with freely, to experiment with, to talk about further with you. This may take the form of make-belief play, as when Peter used a Sellotape tin containing paper clips to be a 'deadly poison gas spray' in one of his many assassination games ! Sometimes a child will repeat one of the musical games you have played, as when Noelle did the paper tearing in the Wendy House to an audience of two dolls, a golliwog, a teddy bear and three large wooden bricks (presumably imported to make the group worthy of her attention). If this happens, you will often find the child doing the game 'wrong' or altering the activity. Don't worry ! This kind of make-belief play has great importance for a child's understanding.

Piaget believes that the child uses such play to come to terms with his experience. He is faced with a mass of new information, some of it baffling, some of it seeming to contradict things he knows, some of it disturbing. By taking the experience and reliving it, by changing it around, by taking parts of it to use in a game of his own devising, he can come to terms with it. Perhaps Peter found the sudden rattle of the paper clips startling ; by making it a weapon that *he* controlled and that startled other people he could manage. Perhaps Noelle, although enjoying the paper-tearing, felt a little anxious and exposed ; by doing the game to her 'audience' she reasserted her own confidence and competence. (It is fascinating that she, and many children replaying an adult game, punished her audience harshly for any failure , as if making explicit a vague feeling of unease that she had experienced during the game.) It is probably significant that this make-believe play is at its peak between two and five, the period when a child is exposed to the greatest amount of new and puzzling material. It is also important to realize that doing something 'wrong' *deliberately* is a very powerful way of asserting your understanding of 'right'. Just think of nonsense rhymes – they are only funny because you understand that they are nonsense. As Chukovsky says about the child : 'every departure from the normal strengthens his conception of the normal.' So don't get worried if your child uses the materials in a different manner.

Another common way in which a child extends the use of the objects from the games is to find other things like them – other kinds of shakers, other things to tap together, and so on. This is paralleled by the way a child will often find objects to make sounds to be fitted into a story with sounds that you've told – 'Mum, I've got a cement-mixer for the story', waving your egg-beater. This tendency is likely to become stronger from about the age of three. The drive to experiment in a more 'scientific' way shows a significant upsurge between three and a half and five years. This is partly because at this age the child becomes increasingly able to put a plan into words, to set himself a goal, to formulate a hypothesis about something. The pattern of words helps him to resist distractions. You know how often a toddler will set out to do something but be distracted by a toy or sound he comes across on the way. When he gets older he will be better able to remember what he told himself he was going to do, and so continue on his way to do it. He is also increasingly able to use words to stand for things. Earlier, only the presence of the objects themselves would have enabled him to remember the sounds they made. Now he becomes increasingly able to collect his experiences mentally, and to make generalizations from them. The young chimpanzee, who was originally superior in his abilities, is being left further and further behind.

As your child's exploration begins to be more systematic, and he begins to show interest in sorting things, in categorizing, in seeing the links between things, there are certain ways that you can help to develop his understanding of sounds. From an early stage some sound-making objects will have a particular significance for the individual child – we have already talked about Katherine and her biscuit tin. It helps if you acknowledge this, and one of the best ways is to have a table, shelf, cardboard box or plastic washing-up bowl for your child's selection of sound-making objects. When this gets too full, you can usually reduce the number by pointing out the congestion to him and asking him to make a selection. If he selects them all (!) it sometimes works to switch tactics and point out that a lot of them make a very similar sound ; which of the shakers makes the most interesting sound and which of the biscuit tins ? If he then demonstrates that they all make slightly different sounds (which makes them special), you are beaten, but you can console yourself with the reflection that you have helped to develop a very sensitive appreciation of sound. You can always provide another washing-up bowl !

The existence of a collection of sound-making objects that have been experimented with enables you to help him to clarify his ideas about sounds, and to generalize. Again, the process is largely one of talking. 'Which of your things do you shake to make a sound ?' 'How many of your things are made of metal ?' 'I've picked up two of your things that make sounds. In what way are they the same ?' 'Show me all the things that sound like bells.' Any question, comment, game, or observation that helps to focus his attention on the similarities and differences between sounds (and the things that make them) will be immensely helpful. As always, the child himself and the things he does and says will give you the best clues. You will also find that he tends to relate the sounds he hears outside to the objects he is familiar with :

'I think that clock bell must be made of metal.'
'Why, Jimmy ?'
'Because it makes a ringing sound, like our metal things.'
'Mum, that hooter sounds like blowing on our big big bottle.'

This is immensely valuable — and all the answering, suggesting, encouraging you can do will reinforce the *bringing together* of experience, verbalization, listening skills and understanding of sounds which is happening when your child makes such comments.

Certain games may be very useful here in enlarging the child's awareness. Take the case of shakers. Given a good experience with rattles, and the chance to see and play with *transparent* pots and jars containing materials, a child will easily come to understand that different materials in shakers will usually make different sounds. It will be much less easy for him to discover that the material of the container itself can make a difference to the sound produced. So it is worth setting up, say, a transparent plastic pot, a different plastic pot, a metal tin and a wooden box, together with one kind of filling (perhaps rice, or small glass beads). The child can put the material into each of the pots, and so discover that the same filling will make different sounds. Your role is to encourage and perhaps to ask questions. The child may ask you directly 'Why do they make different noises ?' It's better, I think, not to give the answer, but to ask a helpful question ; 'It can't be the rice, can it, because that's the same in each pot. What is different about each pot ?' or even 'What is each pot made of ? Do they make the same sound when you flick them with your finger ?' If the child can discover and put the answer into his own words that is much more valuable and satisfying than just hearing it from you. However, remember that it's a game, for fun. It is much better for you to give the answer than for the child to feel foolish or trapped or resentful.

In a similar way I often produce a small group of sound-making objects that are linked in some manner — for instance, a group of eggcups (a wooden, a china, a plastic and a metal one), or a group of different-sized tins, or things that make a scraping sound (perhaps a wire record rack, a shell and a piece of corrugated cardboard), or a set of small bottles. We look at them and talk about their uses, colours and so on, then we make the sounds and listen to them. All this helps to focus the child's attention on families of sound-making objects, the differences caused by different materials, and so on.

Mind you, as I keep saying, you can't always be sure how things will develop. I often use a group of three bottles (a half litre milk bottle, a junior asprin bottle and a small brown pill bottle), and after the usual talking I tap the bottles with a beater, and then blow across the tops to make a hooting sound, much to the delight of children. At least, that's the idea, but I often get deflected. Once ,when I tapped the little bottle it slid across the table, and Tony shouted, 'That's like a Dalek !' We never got back to the bottles ! We found ourselves moving stiffly around, holding our noses and chanting in high-pitched voices : 'Exterminate ! Exterminate ! I am a Dalek.'

On another occasion I got through the tapping, but my blowing into the milk bottle caused condensation. 'Why has it gone white ?' demanded Stephen, and the ensuing conversation about breath on cold mornings, steam from kettles and windows in winter prevented me from blowing the two remaining bottles. Even if we get as far as blowing all the bottles, the activity may develop in any one of a number of ways. Darren, a bright four-year-old, once told me that the pill bottle made a higher note than the aspirin bottle (true ! and quite an advanced awareness for a four-year-old) ; then promptly said 'And I know why – because it's brown.' You can imagine that this took us off on quite a discussion. Another time with a group of children, when I blew the aspirin bottle, Samantha (also four) said, 'That sounds like a train whistle – an old-fashioned train whistle'. We all agreed. The children started making steam noises and moving their arms like wheels, so I talked and bottle-whistled us through an imaginary train journey, starting slowly, getting faster, slowing for signals and eventually stopping at a station. Since I was rapidly running out of puff, I declined the pressing invitation to repeat the journey ! Instead, I said, 'I know a song about a train' ; so we all sang :

Train is a-coming

Train is a-coming, oh yes!   Train is a-coming, oh   yes!

Train is a-coming, train is a-coming, train is a-coming oh yes!

and we made up lots of improvised verses, like :

We start at the station . . .
We slow down for the signal . . .

Eula is the driver . . .
Beverley is the guard . . .
Samantha is the ticket collector . . .
We are all the passengers . . .

and (of course)

David is the whistle, *Oh yes!*

It all goes to show that you need to be flexible. It also reminds us that
understanding sounds is only one aspect of children's learning ; it flows
into and out of many other kinds of play which will give us masses of
opportunities for developing a child's understanding.

In the process of encouraging experiment with sounds a couple of
pieces of equipment will be useful things for you to make. They are both
very simple. The first is sometimes called a xylophone base. It is simply a
piece of *solid* plank (for stability and strength) on top of which are
glued or screwed two lengths of approximately 2 × 2 cm timber.
Along the top of each length you fix a strip of foam plastic self-

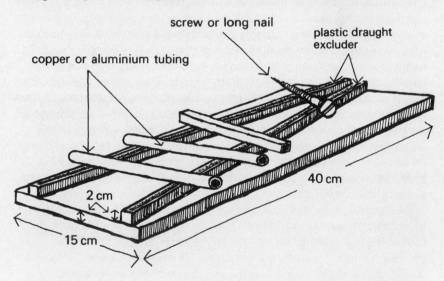

adhesive draught excluder. This base allows a child to put on it all kinds
of rods, strips, lengths of wood or metal or plastic, and to tap them with a
beater to see what kinds of sounds they do (or don't) make. Aluminium
and copper tubing, 15 cm nails, strips of slate, metal curtain track and
strips of hardboard are some that make interesting sounds. Resting the
objects on the foam plastic so that about a quarter of the length
overhangs at each end allows them to make the best sound, but children
will discover this for themselves. They often show great absorption in
this frame and the things you can put on it. Michael, aged four, once
spent thirty-five minutes putting different things on the frame, tapping

them, holding them with his fingers and tapping again, letting them go and tapping again.

The frame also becomes a tool : children finding or playing with an object will say 'I wonder if it will make a sound on the frame', and bring the object to have a go. Objects I have seen tried in this way include a rusty spoon from the sand tray, a knitting needle, a strip of tissue paper, a piece of apple, a biro, pieces of a construction kit, a plastic ruler, a half-eaten jam sandwich and a bar of soap. Much was learnt.

A very interesting and revealing experiment using the xylophone base can be done with three- and four-year-olds. Get hold of a length of soft wood about a metre long. This can be a cheap broom handle, or something rectangular in section, anything from 1 cm to 3 cm wide. You will also need a small saw. Ask the child to cut off a piece of wood (don't specify how long), then get him to put it on the xylophone base and tap it with a hard beater to make a note. Ask him if he thinks another piece will make a note too. Will it make the same note ? You or he can cut another piece, and another and another, and compare the notes made. It is virtually certain that the pieces cut will be of different sizes, but you can suggest that the third or fourth piece be cut longer or shorter than the others. Children are fascinated by the fact that the different lengths make different notes, and seeing all the bars cut off the same length of wood helps to eliminate some of the false trails that can result if you use ready-cut lengths. I once did this with three four-year-olds, using a strip cut from a board. One side of the offcut was blue. Floyd cut a length, then Tony cut one, which he put on the base blue side up. When he found that the two bits made different notes, he said confidently, 'Ah, but mine's blue !' When we turned over Floyd's piece to show that it also was blue on one side, Tony was disconcerted but curious. After another bit had been cut he suggested, rightly, that the differences in length might have something to do with it.

The second piece of equipment is a hanging frame. The value of this frame is that many young children find it extremely difficult to hold up something in one hand and tap it with the other, especially if, like a triangle, it tends to spin round and round. There is another problem with sound-making objects that hang. If you play one, then have to put it down, pick up another and get it still before you can make a sound from the second object, it becomes difficult to compare the sounds the two things make. This is even more difficult for young children. With a hanging frame a number of things that they think will make interesting sounds can be hung up, and the sounds compared quickly and easily. Shelf brackets, coat hooks, china cups, flowerpots and many other objects are good for this. A row of hooks screwed into an old-fashioned clothes horse or any other convenient place will be as good, but a clothes horse tends to be cumbersome to put away and takes up floor space.

If a child gets plenty of opportunity to experiment with the sounds

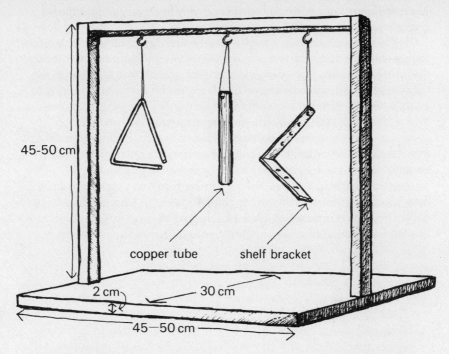

45-50 cm

copper tube   shelf bracket

2 cm   30 cm

45—50 cm

made by ordinary objects, and plenty of talking about the results with
adults, he will build up a very extensive awareness of sounds. He will
understand clearly that patterns of sounds are one of the interesting
characteristics of life and that they are made by objects or people or
machines in the environment. He will have established ways of listening
to and talking about what he hears. He will be alert and curious about
sounds, and he will have had plenty of experience of making them with
familiar objects. A pretty good preparation.

But is this 'music'?

Some of you may be concerned that such a long chapter, covering such a
large amount of experience, seems to be very little concerned with
anything that you can recognize as music. There has been little about
tunes, rhythms, accompaniments, providing instruments and so on.

It constantly astonishes me that in the field of music we expect skills,
awareness and social behaviour that we don't expect from pre-school
children in any other field. We don't expect them to draw recognizeably
or realistically; we don't expect them to play cooperatively with other
children until late in their pre-school years, if at all. We concentrate on
providing them with opportunities to explore at their own pace and in
their own way; to develop confidence in the use of materials; to
understand something about their properties and the ways that they can
be used. Yet so often we assume that young children can listen to music,

use instruments meaningfully and sensitively and can join together in group music-making, well before they are five.

Clearly this is unrealistic. Equally clearly, their later ability to do these things will only come from exploring and developing confidence about the world of sounds. Providing musical instruments will do little to help this. Children will use a saucepan lid in very much the same way as a £15 cymbal, and the cymbal's advantage in sound quality will be balanced by the saucepan lid's advantage in being a familiar and understood object. Of course, if the cymbal (or guitar or piano) is a valued possession of the family the situation is somewhat different, but you certainly won't make a child musical or give him a good musical experience just by lashing out money on instruments. (We will look at how you can introduce conventional instruments in Chapter 8.) All your child's important discoveries about sounds can be made with objects available all around him, provided he has help from you.

5

Singing and making up songs

I wonder how many adults think of children's singing entirely in terms of their joining-in with other people, singing accurately in tune, keeping in time, remembering the words? Rather a lot of them, I expect. But all those adults are making a basic mistake, one that is very commonly made in connection with music. They look at what constitutes adult music and try to see signs of this in the ways young children behave; even worse, they may even try to force children into the adult patterns on the grounds that it will be good for their musical development!

In fact, as we have already seen, young children's singing is playing – playing with sounds, making up patterns with words, making sounds as part of dramatic play and inventing their own songs. Such play becomes a major part of their musical activity once they have begun to talk fluently. Only a certain proportion of such play is singing songs in the adult sense. Again, we tend only to notice a small part of their total musical play – mostly those patterns the child finds so satisfactory as to repeat them frequently – and unless we are researchers with tape-recorders and microphones permanently set up we only manage to remember and record a small proportion even of those patterns we recognize! I am no different from you in this. Inevitably most of my examples come from my own children and are a small part of their output. But in case you think my children are exceptional, I must stress that I have heard exactly the same kinds of songs and singing from many other children – they are simply the kinds of things that children do. All the examples come from between the ages of two and five plus.

First some word patterns, because this is where much of their singing play begins. At three Peter became fascinated with the word 'rectangle'. He used to say it over and over and over, and soon it was being used as a readiness cry – whenever he wanted to leap off something or start a sprint there would be a great shout of 'Rectangle, rectangle!' A little later we realized that it had taken the place of the space launch count-down 'Ten, nine, eight . . . zero! Blast-off!' Now, whenever an Apollo moon-probe was taking off we got 'Rectangle, rectangle, meeooooaaargh!' Such a use of a striking word to make patterns and chants is very common; Kenneth Jameson quotes 'Rho-do-den-dhron, rho-do-den-

dhron'. But often the child just takes sounds that he likes and makes a
pattern with them. Peter had a rhythmic chant that went:

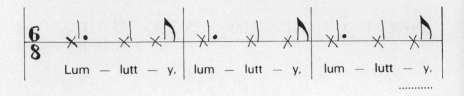

An important feature of such patterns is that once they have been
discovered they are *used* by the child. He gives them great meaning and
importance in his play, and it is only occasionally that you will discover
the origin or the significance (as with 'Rectangle, rectangle,
meeooooaaargh!'). In our house 'Reflection' was a mysterious word of
this kind, a real Word of Power, used with great aggressiveness by Peter
in many dramatic situations. We never identified its significance for him.
Another baffling pattern arose at the time of the 1971 Cup Final. There
appeared in our children's games a strange character called Mr Cholfy,
who was very strong and had many mysterious adventures. We only
twigged some time later, and then quite by accident, that this was
Chelsea Football Club, who were in that Cup Final. Again, children make
up words for things very freely, especially if given the example of adults
who enjoy playing with words. For some time in our family all favoured
puddings were called 'floggy pudding' (could it be anything to do with
the figgy pudding of *We Wish You A Merry Christmas* ?) and had to be
mashed up with a spoon into 'illy gum'.

All this may seem to have a tenuous connection with music, but in fact
it is a crucial stage in singing development and in song- and tune-
making, to which it frequently leads. One example will make the pattern
clear. A common word-play pattern for small children is to say a sound
over and over, changing the initial consonant. Katherine used to chant
'bog, fog, sog, hog, log . . .' and Peter was much taken with 'tail, fail, mail,
sail, bail . . .' For some reason the last two stuck, and he would go around
rhythmically chanting, 'sail, bail ; sail, bail ; sail, bail . . .' One day it
developed a tune:

Then, for no apparent reason, it became:

Sa — il, ba — il, ut — ty sa — il, ba — il.

sung over and over and over again.

Such little songs occur all the time (and don't forget that it is only the occasional particularly memorable one that tends to be repeated often enough for adults to remember it). They are inspired by all sorts of things. Sometimes one of the children's patterns of words will suggest a tune; usually this has a very limited range of notes, like this chant of Peter's (notice the similarity to the 'Sail, bail' tune):

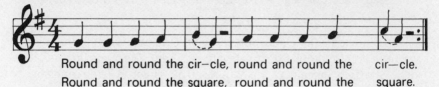

Round and round the cir—cle, round and round the   cir—cle.
Round and round the square, round and round the   square.

It is interesting and, I think, significant, that the way children make up tunes for a pattern of words using a limited range of notes relates so closely to Carl Orff's approach to encouraging children's tune-making, and to the kind of improvised singing on one or two notes that we talked about in Chapter 3, 'Early vocalizing'. Sometimes in songmaking the stimulus is a favourite toy – in the following example a small stuffed camel always very formally addressed as 'Hump-backed camel'. He inspired Peter to create this song, sung, like most play songs, over and over:

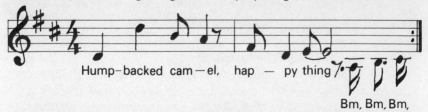

Hump-backed cam—el, hap — py thing
                                    Bm, Bm, Bm,

The pattern also got used for such gems as 'Hump-backed Daddy, smelly thing!' (Incidentally, the 'Boom, boom, boom . . .' was an optional second part, improvised by Peter when Katherine proved able to manage the song herself.)

Sometimes the stimulus is a particular event, like the time Peter was taken, aged five, to the Transport Museum at Clapham, where he saw the locomotive *Mallard*, holder of the world speed record for steam locomotives at 126 m.p.h. This made a great impression on him, but even more did a tape of sound effects of the locomotive at speed that was operated electrically by pressing a button. *Mallard* (or sometimes 'Mannard'!) became another Word of Power, and the following two tunes were widely used in play, always sung in a jocular, parodying, lunatic way :

Oh the Mall — ard, the fa-mous e-lect-ric Mall-ard!

Beep, beep, the Mall — ard, the fa —mous Mall-ard of en-em-y!

Indeed, almost anything may be a stimulus. One day, when Katherine was three, she emerged from the lavatory saying, 'I've made up a lavatory song'. She drew herself up ; we composed ourselves to listen ; and she sang :

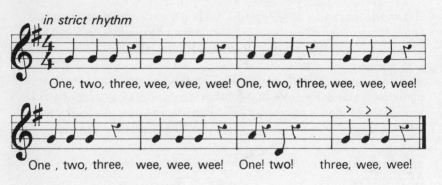

One, two, three, wee, wee, wee! One, two, three, wee, wee, wee!

One , two, three, wee, wee, wee! One! two! three, wee, wee!

She then let out huge guffaws of laughter !

As has already been mentioned, from the age of two most children talk a good deal if they have the chance, and often use such talk to sort out their experiences, organize their play and come to terms with puzzling or complex or unpleasant situations. Naturally, such speech often becomes a chant and can even develop into a song. The following is a classic example. We had mice in our cupboards. A couple of days before, Peter and Katherine (then aged about three and a half) had been talking about mice getting squashed in mousetraps, and Katherine had shown distaste at this. Now she was sitting at the tea table, about to eat a piece of cheese ; suddenly out came :

slowly & freely

There once was a mouse, nib—bl—ing a piece of

rhythmically

cheese. Sud-den—ly the great spring came down and

squashed the mouse and that was the end of the

mouse. Oh the mouse!
(with relish)

She then munched the cheese with appetite !

Another way that young children commonly make up songs is by changing the words of existing songs. This happens particularly if they are used to their adults treating songs in this way and improvising snatches of song, as we described in Chapter 3. It often begins with the child changing a single word – 'Peter hammers with one hammer' becomes 'Peter hammers with one slipper' because he is striking the ground with a slipper while you are singing the song. Later the improvization becomes more extensive. Katherine was particularly fond of this sort of play and used it a lot. When she was just three, and sitting at the breakfast table, she found that Peter had collared the sugar, and no one was paying her any particular attention. So she suddenly sang :

Please me have a soo—der, Please me have a

soo — der, Please me have a soo — der to

put on my fakes!

Another time, a few months later, she was sitting at the kitchen table with a bowl of small apples, arranging them in patterns. At one point she had five on the table, and began to sing (to the tune of *Ten Green Bottles*) :

Five round apples sitting on the wall,
Five round apples sitting on the wall,
And if one round apple should accidentally fall,
There'd be four round apples sitting on the wall.

The participation or stimulus of an adult can be part of this process. Peter and Katherine were talking about dinosaurs, which were a current passion, and were marching about chanting :

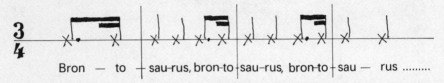

Bron — to sau-rus, bron-to sau-rus, bron-to sau — rus ....

Pauline sang (to the tune of *Happy Birthday to You*) :

Brontosaurus to you . . .

Peter immediately joined in with :

Stegosaurus to you . . .

and within a few seconds had come up with :

Brontosaurus to you,
Stegosaurus to you,
  Iguanadon, Pteranodon,
Triceratops to you.

On another occasion, when he was almost six and splashing violently in the bath, he was told, 'Stop mucking about ; wash your face and your neck and your knees !' The latter phrase delighted him, and he rapidly came up with :

Your face and your neck and your knees, I'm

going to sneeze and catch dis — ease, Your

face and your neck and your knees, oh please don't

tease or I will squeeze, Your face and your

neck and your knees ———!

The link with the playing with words described earlier must be very clear, though this is a very developed and advanced example of such play. It must also be clear how much understanding and practice of the fitting of syllables to notes this kind of play gives, and so how much it improves a child's singing skill.

Encouraging this kind of play can recoil on you somewhat! One morning we were all getting up and getting dressed, except for Katherine, who was sitting meditating on the bedroom rug in a typically four-year-old way. Pauline, who was holding a pair of pants, began to sing (to the tune of *Polly Put the Kettle On*) :

Mummy, put your knickers on,
Mummy, put your knickers on,
Mummy, put your knickers on,
    Put them on.

Katherine, with a delighted sideways glance, immediately chimed in with :

Daddy, take them off again,
Daddy, take them off again,
Daddy, take them off again,
    Take them off.

Sometimes the song is even more of an interplay between the child and the adult. Katherine, then aged four, was having lunch with Pauline, who had peeled a banana for her, removing a brown spot and leaving a hole. Katherine began to sing (to the tune of *There's a Hole in my Bucket*) :

Katherine: There's a hole in my banana,
          Dear Mummy, dear Mummy,
    There's a hole in my banana,
          Dear Mummy, a hole.

Pauline joined in :

Pauline: Then mend it, dear Katherine,
          Dear Katherine, dear Katherine,
    Then mend it, dear Katherine,
          Dear Katherine, mend it.

Katherine: With what shall I mend it,
          Dear Mummy, dear Mummy,
    With what shall I mend it,
          Dear Mummy, with what?

Pauline: With string, dear Katherine . . .

Katherine: Where shall I get the string from . . . ?

Pauline: From the string tree, dear Katherine . . .

Katherine: Where is a string tree . . . ?

Pauline: In the middle of the sea . . .

Katherine: How shall I get to it . . . ?

Pauline: Sail on a banana . . .

Katherine: Where is a banana . . . ?

Pauline: In your hand, dear Katherine . . .

Katherine: *BUT* there's a *hole* in my banana . . .

Peals of delighted laughter from both Pauline and Katherine !

I must stress again — all such song-play and song-making is normal and common with pre-school children. Of course, the more developed and therefore more recognizeable examples depend for their appearance at such an age upon a number of things. The child has to have considerable verbal fluency — hence part of the emphasis I laid on the relationship between talking and singing development in Chapter 3. He has to have the example of adults who not only sing but who use songs and words in fun, for all sorts of games. He has to have built up a large repertoire of songs and song patterns which he can draw upon. Without these advantages he will probably still make his own play songs and patterns, he may even improvise new words, but his development will tend to be delayed and may well not be recognized. Mrs D. M. Day vividly described during a lecture in 1974 the example of a child at the water tray in infant school, pouring water through a funnel and making exactly the same vocal pattern as we described Peter using at seven months old. Another difficulty for a child going through these stages while at school is that he will already have become more self-critical, and he may feel that his improvizations are unsuccessful because they are so primitive. He is also more likely to be criticized or ridiculed by unperceptive parents or teachers for silly or immature behaviour. A child producing the 'Lavatory Song' in a reception class may well not be greeted with the enthusiasm that his achievement merits !

Indeed, we can see the kind of vicious circle that many children are caught in by the time they come to school. They have not heard much singing, so their singing awareness and confidence are limited. Consequently their own play singing has not been recognized and encouraged – so they have lost opportunities to practise. Consequently they still need to do this at school, where it is not recognized and may be discouraged as 'silly'. Instead they are forced to join in songs and formal rhythmic games for which they are not ready, so they become inhibited and don't join in. As a result they don't develop the skills of singing, or develop them very slowly – so they are classed as 'growlers' and often excluded from the singing activity. It would be funny if only it were not so common ! But if a child has had plenty of opportunities to hear singing and to do plenty of vocal play, singing with other people presents few problems.

Learning to sing other people's songs
We have now come back round to the business of learning to sing patterns laid down by other people, I hope with a clearer idea of how this relates to the other important kinds of children's singing. In the normal home situation this learning is going on at the same time as the play singing and the two activities feed each other. All your child's spontaneous vocal play builds up the muscular control and vocal skill that makes it possible for him to join in with your songs when he wants to. In turn, by singing a great deal to your child you show him patterns which he can understand and imitate and give him an idea how, when and where to use them. In turn this makes him more and more aware of what he is doing in his own singing play and experiment. As he becomes more aware of his own patterns he can use them consciously and deliberately. Thus he can make up his own songs ; he can also choose to sing your songs with you. Because he loves you he wants to join in with you – so he does. It's an easy and natural process.

'But what do I do ? what do I do ?' Whenever I talk to adults about their children's singing all sorts of anxious questions flood out. 'Shouldn't I teach him to sing "properly" ?' 'What standard should I be expecting from my daughter ? – she's four years, seven months and three days old.' 'You can't be serious about me singing to him ! With my terrible voice I'll *wreck* his singing . . . won't I ?' 'How can you sing to a child if you can't read music ?' Most of these questions reflect clearly the deep insecurity created in us by our own music lessons. We are so sure that what we do in music must be wrong – it always has been !

I have said it already. Why on earth should learning to sing be considered so complicated ? The answer, simply, is that it's not. If you can 'teach' your child to speak (which you do) you can teach him to sing. He learns to talk through you talking with him a lot ; he learns to sing through you singing with him a lot. Unfortunately, your fears and tensions (or your enjoyment and confidence) transmit themselves to your child ; so does your rigid adherence to set patterns (or your flexibility to experiment). A lot of children suffer from this. A child whose adults are frightened to sing, or who make singing a rigid, right-or-wrong obstacle course, will be inhibited and restricted in his singing. A child whose adults make singing natural, fun, and are not preoccupied with whether the song is sung accurately and in tune, will be encouraged to join in. So you *should* sing cheerfully, however creaky your voice, and with confidence in your value. This will give your child confidence.

Confidence is crucial in getting him to join in ; and his joining in is crucial in developing and refining his formal singing skills. He may sing confidently on his own ; but it is only when he comes to match his voice with someone else's and learns to adjust his part where necessary that he can begin to master singing in tune. So your primary concern must be to encourage and make possible his joining in. *Anything* that obstructs this, however good may be the musical reasons for it, must be avoided. Above all, you must not set out from the beginning to teach the child to sing in any formal sense, or to force him to perform. That is the kiss of death.

Participation or performance ?
The strength of my feelings about this may have surprised you. Isn't music *about* performance – isn't that the essence of it ? Shouldn't our music teaching be geared to getting as many children as possible up on to that platform, at the local music festival, at prize day, whenever and wherever possible ? My answer to all the questions is an emphatic 'No !'

I think music is 'about' making and appeciating patterns of sound. This *may* involve making them for other people to hear. In our own musical culture we stress high quality musical performance to a passive audience, but this is a bias that has developed largely over the last 300 years. It conditions very much our thinking ; it leads us to overvalue the performing skills. Above all, it is a very unsound basis for young children's music-making, especially when it encourages the formal teaching of musical skills like singing.

The danger of formal teaching of singing to young children is precisely that it presumes and demands a performance as its end product. This demand cannot be sidestepped. The only point in getting someone to learn something in this formal way is so that he will be able to perform it, and the implication is always that the teacher will at some point in the proceedings say, 'Now you know the song – do it ! I'll stand here and judge how well you do it.' Although such performance is an essential part of sophisticated musical activity, it always creates *stress*, even among highly competent musicians. Just imagine yourself suddenly asked to do something you do only moderately well in front of a group of adults you don't know, or even in front of one strange person. You may well manage it, but you know that you will experience a good deal of tension and stress. This is of the nature of performance.

Don't be misled. This stress is only slightly the result of embarrassment or self-consciousness, and you cannot dismiss the point by claiming that small children are much less selfconscious than adults. Mostly the stress arises from the fact that as a performer you are up against it. Your options are narrowed down to two : succeed or fail. Either you can do it 'properly' or you can't. Such a narrowing of options is very difficult for a young child in any field. It is particularly stressful in an intensely personal and self-revealing field like singing. Many physical and emotional factors may inhibit him. He may not yet have reached the developmental stage where he can manage to sing a whole song ; he certainly may find it intensely difficult (if not impossible) to sing accurately in tune ; there are dozens of reasons, as you know, why he may not wish to sing at a particular time.

Because of this the effect of formal singing teaching with young children is always to present the child with a series of demanding hurdles. If he is musically able and has had a good musical background he will succeed at the majority of these. His confidence will go up by leaps and bounds ; he will be increasingly eager to tackle new hurdles ; he will get plenty of practice and so refine his skill. It will not be long before adults are saying, 'Thomas is a very musical child, you know,' and giving him lots of praise. This further boosts his confidence and increases his ability to cope. Soon he, and the smallish proportion of children like him, will have become the musical élite. They will be given the opportunities and encouragement at school to become musicians. Perhaps, eventually, they will become the music teachers who create a similar obstacle race for the new generation, confident that such an approach must be right because *they* have succeeded in it.

In contrast, the child who is less musically able, less advantaged in background, will fail at many of the early hurdles. His confidence will go down, accelerated by the disappointment or disapproval of his adults ; he will be less eager to tackle the next hurdle ; he will get less practice ; the adults will begin to say, 'Poor, Billy, he's not got a note of music in him.'

He will be embarked, with the majority of his contemporaries, on the path of not being given an instrument in the music lesson, being criticized for not singing in tune, being rejected from the school choir for growling, asked to sit with a book in the library instead of coming to music — all the kinds of treatment that have destroyed the confidence of most adults in *doing* anything musical, despite their love and enjoyment of music they listen to. Have you ever read the Schools Council *Enquiry One* into secondary schools? It contains the shattering information that music as a subject is considered the least useful, the least enjoyable and the most boring subject in the curriculum! It is a crushing indictment of most music teaching. In my view the overstressing of early performance is largely responsible because it destroys the confidence of so many children early on. Even at the age of six you frequently find children who in the music lesson open and shut their mouths without making a sound — frightened of being wrong — or who pretend to clap rhythms but don't let their palms touch — frightened of making a mistake — or who just opt out of the activity completely — which in some ways is better than faking! Performance-oriented music teaching can be immensely destructive with young children.

This ought to make us question such teaching for under-fives even if it were necessary in order to get them to sing. The really tragic thing is that it is not! At this age you are not trying to train a formal choir (if you have any sense). You are trying to develop a child's musical confidence; you are trying to get him to join in; you are trying to get him to learn songs; and so on. But you can make these things happen pre-school without any formal teaching. If you do things that you enjoy doing simply for your child's enjoyment, the strong human instinct to join in with things in a secure situation will ensure that he does. Of course, this participation may be at any one of a wide variety of levels. A child is an individual. But the lower levels of participation lead naturally and inevitably to the higher ones, provided the child is allowed to find his own level in the first place, and provided that he is enjoying his singing.

Let's look closer at this process in operation with a simple song:

The Wheels on the Bus

84

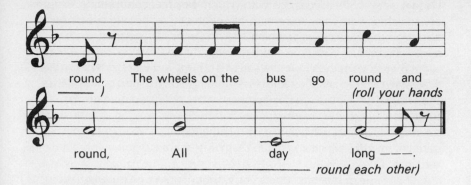

round, The wheels on the bus go round and
_____) *(roll your hands*

round, All day long ———.
————————————————————— *round each other)*

The horn on the bus goes beep, beep, beep . . . (*toot horn*)

The windscreen wiper goes swish, swish, swish . . . (*hand waves across face*)

The people on the bus bounce up and down . . . (*do so*)

The bell on the bus goes ding, ding, ding . . . (*pull the bell*)

When you sing this song with different children you see many ways and levels of participating. Some children will only participate by being with you and the song : they listen and are clearly involved, but don't do or sing anything. Some children will only do an occasional action without saying or singing anything ; it is quite common for a child not to do anything until the verse about the people and then to bounce vigorously throughout the rest of the song – and even beyond ! Certain children will do all the actions quite confidently but won't say or sing any of the words – though you sometimes see them whispering or mouthing the words to themselves. Other children may 'strip' and sing certain selected bits ; the final note 'long' is a popular one, or the whole of the final phrase 'all day long', or 'Round and round' (sometimes sung in the right place but in every verse). Some children will attempt to sing the whole song but not be able to carry the tune properly, so they may well just hum the tune or say the words. Even children singing confidently may well be 'thrown' in the windscreen wiper verse or the people verse, where the actions distract or totally involve them. Some children, even at the age of three, will sing and do the whole song with the greatest of ease, and some may even suggest new verses and actions to extend the song. *This is the normal spectrum of young children's participation*.

I emphasize this because it is vital for you to realize that a young child who does something seemingly very limited may be functioning at his highest level musically. To demand a fixed standard of *performance* will inevitably condemn such a child to failure and create stress for all the children except a favoured few, and maybe even for them. In contrast, the children joining in with *The Wheels On The Bus* are being invited to choose a level of *participation* with which they feel comfortable. Children are sensible, well-balanced creatures; each of the children I describe above has chosen a level at which he can succeed. This may seem a surprising remark about the children who 'do nothing', but if we examine what they have gained from the activity I think you will see what I mean. They have shared an enjoyable experience with you (and perhaps with the group); they have not been picked upon, criticized or made to feel they have failed; they have experienced the pattern of the song and seen a number of simple ways they may be able to join in. Above all, this has given them confidence and made them better able to join in more fully the next time.

If this is true of the 'non-doers', how much more true is it of those children who have done something successfully? The striking thing about doing such a song in the way I describe is that if you do it three or four times without 'teaching' it at all, you will find that each child is likely to have increased the extent and skill of his contribution. If you listen to individual children during their play or talk to their Mums you will often find that, freed from the pressure of the group 'audience', able to do it at their own speed, many of them can sing the whole song quite comfortably. 'Teaching' in any formal sense is unnecessary as well as dangerous with the under-fives. (It tells us something about the oddity of our attitudes to music that it is virtually the only area of activity with under-fives where such a remark is not so obvious as to be not worth making!)

How, then, should you proceed at home? If you are not expected to 'teach' your child to sing, what should you do? The first thing clearly is to sing a lot with your child – and if you want him to join in then a good number of the things you do should make it very easy for him to participate, at whatever level he can manage. Part of this process should be to continue the fingerplays and little action rhymes we have already talked about. Even though they don't have tunes to sing they are very useful in encouraging participation. Here's one I like:

Fingers Like To Wiggle Waggle

Fingers like to wiggle waggle,   (*do the actions*)
Wiggle waggle, wiggle waggle,
Fingers like to wiggle waggle
Right in front of me.

> (*Each time you say the rhyme you change the final line so as to wiggle in a different place*)

... up above your head.
... underneath your knees.   (*and so on ...*)

Here's another:

Two Little Feet

Two little feet that go tap, tap,   (*tap feet*)
Two little hands that go clap, clap, (*clap hands*)
Two little eyes to see who's there – (*make 'spectacles'*)
Oh my goodness, it's a bear !   (*jump with surprise*)

(This rhyme can be adapted to use other animal names—or to use the name of your child.)

Two little feet that go tap, tap,   (*tap feet*)
Two little hands that go clap, clap, (*clap hands*)
Two little eyes to see who's who – (*look around very slowly*)
Samantha Griffiths, I see you ! (*point at the child*)

This one too is a particular favourite – it does have a tune, but is very much the same kind of game :

Little Fish

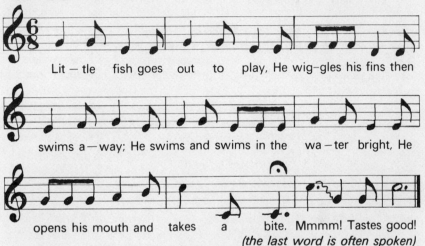

Lit — tle fish goes out to play, He wig-gles his fins then swims a—way; He swims and swims in the wa—ter bright, He opens his mouth and takes a bite. Mmmm! Tastes good!
(the last word is often spoken)

(*Put your left hand out, palm down, fingers together, thumb sticking out. Put your right hand on top of the left, palm down, thumb out. Now you've got a fish with fins at his sides. Wiggle your thumbs and make the fish swim by moving your hands up and down. Now make the fish swim and wiggle his fins at the same time. Make his mouth open by raising your right hand fingers, then snap his mouth shut. At the end, on 'tastes good', you can rub your tummy appreciatively.*)

In the early stages joining in tends to be a matter of doing the actions, but quite soon your child will begin to say or sing the words too ; this is important and you can encourage it without pressing.

Extending this kind of activity into songs you come to the simple action song. Here is a favourite of mine :

Tidey-oh!

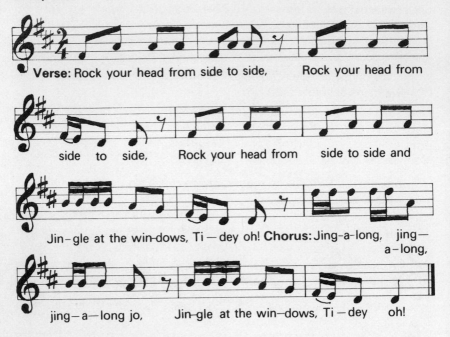

Verse: Rock your head from side to side, Rock your head from side to side, Rock your head from side to side and Jin-gle at the win-dows, Ti—dey oh! Chorus: Jing-a-long, jing—a-long, jing—a—long jo, Jin-gle at the win—dows, Ti—dey oh!

Put your hands on your head,
Put your hands on your head,
Put your hands on your head,
   Jingle at the windows, Tidey-oh. *Chorus*

Nod your head up and down,
Nod your head up and down,
Nod your head up and down,
   Jingle at the windows, Tidey-oh. *Chorus*

Flop your shoulders up and
   down . . .   *Chorus*

Stretch your arms up in the air . . . *Chorus*

Pull your ears with your fingers . . . *Chorus*

Tap your hands on your knees . . . *Chorus*

Put your fingers on your nose . . . *Chorus*

Put your head right down on your
   knees. . . .   *Chorus*

So many things can be said about a song of this type. It is simple and repetitive, with a chorus, and the child hears the patterns over and over — so it's easy for him to 'strip' and so to imitate. Even if he can't sing accurately there are plenty of rhythmic actions for him to do, so that he can join in and gain confidence. It is also a valuable kind of song in that it need never be sung the same way twice – you can suit the verses you sing to your child's interests and abilities. This encourages him to make up his own verses and stimulates his song-making, as we have seen. This also means that the song can grow with the child. When he is used to doing one action in each verse he loves being asked to do two or even three :

Hold your ear with your hand,
Hold the other ear with the other
    hand,
Now nod your head up and down
    And jingle at the windows,
      Tidey-oh.   *Chorus*

However, although this variety is very exciting and valuable for the child, we must not forget that he loves the security of something familiar, of a pattern he sees repeated each time. Because of this I find it useful with songs of this type to have a fixed final verse which we always sing last of all, regardless of how many new verses we have had. My final verse is :

This is going to be the last verse,   (*slap your thighs*)
This is going to be the last verse,   (*slap thighs*)
This is going to be the last verse,   (*slap thighs*)
    So jingle at the windows,
      Tidey-oh.   *chorus*

But you can invent your own special final verse.

Why do actions ?
Combining actions with young children's singing is particularly important. Firstly, young children don't naturally separate one sense from another. Their instinct is to move when they make sounds, and to make sounds when they move, as many a harassed mother knows ! Expecting them to sit still during musical activity is unrealistic ; it tends to build up a tension which suddenly explodes ! Much better is to provide opportunities for the discharge of nervous impulse by including actions in many of the songs and rhymes we do. This discharges the tension and the action becomes purposive, conscious, controlled, instead of just being an involuntary nuisance. Secondly, young children understand and come to feel things very much through their bodies, so actions actually heighten their intellectual understanding and the emotional release of a song. (In fact this is not just true of children. I have sung *Little Fish* to groups of adults without doing the actions and it has been very flat and unsuccessful – but add the actions and their delight is plain to see !) Thirdly, the *integration* of sound and movement is crucial in building a child's sense of pulse, rhythm, phrasing and musical shape,

and we shall see in a later chapter how this relates to more formal rhythmic development. Fourthly, movement is often an easier way for a child to join in than speaking and singing, so songs and fingerplays that allow and encourage actions help to develop confidence and musical skill, because any child, however inhibited, can take part. The confidence gained from this will lead him to join in vocally.

Consequently, many of the best songs for young children contain actions, included in the kinds of simple structures that help them to participate. The classic book, worth every penny of its now considerable price, is *American Folk Songs for Children*, which I have already mentioned. You can find a list of other useful books in the bibliography at the end of this book.

One of the nice things about a lot of the action songs is that, because the essence of the song lies in the physical participation, they do not demand from the adult particularly 'good' singing. Many of them are chants, like *Hickety Tickety*. The chorus is chanted with clapping or knee-slapping, and then the adult holds up a certain number of fingers. When the child says how many fingers are held up, the adult *speaks* the appropriate verse in rhythm, and then the chorus is chanted again. The same number can be used several times with different verses:

Hickety Tickety

Chorus: Hick-e-ty tick-e-ty rump-a rick-e-ty hor — ny cup,

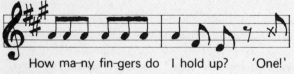

How ma-ny fin-gers do I hold up? 'One!'

Verse: You said one, we've just be — gun! *(to chorus)*

(spoken)

[*Repeat the chorus before each verse*]

ONE! You said one, a sugar bun. We've just begun. Shoot with a gun. Look at the sun

TWO! One for me and one for you (Dip the fingers in the stew. This one's green and that one's blue.)

THREE ! One for you and two for me. (One on my nose and two on my knee. One on the grass and two up a tree. Two on the beach and one in the sea.)

FOUR ! Two through the window and two through the door. (Two on my head and two on the floor.)

FIVE ! Get in a car and away you drive. (You said five, bees in a hive.)

TEN ! You said ten, we'll start again.

With very young children it is a good idea to stick to three or four fingers, or at the most the numbers given above, but with older children you can improvise further verses for the numbers six to nine – a song like *This Old Man* will give you ideas. Incidentally, the usual ending to the game is :

FOUR ! I held up four . . . and I won't hold up any more !
    (*hiding the four fingers away in your armpit*)

Any adult (yes, *any* adult) can do a chant like this, and any child can join in with it in his own way.

Learning to sing in tune

You may well be happy about this approach in encouraging and developing your child's confidence and willingness to participate – but will it be helping him to sing 'properly' (that favourite word of musicians) ? How do you get him to sing in tune ? If your own singing is not very good, will you be doing harm ? It is time to look more specifically at how children learn to sing in tune, since this causes more misconceptions and anxieties than almost anything else.

The basis of learning to sing in tune is the way adults make patterns of sound and encourage the child to imitate. In trying to imitate what he hears he gradually comes to *know* with his body, his throat, his vocal chords, what it feels like to make a certain sound. Thus when he hears a sound his 'body' will automatically take the shape and do the actions that will produce the same sound. This is a matter of building up habits and skills through a gradual trial-and-error process. It is not a matter of adults feeding in the correct techniques and sounds. Naturally, the wider a repertoire of his own sounds the child has mastered and become aware of, the more likely he is to be able to match a vocal sound he hears you make and so to be able to imitate it with confidence. The more he sees and hears you making singing sounds, the greater this confidence is, the more he tries to imitate singing and so the more refined his skill becomes.

We ought to remind ourselves of several important points about this imitation process ; all of them affect the way he learns to sing :

● In all forms of children's artistic experiment and development the *process* of experimenting is far more important to them than the *product* of their experiment.

● All of a young child's singing is play.

● In the early stages of his singing development a young child can only relate to a person. This is why recorded music is of no use in helping a child to learn to sing – if it were, children nowadays would all sing like nightingales ! (Later on, of course, it can extend their range and awareness.)

● We have noticed in connection with language development that a child doesn't imitate just the exact sound that is made ; he also imitates how, when and where it is made. The context and atmosphere surrounding singing is just as important as the sounds made.

The fact that young children are not necessarily interested in the product of their singing is very significant. To start with, they usually do not listen to themselves critically (in an adult sense). If they join in with singing they may well not be in the slightest bit bothered that what they are doing doesn't really fit, even though they may well be able to tell the adult that someone else is not singing the 'right' tune ! You may well think that if they can do this, then to point out their own inaccuracies will make them conscious of them, and so help them to correct themselves. Alas ! no. At this age it is common for a child to be egocentric about his own products but to have a growing social awareness when he examines the products of others. Until he becomes fully conscious of his own products in the same way, pointing out his 'mistakes' will only make him *selfconscious* and so inhibit him in his singing. Left alone, he will naturally correct himself when he reaches that developmental stage.

There is another important reason for not correcting him. You will remember how we commented on the fact that young children can understand language and may in fact be 'speaking' meaningfully long before what actually emerges from their mouths is recognizable to the listeners as speech. The same is true of singing. A child who joins in with a song out of time and out of tune may well *know* the song ; he may well be able to sing the song accurately inside his head. Thus in a very real sense getting him to sing the song 'correctly' is concerned only with performance, not with the more important aspects of learning to sing.

We need to remind ourselves constantly that all a young child's singing is play, and like all play it can be idiosyncratic, personal and highly variable from day to day. He uses his songs in whatever way he pleases. Sometimes he repeats them exactly ; sometimes he alters them. It is only with a growing social awareness and a decrease in egocentricity that he sees the point of conforming to a set pattern. Thus a child with whom you are singing may not *choose* to repeat patterns he hears or makes or discovers. If he does 'repeat' at your request, it may turn out a completely different pattern ! Even if he volunteers to sing you something familiar this may still happen. A child will frequently say, 'I'll sing you *Baa, baa, black sheep*' and then sing a tune with little or no resemblance to the original. He may well be able to repeat his own tune note for note (so he is not just improvising on the spot) ; and he will certainly recognize the original tune if you hum it to him (so it is not ignorance). Nor is it incompetence ; indeed, it has nothing to do with his singing skill or lack of it. It is largely related to the young child's inability to do a *mental* check before doing something ; he has to *try* it and see how it comes out. A tune he has become completely familiar with, or that he has made up, may well come out the same each time, but he can't hold a mental image of the tune and check his own against it as he goes along. Thus his own *Baa, baa, black sheep* doesn't clash in his mind with the authorized version. Once again, correcting him is worse than useless. It is only through growing maturity and through frequent singing with other people that he will become able to compare and thus to standardize his singing. Here again lies the importance of adults sharing singing with the child and encouraging him unstressfully to join in.

I say that a child will frequently do this, and you will find plenty of examples of it at playgroup and even in the infant school. However, I think it is worth emphasizing that by that age it indicates a considerable backwardness in his singing development. By the time a child is three – if he has heard plenty of singing from his adults – he will be perfectly capable of recognizing and reproducing a simple tune well enough for it to be easily identified, and when he does something different it will usually be as a joke ! This should remind us again how low are our expectations about children's singing.

From hearing a lot of adult singing in a secure and intimate situation the child builds up an awareness too of the latent structure of singing – things that fit and don't fit, patterns of melody, qualities of singing that express emotions, and so on. He uses this awareness to help him understand the novel singing he hears ; he uses it to direct his own spontaneous singing. Clearly, the more awareness a child develops early in all the ways we have described, the greater will be his singing competence. Indeed, much of what we class as 'musical ability' in children may simply be that the child in question has had his potential for making and understanding sounds *unlocked* in this way. We all of us have a lot of musical ability – most of us can't use much of what is there.

The significance of this awareness of the latent structure may be even more far-reaching. It is very debateable whether there is a music acquisition system in us that corresponds to our language acquisition system ; it is significant that very few music educators have even begun to think in these sophisticated and child-centred terms. Nevertheless, it seems likely that some instinct for musical structure must be developed early. Perhaps the American psychologist George Miller's theory about listening suggests one approach. He postulates :

that when we listen to someone speaking, or read a book, we are able to take in the syntax of the sentences spoken or read because we ourselves are generating alternative possible sentence structures and matching with what we are given.

If this is true in music also – for instance, if when we listen to music we are constantly creating in our minds patterns of the possible ways the tune may turn – it explains a number of things. It explains why it is so difficult to learn a tricky song (for example one which has unusual intervals). Because we are not 'expecting' the interval or pattern which comes we don't take it in, and so cannot reproduce it until a number of repetitions have made it familiar enough for us to anticipate it. It also explains why we have such difficulty in listening to a 'new' musical composition, particularly in an advanced or unfamiliar style, and why we find ourselves shaking our heads in confusion or cutting out. (This must be why many eminent contemporaries of famous composers like Beethoven found their music raucous, ugly and incomprehensible when they first heard it, even though we find it tuneful and easy to understand.) It explains finally, how and why children are able to join in with certain bits of songs, as we have seen them do. Clearly, if a theory like this is true, children who hear a lot of singing and therefore can imagine a wide range of alternative possible structures, find it much easier to imitate and so to sing in tune.

Games to develop singing skill
What are the practical consequences of all these points? For instance, does it mean that it is wrong to encourage the development of musical skills in young children? I think that this really depends on what you have in mind. If you mean demanding certain standards of achievement from children and pressuring them to practise the skills required, then I feel it is completely wrong, unless you know from close and lengthy observation of an individual that he is able and willing to undergo such pressure. Musical prodigies like Yehudi Menuhin clearly come into this category! However, there is nothing wrong with providing experiences that will make possible and encourage a child's further development – indeed, adults have an obligation to do just this.

First, with under-fives you should sing at close range, and largely without accompaniment; the simpler and more personal the patterns of sound are, the easier children find it to copy. People do not realize nearly enough how very confusing small children may find instrumental accompaniment, particularly if played on the piano. The piano is a loud and bossy instrument unless played very delicately; its sound is full of overtones and resonances. This often confuses young children (and may even frighten those who are unfamiliar with the instrument – I have seen several cases myself). Again, it may surprise the adults who enjoy the richness of harmony and the interest provided by bass runs or arpeggiated chording in a piano accompaniment to learn that before the age of eight or nine very many children can't hear such things except as a muddly background which tends to distract them from the tune. It may also surprise adults to know that giving a starting note on the piano and playing the melody loudly are of little help to children in singing in tune until they have already developed quite considerable skill at singing in tune with a human voice. In other words, the piano accompaniment hinders more than it helps. It also cuts off the adult from the crucial, face-to-face contact with the children. It is interesting to speculate why piano accompaniment is so widely thought to be important with young children's singing. It may be a cultural hangover (musically it is the done thing from the Wigmore Hall downwards) but I suspect that the main reason is that it makes the sound of a group of young children singing a little more acceptable to adult ears ! Less powerful and bulky instruments such as the guitar, which tend to be used just as a light support for your voice and don't cut you off from the children, are better than the piano, but the unaccompanied human voice is the main instrument in learning to sing.

A second important contribution you can make is to play lots of the simple sound patterning games that we have already talked about several times. These often arise spontaneously ; they may be inspired by the child's play or by something in a story. With my children one such game arose from a Noggin the Nog story (*The Flying Machine*) in which Olaf the Lofty, inventor of a flying boat, and Graculus the talking bird are arguing about the best material to cover the wings :

Down beside the harbour, Graculus, the green bird, and Olaf the Lofty were arguing furiously.
'Feathers !' shouted Graculus.
'Leather !' shouted Olaf.
'Quiet !' shouted Noggin. 'Is the machine finished yet ? I want to show it to Thor Nogson !'
'All but the wing coverings,' said Olaf. 'We shall use leather.'
'Feathers !' muttered Graculus . . .

My children loved the rhymed shouting and went about chanting :

Feathers !
Leather !
Feathers !
Leather ! . . .

over and over again. It was considered particularly splendid if either Pauline or I would chime in with a 'Quiet !' (the first time it happened by accident, when we couldn't stand the row any longer). The children also liked starting very quietly, in low voices ,and getting louder and higher, louder and higher, until our shout of 'Quiet !' sent them back to the beginning again.

Such idiocy may seem some distance from learning to sing in tune, but the confidence and skill gained from controlling the pitch and loudness of your voice is basic. Any kinds of imitating sounds that arise spontaneously are valuable in this way – do you remember how we discussed talking with children about everyday sounds and things around the house that make sounds, and then imitating them (pp. 52–54) ? A child who can do that is ready for other sound-imitating games, perhaps slightly more formal ones like the following. I sometimes say to a child, 'I'm going to make some kind of a sound, perhaps with my body, perhaps with my voice. It may be loud, it may be soft. You listen and then see if you can make one like it – or the same sound if you can. That would be very clever.' Then I make sounds, one at a time, whatever kinds I fancy – maybe a clap, then a squeak, then a noise like a siren, then a letter sound like 'B-b-b', then a slide of my voice from high to low, then a growl like a bear, and so on. (Any kind of sound that I think the child will have the confidence to attempt may be included, sometimes loudly, sometimes softly – even sung notes are not forbidden !) After making each sound I wait for the child to make his own imitation. This may be exact or very approximate, of course. I stop as soon as I think we've had enough. Because this game practises careful listening and encourages the child to attempt an imitation of the sound he has heard it develops awareness of a wide range of vocal sound-making and the way it feels, which is the basis of in tune singing. However, the demands are much simpler and less rigid than those of conventional singing. Because of this it develops confidence, and indeed is a particularly valuable kind of game for the older non-singer who may already be very inhibited by what he considers his failure to sing.

Related to this is the use of the kind of improvized singing patterns we talked about in Chapter 3. Now you are using them not simply to make the child aware of vocal patterning but more directly to encourage him to make a simple vocal response, to get him to sing patterns back to you. For instance, I try things like :

Pe — ter, Pe — ter, do you like ice — cream?

to which he can respond, using the one note :

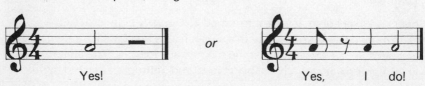

Yes! or Yes, I do!

96

or what he chooses. If he speaks the reply, or sings it out of tune, I usually sing, using either the original note or his note, something like :

I know you like ice cream. Do you like   crisps too?

However, I'm very careful about appearing to criticize the child's inaccuracy. I *never* point out directly that the child's pitch is inaccurate, and may well not 'reply' to the child's response if I think there is any possibility of him being put off. There's no point in reducing his confidence. After all, either he has not reached the stage of being aware that his pattern doesn't match yours, or he's all too aware ! !

You can do such question-and-answer singing about anything, as long as your child knows the answer to the question without having to think about it, because that would inhibit his singing fluency. I use questions like :

'What are you playing with, Samantha ?'
'What can you see out of the window ?'
'What are you making, Bayo ?'
'What's your name ?'
'What day is it today ?'
'Where are we going after breakfast ?'

but I am sure you can think of lots of possibilities yourself. They don't have to be questions, either ; I use this technique to abuse my children, with such patterns as :

Kath—er—ine is a sog—gy   dough — nut!

Naturally I get a response ! It may be as simple as :

Rub — bish!

but usually comes back a cry like :

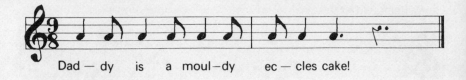

Dad — dy is a moul—dy ec — cles cake!

or it may be a different pattern, like :

Dad dy is an id — i — ot! *(clap, clap)*

Singing such patterns on one note is fine, but as you get more confidence yourself you're likely to find yourself using other simple tune patterns as the basis for your improvisation — maybe two notes, or snatches of existing tunes familiar to the children (as we discussed earlier) :

What's your name? (Pe — ter Ro — bert)
(using two notes)

Ma — ri — anne, where are your pants? (Here!)
using 'Ding Dong Bell'

What are you play — ing with, Sa — man — tha?
(using 'Drunken Sailor')

With the more complex improvisations you may well find that the child just speaks the answer, or sings it on one note, as in the second example above. For him to use your tune to reply is quite a sophisticated skill, dependent on a lot of singing experience and a long familiarity with you singing and improvising — but I must stress that experienced three-year-olds are quite capable of answering the third question above with :

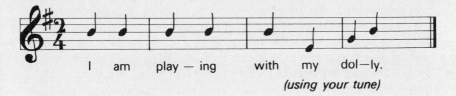

I am play — ing with my dol—ly.

(using your tune)

or even with :

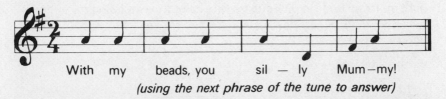

With my beads, you sil — ly Mum—my!

(using the next phrase of the tune to answer)

Such singing is very close to the kinds of play songs that children make themselves, so it is not necessarily such a big step. As always, feeling secure with you and getting examples from you are the key factors in making it possible.

But I couldn't possibly improvise!

The kind of improvisation I am describing and encouraging you to try may appear very daunting, but it is much, much easier than it appears. It is only play with sounds, after all ! The key is having the confidence to try, and not to be worried about making mistakes. This is, I think, where the real problem lies. We are all conditioned to think that we have to do musical things perfectly. Forget that — if a thing's worth doing it is worth doing badly ; and improvising gets easier and easier with practice.

If you are still worried about making mistakes, and can't possibly face it, just reflect that this is exactly the kind of pressure we put on small children when we try to teach them formally to sing ! A sobering thought, isn't it ?

One tip that may prove helpful to you is that a number of books contain simple songs about small children's domestic and personal activities. Many of the best books of this kind have been compiled for use by those working with mentally handicapped children. Don't be put off by this — remember that a song written for an eight-year-old with a mental age of three will probably be ideal for your normal three-year-old. Try some of the songs in books like *Music Activities for Retarded Children* by D. R. Ginglend and W. E. Stiles or *Children's Play Songs* by Nordoff and Robbins, and, of course, look in *This Little Puffin* and *American Folk Songs for Children*. You can also get a lot from the television programmes for small children. *Play School*, *Play Away*, *Rainbow* and all the others have started making much more use of the kinds of songs I have been talking about. Even if you can't remember a whole song, you will often get a phrase or an idea which you can use in your improvised singing.

You can see, I am sure, how this all links up with what we have seen about the way young children begin by joining in with snatches of songs or rhymes and, as they master these, gradually attempt more and more of a song. The simple games described above offer them very simple and short patterns to imitate and so develop confidence and skill. You will make up lots of your own, I hope. This confidence and skill naturally carries over into singing snatches of songs, and the sort that offer simple patterns for children to pick out are very helpful in extending this. The following song, which was made up by two six-year-old children, is a good example:

Johnny writes

Baby plays, plays, plays,	(*wave your arms and legs*)
Baby plays, plays, plays,	
All day long.	
Johnny writes ; Susan skips ;	
Baby plays	(*do appropriate actions*)
All day long.	
Mummy cooks, cooks, cooks . . .	(*stir a pot*)
Daddy works, works, works . . .	(*lift a heavy load, or saw wood, or . . .*)
Nanny knits, knits, knits . . .	(*'knit' with your index fingers*)
Grandad dozes, dozes, dozes . . .	(*doze, singing slowly and sleepily*)

(Of course, when you sing this with your own child, you will want to sing about your own family and the things *you* do ; you may also want to avoid the kind of stereotyped view of female roles that the writers have.) When you sing this song with a young child he will become involved in several ways. He will do the actions ; he may make suggestions about people in his own family to sing about ; he will probably pick out bits to sing himself. One obvious one is :

All   day   long ......

Another (though less commonly) is :

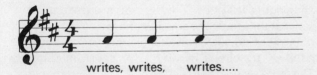

writes, writes,   writes.....

Confidence in singing these fragments in the right places leads rapidly to attempting the rest of the song. Clearly, any song that has a very simple refrain or chorus will be very suitable for this, and it is not surprising that such songs have always been a staple part of folk music, where much music-making is essentially a social activity which has to cater for all ages and all levels of musical skill. If your child can sing a whole chorus, you need have no further worries about his singing ; he will sing complete songs whenever the social situation or his own feelings demand it.

Let me reiterate. The development of singing skill, like the development of speaking skill, is a natural process. It will happen inevitably at the child's own pace, provided that he is given lots of opportunity to hear and join in with singing. There is no set speed or pattern ; indeed, you may find that your child doesn't begin to join in accurately with singing until he goes to playgroup, or even to first school, when he feels it is expected of him ! However, it is the period of singing with you when he was not pressured that will have made it possible for him to sing confidently.

When we compare what happens so naturally and easily in an ordinary home situation with the tensions and inhibitions about singing that so many schoolchildren experience we are forced to wonder what goes wrong. Maybe we have *created* most of the problems ourselves. John Holt quotes his friend Bill Hull talking about children's speech : Bill once said, 'If we taught them to speak, they'd never learn.' He was commenting on the limitations of our teaching of reading (another formally taught school skill), which we see as an activity in which young children require training, pressuring, testing and retesting in order to bring them up to an appropriate standard (how often this is true of children's singing !). He goes on to say, referring to learning to speak :

Suppose we tried to do this ; what would happen ? What would happen, quite simply, is that most children, before they got very far, would become baffled, discouraged, humiliated and fearful, and would quit trying to do what we asked them.

I have never found a better description of what happens to most people in their music lessons !

Let me say again, the tragedy of formal teaching of singing to young children is that such an approach is not only destructive but totally unnecessary. The great genius of young children is that they don't feel the need to get everything right all at once. They accept the insecurity of incompetence, provided that they have the security of a loving relationship. They try things out, check them, alter or modify what they're doing . . . try, check, modify . . . try, check, modify . . . try, check, modify . . . until they get it right. The more secure they feel with us, the more chance we give them, both in speech and in singing, to hear models, to practise by hearing themselves imitating the models, and to be approved in this process, the quicker they will refine their skills, and the more pleasure they will get from singing. And at this age the pleasure is more important than the skill.

6
Patterns of rhythm

In view of my approach to singing, is there any need to do anything about developing other musical skills? What about rhythm? Don't you need to give your child lots of rhythmic practice? or can it all be left until the infant school percussion band?

If you listen to some music teachers you get the impression that they have to do it all. It always amuses me to hear them talking about 'introducing rhythm activities' to young children in school. I am never sure whether the implication is that children won't have experienced any rhythmic activities before coming to school (!) or whether the implication is that it is now time for the children to have some 'proper rhythmic experience'. Either way it is obviously a nonsensical idea.

There is no need to 'put rhythm in'. Children's early years are full of rhythmic experience. Even in the womb they sense the pulsation of their mother's heartbeat (and we have already seen how this sound, recorded, will soothe the crying of newborn babies (p. 6)). From birth they are exposed to a wide range of rhythms. Their sucking usually follows definite patterns; they feel the rhythms of hunger and satiety, of feeding and excreting, of night and day. Everywhere tension and relaxation, strong and weak accents are an integral part of life, and this is the essence of rhythm. In the country the slow rhythm of natural things and of the everyday agricultural routine become a part of every child's experience. In the city a child is surrounded by highly rhythmic patterns – chugging motors, chiming clocks, ambulance sirens, the rattle and roar of passing trains, and much more.

Rhythmic patterns and experiences surround all of us all the time. As I write this, in a hotel bedroom, the mill-stream rushes past continuously; my travelling clock ticks in a rapid pitter-patter; my sleeping daughter breathes lightly and slowly; occasionally someone walks down the corridor outside; in the bathroom my wife squeezes out her smalls. In this sense no child ever lacks rhythmic experience, but, as with the matter of understanding sounds, the extent of his awareness of rhythmic patterns will depend on a number of factors. In the same way all children make many rhythmic sounds and patterns, but their ability to do them to order or to fit in with other people will vary. You see your baby doing things rhythmically from a very early age. Since he has control of his mouth earlier than of his limbs, we usually see it first with his sucking, his rhythmic babbling and his other vocal sound-making. For instance, I recently saw Daniel, aged eight months, lying on a blanket on the floor, blowing raspberries in this rhythm, which he kept quite strictly :

slowly

As babies get more control of their bodies you see the same kinds of rhythmic patterns emerging in their movements. As a very small child Mick always used to turn and roll his head from side to side before going to sleep – the regular rhythm soothed and reassured him, and he had an even larger bald patch on the back of his head than babies usually have ! Similarly Peter, when about eight months old, loved being sat up on the sofa ; he used to bang his head and body against the back of the sofa in a regular rhythm for long periods. He got so enthusiastic about this game that we used to have to wedge the sofa against the wall or another piece of furniture for fear that it would overturn. You will also find that any sort of rhythmic stimulus (singing, clapping, humming, etc.) within his field of attention will often start your baby bouncing or banging or shouting *to his own rhythm*. Children's play with their toys shows rhythmic patterns – we mentioned earlier Katherine's banging with biscuit tin and wooden spoon. Often you see it with a baby who is beginning to use a spoon to eat with. Once his initial hunger is satisfied the urge to experiment takes over. The food makes a satisfying sound when hit, and hit it he does, until his Mum leaps in and stops him. (I am not suggesting she shouldn't, by the way – I am just remarking on his rhythmic experiment !) If you look closely at what babies do I am sure you will need no convincing that they have a rhythmic sense. But you may well be wondering why, if this is so, a child won't just be able to clap and echo rhythmic patterns, to keep a beat going, to play in an ensemble with other people, and so on. Clearly it is not that simple, otherwise all children would be rhythmically skilled and confident – which many are not ! What is missing ? Why, for instance, should a child who skips and chants rhythmically on her own sometimes be unable to fit in with the rhythmic patterns of others ?

I think the first thing to stress is that most early rhythmic activity is totally individual, egocentric and idiosyncratic. The baby banging her dinner does so *in her own rhythm*. Before her innate rhythmic sense can be used musically with other people she has to become conscious of it. She has to learn to control it, developing in the process certain specific skills. She has to learn to recognize the rhythmic patterns she makes and be able to repeat them exactly ; she has to go through the process of synchronizing her movements with her own vocal sounds ; she has to have frequent opportunities to join in with other people's music-making informally so as to build up her rhythmic skills. As with the development of her singing, she will only see the need to make her rhythms fit with other people's when she wants to join in with them. All these processes of growing awareness and skill will for most children be going on throughout the age range with which we are concerned.

But doesn't the development of these processes depend on the adult doing 'rhythm activities' such as getting the child to clap the pulse of music, to echo fixed rhythm patterns that the adult claps, to learn the French time names, and so on ? No, it doesn't ! Indeed, such 'rhythm activities' are inappropriate and potentially dangerous for under-fives (which is a great relief for those of you who, like me, always got mixed up in the French time names !) Kenneth Jameson suggests a reason — even though he is not talking about music :

An example of misguided stimulus is the frequently met-with over-insistence on formal pattern-making.

Conventional rhythm activities tend to demand a fixed and very limited 'correct' response. Usually they isolate the one element, the rhythmic, and treat it in isolation, which is always a dangerous thing to do with young children. They are a very limited and limiting stimulus to rhythmic awareness and skill, yet many teachers still insist on trying to use them as the main opportunity for children to build up their rhythmic experience. Really they are a test of the child's level of competence and unless handled with the greatest care and sensitivity by the adult they become a rigid performance demand, with all the dangers we have already discussed in connection with singing.

In contrast, as with singing, the natural process is so easy and so inevitable. If a child gets a rich range of basic rhythmic experiences he has a *resource* on which he can draw whenever social activities demand certain rhythmic skills. In the natural situation of joining in with older people the child will never be forced to attempt something beyond his capability, though he may well cheerfully attempt something he can't yet manage. The act of taking part at a level where he can manage makes him more aware and practises the skills in an atmosphere of security and encouragement, and this in turn goes to build up his rhythmic resource. The ridiculousness of formal rhythm activities with this age group can be clearly seen if you equate it with demanding that four-year-olds draw realistic human figures in order to develop their figure drawing. We don't do this ! Instead, we give them lots of opportunities to paint and draw in their own ways ; we talk about their pictures ; we look at a wide range of pictures of people in books and magazines. By the time the child becomes interested *himself* in the realistic portrayal of a person he has the basic skills to attempt it, and his attempt motivates him to improve his skills.

The same kind of natural process should happen with rhythm. We should only impose formal rhythm activities when we know that the child has the skills to cope, not when we are trying to develop those skills. But there are many less formal things we can do to help the development. You will not be surprised to hear me say that the interaction between you and your child is crucial in his becoming aware of patterns and gaining confidence in making them himself. From the beginning you can contribute by doing various kinds of rhythmic playing with him. We described in the early chapters the ways adults can rock babies, dance with them, croon and chant and sing to them. These things will make a big contribution to a consciousness of rhythm, as will the 'Boo' and 'Aaaaah-bubble !' games, nursery rhymes, finger plays and so on. Some children, of course, will get very special and specific rhythmic experiences. I remember seeing a father sit his six-months-old son in a baby chair and say very seriously to him, 'Now, I'm going to play you a dance.' He played a galliard on his lute, and the baby sat fascinated, watching his father's hands moving on the instrument, until the tune was finished. But such special experiences, however valuable, are not essential. Your baby will grow and develop rhythmically through the ordinary kinds of experience any adult can provide. At first this will be through playing, talking, moving and singing with him. Gradually this links up with his own solitary exploration of his environment and practising of skills, such as shaking or babbling. Later the playgroup leader or teacher takes over part of your role ; later still cooperative musical activity with other children and adults becomes more and more important to the child. In the process he develops the skills he needs to perform rhythmically.

Rhythm things to do with a child

Let's look in more detail at some of the things you can do with your child that will help his rhythmic development. One of the earliest activities is to bounce or rock him in little repeated patterns, perhaps like this one :

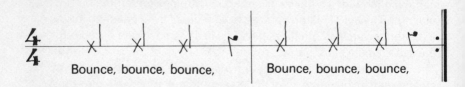

You do it over and over and over again. The baby feels the pattern and has plenty of chance to get to know it through the many repetitions. As I have said before, it helps if you make a sound — grunt, speak, sing — in time with the bounces. Any rhythmic patterns that arise spontaneously are fine for this. Some of them may be suggested to you by sounds or movements the baby makes himself. For instance, a baby will often make two or three downward movements of his whole arms from above his head to his lap. You can take his hands and repeat the movements yourself, adding a vocal sound. As with talking and singing, this kind of copying is very powerful in making the baby aware of patterns he can make. It leads obviously into all the kinds of rhythmic games we have already quoted, like *Pitty patty polt* (p. 7) or *See saw, Margery Daw* (p.7). Another very familiar one is done with your baby sat on your knees, facing you :

Pat-A-Cake

Pat-a-cake, pat-a-cake, baker's man,	(*clap the baby's hands together rhythmically*)
Bake me a cake as fast as you can,	
Pat it and prick it and mark it with B	(*'pat' and 'prick' one hand with a finger of the other – mark a 'B'*)
And put it in the oven for baby and me.	(*clasp his hands in both of yours*)

When you do a rhyme like this he is hearing a rhythmic pattern of words ; he is also *feeling* corresponding patterns through his body ; at the end of the rhyme you stop his physical participation by clasping his hands in yours, and then start it again when the rhyme restarts. His rhythmic experience is being reinforced in every sense. After hearing and doing the rhyme several times with you he will naturally want to do it himself, and if you begin the rhyme he will often begin the clapping. Mind you, he probably won't be able to coordinate his clapping (his hands may miss each other, for instance) and he will almost certainly be out of time. Matthew tried to perform the clapping before he was a year old, but he was sixteen months old before he could do it more or less in time with his Mum.

We have talked a lot about improvised games and songs to do with rocking and see-sawing, on swings and rocking boats and rocking chairs. These are enormously important rhythmic experiences, and babies and young children love them. They also love to be jigged up and down on your lap or crossed legs, and there are lots of good rhymes for this, like *Ride a cock horse* and *This is the way the ladies ride*. One of my favourites is :

Father and Mother and Uncle John

Father and Mother and Uncle John	(*jig the baby up and down, holding his hands*)
Went to market, one by one.	
Father fell off !	(*Let him slip off to one side*)
Mother fell off !	(*Let him slip off to the other*)
But Uncle John went on and on And on and on and on.	(*Pull him back on, and jog him faster and faster to the end*)

Another good game is leg-shaking or leg-waving, where you sit the baby on your lap with his back to you, leaning against your chest, and you take hold of his ankles. Here are two splendid rhymes of this type from Norah Montgomerie's book *This Little Pig Went to Market*:

Old Farmer Giles

Old Farmer Giles,	*(lift his legs up and down in time*
He went seven miles	*with the rhyme, getting faster and*
With his faithful dog, Rover.	*faster)*
Old Farmer Giles,	
When he came to stiles,	*(at 'jumped' lift both his legs sharply*
Took a run and jumped over !	*as high as they will go)*

The Fight

This is Bill Anderson,	*(lift left foot)*
That is Tom Sim.	*(lift right foot)*
Tom called Bill to fight	*(lift right foot across over left foot)*
And fell over him,	
Bill over Tom	*(lift left foot across right)*
And Tom over Bill	*(right across left)*
Over and over as they	*(repeat faster and faster)*
Fell down the hill !	*(part your knees suddenly and let*
	the baby slip down between them)

With all these rhymes and games you are building up a powerful awareness of patterns of rhythmic sounds being related to physical sensations and movements. You are 'feeding in' the experience that he will use when he sets out to play his own rhythmic patterns. If you are tempted to undervalue this, remember that a child's ability to imitate is in full force between twelve and twenty-four months, and that the period between ten and eighteen months is highly significant in his development of later competence (p. 30). These early rhythmic experiences are immensely powerful.

As well as stressing rhythmically regular patterns, these games include many other important rhythmic experiences, such as slowing and accelerating, strong and weak stresses and the building up to the climax of a sudden slip or fall or stop or boo or clap. These are particularly important as a contrast to, and therefore a clarification of, the regular rhythms ; in order to come to a full understanding of regularity he needs repeated experience of such variations from the basic pattern. The development of a rhythmic sense and skill is not a matter of drumming in regular patterns of crotchets and quavers ! It lies in making the child aware of the complex patterns of life. Alice Yardley puts it beautifully :

A child's love of rhythm may be expressed in beating a drum, but beating a drum doesn't teach a child rhythm, since rhythm doesn't need to be taught; it exists in the child as part of his life. This natural love can be encouraged and deepened; it cannot be imposed. (*Sense and Sensitivity*)

Interestingly, the beating of the drum doesn't necessarily even *refine* the child's rhythmic skill; for this to happen he has to be *aware* of the patterns he is making. Naturally, you can help him to be more aware of rhythm and you can give him opportunities to practise appropriately. But the basis for all this must be his own rhythmic experience, not your expectations of him.

We can see that many games not obviously musical are very important musically with young children — games like 'Aaaaaah-bubble!' (p. 8), with its slow build-up to the sudden climax, or more complex versions, like:

The Tickly Bird

The tickly bird is coming for Paul   (*'flying' your hand all round the*
Flying here, flying there,   *child, but never quite touching*
Flying in the kitchen,   *him*)
Flying in the hall,
Flying, flying everywhere.
    Perhaps he's not coming for Paul   (*'fly' your hand away behind your*
    At all...   *back*)
    But...   (*wiggling your shoulders and head*)
The tickly bird *is* coming for Paul,   (*'fly' your hand all around*)
Flying here, flying there,
Flying round his trousers,
Flying round his vest,
Flying, flying everywhere.
    Perhaps that bird will choose...   (*make your hand hover*)
    His shoes!   (*grab his shoe*)

In a very general sense the pattern of games like this — the repetition, the ebb and flow — are an important part of the child's growing rhythmic awareness.

Another kind of game arises from the way that adults link sounds to patterns of actions, or imitate the rhythmic patterns of sounds that can be heard in the environment (we have seen lots of examples in previous chapters). One obvious but very basic game is to say 'Left, right, left, right, left, right...' in time to the child's walking, or to sing, or clap, or click, in time to *his* steps when running or skipping or walking. Children love this kind of pattern — it is frequently a successful way of getting a small child to walk the remaining distance home when he isn't very keen. One warning, though; you are not trying to get the child to fit his steps to a rhythm that you fix, which is something he may well not be able to do. You take your time from *his* speed of step. This experience leads directly to footstep patterns in stories you tell (see later in this chapter) and from this to a clear understanding of some of the basic rhythms of music.

Many of the most valuable kinds of rhythmic experience arise out of little movement games with an adult. They can be ridiculously simple patterns and many of the best will be improvised on the spur of the moment. For instance, one of the most successful I've tried, whether with an individual child or with a line of children holding hands, is to go :

Jump ! . . . Jump ! . . .	(*with feet together*)
One, two, three . . .	(*take three big steps*)
Jump ! . . . Jump ! . . .	(*with feet together*)
One, two, three . . .	(*take three big steps*)

This is repeated till we reach the end of the available space – then we shout 'Turn around !' and we 'Jump ! . . . Jump ! . . .' back again. After a large number of repetitions we may alter the pattern of movement. We may go :

Wiggle ! . . . Wiggle ! . . .	(*wiggle your bottom and shuffle your feet*)
One, two, three . . .	(*take three big steps*)
Wiggle ! . . . Wiggle ! . . .	(*wiggle your bottom and shuffle your feet*)
One, two, three . . .	(*take three big steps*)

We may change to hopping (though small children tend to fall on their noses doing this, so watch out) or tiptoeing right across the space, then we turn round with our shout and do it back again. The children usually suggest different things we can do, once they have got hold of the pattern. It is very interesting that they often have great difficulty in doing the pattern in time with me when they start, but this doesn't worry them. They jump and stumble and giggle along, perhaps doing three jumps and four steps ! As the game is repeated over and over you see them mastering it. As with their singing development, you see them get a bit right ; they keep trying and modifying ; and by the time we stop (usually from my exhaustion) they have got it completely right. Once again this suggests that we should be very hesitant to 'correct' or 'teach' children when doing these activities. It also reminds us of the value of doing something lots and lots of times, provided the child is enjoying it.

Lots of simple household jobs are very good for improvising rhythmic patterns, so are jobs in the garden or connected with 'do-it-yourself'. Margaret Shephard quotes the blanket-shaking (or rug-shaking or tablecloth-shaking or doll's mattress-shaking) pattern :

Shake the bed, shake the bed,
Turn the mattress over.

What about making up something like this?

Flip, flop, flippety-flop,
Shake the ⎰crumbs
　　　　　⎱feathers all off the top.
　　　　　⎰dust

or like this?

Bang, bang, bang the nails,
Bang them with my hammer.

Scrubbing, sweeping, sawing, rolling out pastry — the list of possibilities is enormous. Do you remember Doc Watson listening to his mother singing while she churned the butter? That may not be one of your usual tasks, but I am sure you can find some other job to sing at!

Another thing you can do with children from an early age is to make your own little rhythmic patterns of claps, stamps, pops, clicks, whatever. Mind you, this is not so that your child can copy them directly. It is much more that he becomes aware that making rhythmic patterns is an acceptable and enjoyable thing to do, and he gets experience of the ways that adults fit in rhythmic patterns and put them together. The sort of chanting and clapping you get in football crowds is one possibility:

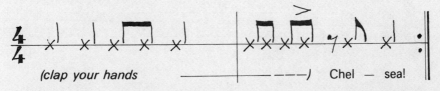

(clap your hands —————————) Chel — sea!

and you can put words to it:

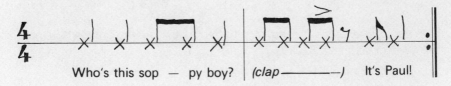

Who's this sop — py boy? (clap————) It's Paul!

Any little pattern of clapping will do — like this one:

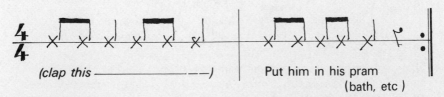

(clap this —————————) Put him in his pram
　　　　　　　　　　　　　　　　(bath, etc)

It can easily be adapted to all sorts of feeding, dressing and so on.

Clearly, this kind of play will often occur in songs or fit into them. Do you remember the 'Ole' in the *Burping Song* (p. 11)? It is a kind of improvising, and links up with all the singing games; perhaps I should stress again that musical experience for young children cannot be put into rigid compartments, despite the efforts of some music teachers. A colleague of mine once asked a six-year-old girl at a very musical infant school whether she ever played any tunes on the instruments. The little girl looked very shocked. 'Miss plays the tunes,' she said firmly. '*We* don't play any tunes until next year.' Oh dear!

Improvised songs with a strong rhythmic emphasis often come out when you are doing very physical things with your child, like pushing the pushchair. One of my children's favourites was the old standard pattern :

(clap,   clap)

and it got lots of different words put to it at different times :

What a load of rub — bish!	(clap,	clap)
Where is my Kif — fen?	(clap,	clap)
Who is in the lav – a – tory?	(clap,	clap)
What is for din — ner?	(clap,	clap)
You're a sil – ly saus – age!	(clap,	clap)

As the children got older they would frequently use the same pattern to answer or comment back :

| I am in the bath — room! | (clap, | clap) |
| Dad–dy is an id–i — ot! | (clap, | clap) |

This kind of rhythmic awareness will also show itself in their own song-making, as with the '*Boom, boom, boom . . .*' in the *Hump-Backed Camel Song* (p. 75). You also find that such things arise spontaneously, either from you or from the children. I was playing with a small group of young children in a nursery class and Sharon suggested that we should sing *The wheels on the bus* (p. 84). We did this, complete with the actions, and then passed on to looking at some objects that made sounds. One of them was an aluminium coat hook that made a beautiful, bell-like sound. As soon as he heard this David (nearly five) said, 'That's the bell on the bus – sing it again.' We sang the bell verse, with the children singing 'Ding, ding, ding . . .' and me playing the coat hook. On the spur of the moment I put in an extra two dings at the end :

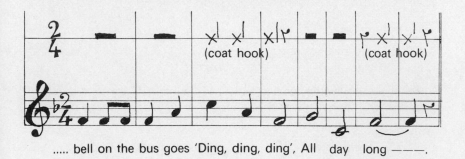

..... bell on the bus goes 'Ding, ding, ding', All day long ———.

There was a moment's astonished silence, then peals of laughter. 'Do it again !' they cried. We sang the verse again, then the whole song again, and they spontaneously put in the new rhythm at the end of each verse, using the appropriate action or sound.

It is a good story, I think, to remind us how unreal is the breaking-up of children's music into rigid sections that even a book like this encourages. The activities you do naturally and spontaneously with young children cut across boundaries and their value for the children lies in many different (yet related) areas. As children get older one activity leads gradually into another, more complex one. It is not a conscious process of you saying, 'Now I think Jane has passed out of the stage of simple rhythmic experiences ; I must do some more sophisticated patterns,' any more than when playing ball you consciously say, 'Jane is beginning to track and grasp the ball with her hands, so I must stop throwing the ball into her cradled arms.' In both cases, when playing games with a child you know well, you instinctively extend the range of the activity to suit the growing needs and skills of the child. You don't have to worry about what comes next, in playing ball or in playing music.

Let's take as an example the way I suggested you should dance with your baby in your arms. You will find that as you sing or listen to music with the baby on your lap you will jog or rock him. As he gets bigger, you will jog or wave or tap individual parts of his body. You will clap his hands together in time, or wave his legs, and this links up strongly with the Norah Montgomerie games we quoted earlier. As he becomes a toddler and is able to sit or stand on his own, and to clap or tap for himself, you will tend to use more fingerplays and games where he can join in with rhythmic patterns himself. Here's one:

I Can Knock

I can knock with my two hands,	(*spoken rhythmically*)
Knock, knock, knock.	(*knock with one fist on the palm of the other hand*)
I can rock with my two hands,	(*join your hands 'in prayer'*)
Rock, rock, rock.	(*rock them in front of your face*)
I can tap with my two hands,	(*spoken quietly*)
Tap, tap, tap.	(*tap with one finger on the palm of the other hand*)
I can clap with my two hands,	
Clap, clap, clap!	(*loudly!*)

Another very enjoyable game is 'Roly-poly', which you speak in much freer rhythm, fitting it in with the speeds your child can manage:

Roly-poly

Roly-poly, ever so slowly,	(*roll your fists slowly round each other*)
Ever . . . so . . . slowly . . .	
Roly-poly up, up, up, up, up . . .	(*roll your fists upwards, making your voice higher and higher*)
Roly-poly, down, down, down!	(*roll your fists and your voice suddenly down to your boots*)
Roly-poly out, out, out, out . . .	(*roll your fists away from your body*)
Roly-poly into your tummy!	(*roll them back fast*)
Roly-poly up on my nose . . .	(*do it*)
Roly-poly down on my toes . . .	(*do it*)
Roly-poly ever so slowly . . .	(*exaggerated*)
Ever . . . so . . . slowly . . .	
Roly-poly faster, faster, faster,	(*accelerate*)
Faster, faster,	
And stop!!	(*with a slap on your knees*)

When doing *Roly-poly* you don't have to do all the sections, of course, and you need to repeat each section you do two or three times, so that the child has a chance to get into the swing of the game. Here is another strongly rhythmic game:

I can hear my feet

I can hear my feet go tap, tap, tap.	(*tap fingers on palm*)
I can hear my knees go slap, slap, slap.	(*slap knees*)
I can hear my hands go clap, clap, clap,	(*clap hands*)
But I can't hear my head go ——,	(*nod your head silently three times*)
——, ——.	

When your child begins to do and say with you such fingerplays as these he is having an enjoyable experience. I am sure your main concern when you do them is to have fun, not to do rhythmic training. Yet, imperceptibly, he is extending and practising his rhythmic skills and learning some very important musical ideas:

● He is speaking rhythmically. That may sound like an anticlimax, but speaking in rhythm is a crucial lead-in to playing in rhythm. Young children can speak a rhythm accurately before they can clap it or play it on an instrument, so through speaking they can learn rhythmic skills and develop their rhythmic awareness long before being able to do conventional percussion band work. And remember – children today don't get as many opportunities for chanting and speaking in rhythm as perhaps they used to do (and still do in less mechanized and sophisticated communities).

● At the same time the fingerplays are enabling him to use the spoken rhythms to support and refine his skill at 'playing' the rhythm with his body. Words and movements reinforce each other, and together they develop a strong rhythmic sense.

● He is assisting a very crucial stage in his rhythmic development. We have seen how early rhythmic exploration is purely individual, not necessarily fitted to anyone else's rhythms or restricted in any way. Before a young child can synchronize his own 'playing' of rhythms with other people's playing he must have learned to synchronize his own movements with sounds he makes himself; for instance, he must be able to do a movement like marching or banging and fit with it a sound made with his own voice. Given plenty of play opportunities he will do this in lots of ways. You've seen children lying on the floor with a toy car, going 'Brrrmm, brrrmm, brrrmm !' rhythmically and pushing the car in time ; you've seen them stomping around a space in time to their own shouting or chanting. The simultaneous speaking and moving involved in doing the fingerplays obviously helps and refines this process. Through hearing and seeing the different actions and words done by someone else at the same time he is helped to separate them consciously and so become aware of how they fit together. The importance of this growing awareness is clear if we think of the difficulties some children have at school with rhythmic work. I remember seeing a class of six-year-olds organized into a conventional percussion band. One little boy called Wilberforce stood out amongst them. It was clear that he was not thought to be very musical as he wasn't allowed a tambourine or cymbal or drum ; he just had a pair of sticks and his job was to play the beat. The band raised their instruments, came to attention and were off, to the accompaniment of Beethoven's *Ode to Joy* on the piano. Off too went Wilberforce, getting faster and faster, totally engrossed in himself. The teacher endured for a few bars and then, 'Wilberforce ! You're not keeping the beat ! Listen to the music ! Keep in time with the others !' (all the usual remarks we use so easily). But it was clear that Wilberforce was not aware of the others, or of the music. Indeed, if he had not yet reached the stage of self-synchronization described above, probably he *couldn't* hear the others while he was playing.

● The child who joins in with a fingerplay like *I can knock* is able to try rhythmic participation at whatever level he chooses, in exactly the same unstressed way as we described with his learning to sing. Many very young or immature children only do the final clapping, since that is the easiest action and it comes at the end of the fingerplay, when they are getting into the swing of things. Even if they try to play all the patterns, at first their joining in may be very inaccurate – children often 'knock' four or five times, for instance – but through repetition and the development of confidence they come to master the techniques without any pressure or stress being involved. (The loud clapping at the end is a great releaser of any tension that may have built up.)

● Although such fingerplays may seem to be no more than fun, and so to have little to do with extending a child's musical education, they help to make a child aware of many basic musical concepts and skills. For instance, *Roly-poly* involves contrasts of speed, and the child has to follow them carefully, in exactly the way he will have to follow a conductor in later ensemble music-making. The different sections are repeated varying numbers of times, and sometimes in a different order, so he has to listen, watch and follow very carefully. *Roly-poly* also helps children to understand our very difficult convention of using the terms 'high' and 'low' to describe pitch and it clarifies increase and decrease in speed – another potentially tricky concept. (Some children still have problems with this when they are six or seven, though those who have had plentiful experience of games like *Roly-poly* have no trouble.) Again, when in *I can knock* a child does quietly 'I can tap with my two hands, tap, tap, tap . . .' it helps him to be aware of the contrast between loud and soft in a musical setting and it gives him *meaningful* practice in playing quietly. This is an important point. Before a young child can obey a purely verbal instruction to play quietly he must have become aware of what playing quietly involves. He develops this kind of awareness through extensive talking about and experimenting with sounds, but also through seeing and hearing people making quiet sounds where the situation demands it, as in this fingerplay. Another source of such experience is the kind of story with sounds given later in this chapter, and in Chapter 4, 'Understanding sounds' (pp. 49–72). The significant thing is that it is the nature of the fingerplay or story which dictates the volume, not an arbitrary command by the adult ! In *I can hear my feet* you have the usual values of the rhythmic speaking and moving, but there is also the interesting experience of playing a rhythm by nodding without making a sound to go with it. This is exactly the skill a musician needs in order to keep the rhythm going when he has a rest and isn't playing or singing for a few beats. Many young children can't at first do the nods silently – they grunt or squeak at the same time.

I could go on about the musical value of fingerplays and action rhymes for young children, but I think you will have taken my point by now ! The same value attaches to songs with actions, like *The wheels on the bus* (p. 84), *Little fish* (p. 87), *Tidey-Oh* (p. 88), *Johnny writes* (p. 100), or this one :

Five Little Men

Four little men in a flying saucer . . .

Three little men in a flying saucer . . .

Two little men in a flying saucer . . .

One little man in a flying saucer   (*do actions as before*)
Flew round the world one day.
　He looked left and right
　But he didn't like the sight
So then . . . he . . . flew . . . a-way.   (*slowly*)

As well as the value of doing actions in time with the sound (and we've talked about this a lot), the child gets practice in remembering and playing different patterns - the slow 'round the world' and the quick 'looked left and right', for example .   And if you are afraid that the concept of spacemen in flying saucers is too sophisticated for the under-fives, how about this snippet from a nursery class?

Teacher (*sings*):   'So then ... he ... flew ... a-way.'
1st four-year-old: 'And it crashed ! It crashed ! Boom ! !'
2nd four-year-old   (*with a contemptuous dig in the ribs*) 'No, stupid !
                           He put it on automatic pilot !'

Another action song that children greatly enjoy, both because of the rhythmic actions and because of the contrast between the slow, freely sung first line and the highly rhythmic remainder of the verse, is this one :

I'm a Dingle-Dangle Scarecrow

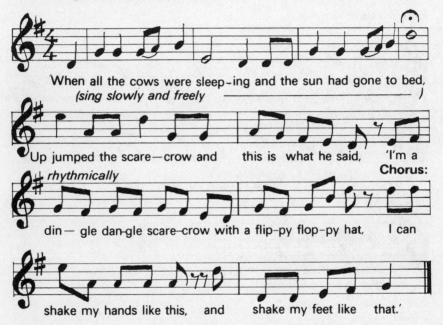

When all the cows were sleep-ing and the sun had gone to bed,
(sing slowly and freely ——————————— *)*

Up jumped the scare—crow and this is what he said, 'I'm a
Chorus:

rhythmically

din — gle dan-gle scare-crow with a flip-py flop-py hat, I can

shake my hands like this, and shake my feet like that.'

When dogs were in their kennels
And the pigeons in their loft,
Up jumped the scarecrow
And whispered very soft ...   *Chorus*

When all the hens were roosting
And the moon behind a cloud,
Up jumped the scarecrow
And shouted very loud ...   *Chorus*

There is also the great fun of the very quiet second chorus and the very loud third chorus. If you find that your child tends to fall over when he shakes his feet (or if you're doing it sitting on the floor) you can always make the last line of the chorus '... and shake my head like that.'

118

An important rhythmic experience which is a further extension of the principle of dancing with baby or doing fingerplays is the simple business of clapping or tapping or stamping or waving in time to a song or a piece of music. This is the basis of a great deal of the rhythmic skill of Africans, West Indians and others whose social patterns encourage a physical response to music. I must stress, though, that when I talk about this activity with young children I am thinking of *you* doing it as something you enjoy and that your child can join in with if he wants to. It mustn't become something you *demand* that the child does and you mustn't fix a pattern for him to perform in time to the music. By now I shouldn't need to explain why ! In any case, making such demands will almost certainly be unsuccessful. I well remember Peter, who at the age of two and three-quarters would sing and clap very loudly when someone was singing a song he liked, but would stop instantly in a fury if he was left (or asked) to sing or clap on his own. The main value of doing such clapping with a child is to let him see your own enjoyment and lack of embarrassment at such joining in.

Another valuable rhythmic activity may arise out of the collection of improvised instruments we talked about in Chapter 4 (p. 66) ; see also p. 140). Your child may well use one of his instruments to 'accompany' music that is playing on radio or record-player. Sometimes he will just play at random, parallel to the music — there may be no obvious connection between the two except that they are happening at the same time. This is very similar to other kinds of parallel play at this stage. Sometimes he may play the pulse of the music, or something close to it ; sometimes he will play little rhythmic patterns from the music. Whatever he does, it is an important experience that should be encouraged.

When he has had some experience of clapping and tapping and stamping sound patterns in these various ways you may be able to play some other games. One is a very simple copying game which also reinforces basic musical concepts. I say to the child, 'Can you clap with me ? We'll start very loudly and get quieter and quieter.' So we do. Then perhaps we do it getting faster and faster, or louder and louder. This helps to build control and awareness and also to clarify the basic musical terms. It also gives you an idea of the extent to which he has managed the synchronization of his own sound and movement. I shouldn't need to say that if he is having any difficulty with the game you should stop it instantly.

There is another kind of action song that gives very useful practice. As well as learning to play all through a song or piece of music, your child needs to get used to playing patterns *within* the song at the appropriate places. Fingerplays and action rhymes help this ; so do all action songs ; but songs that encourage the clapping or tapping of specific rhythms at specific points are very useful too. Here's a lovely simple one :

Clap Your Hands

Clap your hands (clap, clap, clap, clap), Clap your hands (clap, clap, clap, clap), Clap your hands (clap, clap, clap, clap), Clap your hands with me (clap, clap).

Slap your knees (slap, slap, slap, slap),
Slap your knees (slap, slap, slap, slap),
Slap your knees (slap, slap, slap, slap),
Slap your knees with me (slap, slap).

Stamp your feet (stamp, stamp, stamp, stamp) . . .

Tap your toes (tap, tap, tap, tap) . . .

Naturally you can sing about any movements you can do in time to the song. Don't hesitate to sing a verse more slowly if it helps, and make sure you do the actions yourself — your child may need this help at first.

Another excellent song of this kind, a little more complex but always much enjoyed, is *Let Everyone Clap Hands Like Me* :

Let Everyone Clap Hands Like Me

Let ev – ery – one clap hands like me, (clap, (clap, Let ev – ery – one. clap hands like me, (clap,

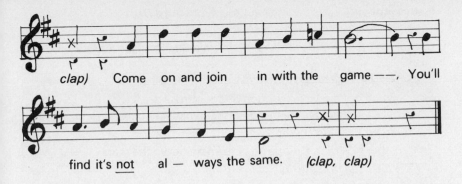

(clap)   Come   on and join   in with the   game ——, You'll

find it's not   al — ways the same.   (clap, clap)

Let everyone wiggle like me,   (do the action)
Let everyone wiggle like me,   (do the action)
   Come on and join in with the
     game,
You'll find it's not always the same. (do the action)
Let everyone tap knees like me . . .   (do the action)

Any action or sound can be used – jump, yawn, sit down, nod, laugh,
stand up, whistle, cry, sneeze and so on. Also very good fun is to play the
rhythm on different parts of the body, as in *Clap Your Hands* ; or to sing

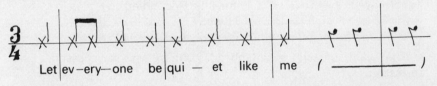

Let ev—ery—one be qui — et like me (——————)

and have a silence instead of playing the rhythm. As we saw with
I can hear my feet, this is difficult for some young children, but very
valuable practice.
   Another valuable source of practice is found in stories including
rhythmic patterns of sounds for the child to join in with. These may use
just the body sounds or may use sound-making objects, as in *The
Building Site* (p. 55). In either case they are very important in developing
a child's rhythmic sense. I'll give an example of each type. First of all the
body sounds – here is how I tell *The Little Indian Boy* :

The Little Indian Boy
One morning the little Red Indian boy
   (*put one finger up behind your head to represent a feather*)
woke up, stretched (*stretch*), yawned (*yawn*),
got out of bed and said to his Mum, 'Oo-oo-oo-oo-oo-oo-oo !
   (*wobble your finger in your mouth to make a war whoop*)
Mum ! I'm going out for a walk.'

So he went out of the hut and shut the door with a *BANG* !
   (*slap hands loudly on your knees*)
He walked off down the road, and his feet made footstep sounds, like this.
   (*tap your fingers on your palm*)
After a while he came to a wooden bridge across a stream.
When he walked across the bridge his feet made a hollow sound, like this.
   (*clap with cupped hands*)
On the other side of the bridge he walked on down the road
   (*tap with fingers again*)
a long . . . long . . . long . . . way.
   (*continue tapping throughout*)
At last he came to a wide, deep river, and he stopped.
There was no bridge to go across !
The little Indian boy looked up the river,
   (*look left, shading your eyes with your hand*)
but there was no bridge that way.
He looked down the river,
   (*look right similarly*)
but there was no bridge that way.
'I shall have to swim across,' said the little Red Indian boy.
He dived into the river with a splasssshh !
   (*make a diving movement with your head and hands*)
and he swam, splissshh, splassshh, splissshh, splassshh, splissshh, splassshh,
   (*elegant crawl stroke actions*)
all the way to the other side of the river.
He climbed out on the bank and he was very, very wet.
So he shook off the water, brrrrrrrrrrr !
   (*shake all over, like a dog and make a wiggly sound*)
On the other side of the river there was a big forest of trees.
The little Indian boy walked into the forest very slowly and carefully because he didn't know what he might find.
He walked like this,
   (*tap with your fingers very slowly and softly, looking from side to side*)
until he came to a very tall, very wide tree
   (*show with your hands how big*)
and he couldn't see whether anything was behind it.
So he looked round one side of the tree
   (*peek left*)
but he couldn't see anything.

He looked round the other side of the tree
    (*peek right*)

but he couldn't see anything.
He listened very carefully . . .
    (*with your hand to your ear*)

but he couldn't hear anything.
So he was just going to walk round the tree when he heard
'Grrr ! Grrrrrrr !'
It was a big, brown bear ! !
The little Red Indian boy ran back through the forest
    (*repeat all the actions and sounds in reverse order, as fast as your child can manage*)

until he came to the river.
He dived in with a splassssshh !
and swam to the other side very fast, splissshh, splassshh . . .
He jumped out on the bank and shook off all the water, brrrrrrrrrr !
He ran back along the road . . .
(remember, it was a very long way),
across the bridge . . .
and all the way back to his hut . . .
He ran inside and shut the door with a *BANG* !
and he said to his Mum,
'Oo-oo-oo-oo-oo-oo !
    (*very breathless and wobbly*)

I'm home again, and the big, brown bear didn't catch me !'

This story, like the action songs, will show you very clearly the wide range of young children's participation, if you do it with a group. Some may be unable to join in at all with the actions, though they follow the story intently (if you do it again you may well find that they begin to join in). Some may just manage one or two of the obvious things — the '*BANG*' of the door or the 'splassshh !' of the dive. You often see children who make ready to tap the footsteps, but at the last moment withdraw their hands shyly, or who tap inaudibly. You will find children who join in vigorously but with very little control (they may clap fast and loudly when the little Indian boy is creeping through the forest, for instance) and you will find some three-year-olds who do everything with the greatest competence. Just as with a song like *The wheels on the bus*, you will see a rapid development of confidence and control as you do this and other stories with sounds over a period of weeks.

    Another useful type of story for developing rhythmic awareness is the kind about about children's everyday lives (often made up by the parent or teacher). This sort of story can well include simple sound effects and rhythms played on percussion instruments, often the improvised or found kind. Musically this is a more sophisticated stage than *The Little Indian Boy*, but it is enjoyed by very young children, provided one of their adults is telling the story. The following is one I made up – but if you use it you will have to adapt it to fit the experience of your child. It is no good talking about tower block flats to a child brought up in a suburban semi!

Floyd Goes to Playgroup

This is a story about a boy called Floyd, who lives in a flat with his Mum and his Dad and his two big sisters.

Well, Floyd woke up one morning, and he was very, very sad for no reason. Do you ever wake up feeling sad, like Floyd? Floyd was very miserable on this morning.

He got dressed very slowly and sadly

(mime putting on a pair of trousers very slowly)

and he still felt miserable. His Mum cooked him a lovely breakfast of egg and fried bread, but he ate it very slowly and sadly

(mime very slow chewing and swallowing)

and he still felt miserable.

His Mum said to him, 'Come on, Floyd! Time to go to playgroup. You like that, don't you?'

They walked out of their flat, down the stairs and out along the road. Floyd walked along with his head down, very slowly and sadly.

(clap with two fingers on your palm, or knock on the chair, or tap with a beater on a drum or woodblock, to the rhythm of Floyd's slow walk. You can encourage your child to join in gently)

Suddenly he heard a different person's footsteps coming from behind, but this person wasn't walking slowly and sadly.

(clap or knock or tap a skipping rhythm)

He looked around and there was his friend Eula skipping along the pavement after him.

(play the skipping rhythm again)

'Hello, Floyd,' said Eula. 'Why, what's the matter with you?'

'I'm sad,' said Floyd. 'I don't know why – I'm just sad.'

'Never mind,' said Eula. 'Come on, run with me. That'll make you feel better.' So they ran along the pavement together.

(play a running rhythm)

But just as they got to the corner of the street they stopped! They could hear a strange sound, rather like this . . .

(on your chest, or your thighs, or, better still, on a large cardboard box, or on a tambour, beat a slow, regular, heavy pulse. Your child can join in)

'What's that?' whispered Eula.

'I don't know,' said Floyd. 'Let's go and see.' So they tiptoed round the corner.

(*play footsteps very slowly and softly*)

There, in front of the playgroup hall, was a strong workman with a big sledgehammer, and he was knocking a wooden post into the ground. It was a very big hammer, so the workman hit very slowly and heavily.

(*repeat the heavy pulse with hammering actions*)

The post went further and further into the ground, and Floyd and Eula watched with great interest.

Suddenly they heard another sound. It was the church clock striking the time.

(*on a steel egg-cup, or a bell, or a chimebar, or anything that makes a bell-like sound, strike ten*)

One . . . two . . . three . . . four . . . five . . . six . . . seven . . . eight . . . nine . . . ten. Ten o'clock.

'Listen, Floyd,' said his Mum, 'it's ten o'clock. If we don't hurry up playgroup will be finished.'

So Floyd and Eula ran in as quickly as they could.

(*repeat running rhythm*)

Outside the workman went on hammering until the post was firm and strong.

(*repeat hammering rhythm*)

Then he put down his hammer and walked off to get a cup of tea.

(*repeat walking rhythm, but more heavily than before*)

And do you know? Floyd had so enjoyed watching the workman that he found he wasn't sad any more. So he had a really nice morning at playgroup.

This is, of course, a long and complex story — it may be too long for a pre-school child or a playgroup, though I have done it successfully with many such groups. I include all the details to show the sort of things that are very simple to do in such a story. With a very young child you would make it very much simpler, with fewer rhythms and sounds. You would also make sure that he'd had plenty of experience of rhymes and fingerplays, as well as opportunities to experiment with sound-making objects. As always, it is up to you to make something suitable for your own child.

Another special advantage of a story including footsteps is that it's an excellent way of making children conscious of the basic rhythms of all music :

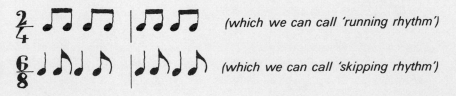

(*which we can call 'running rhythm'*)

(*which we can call 'skipping rhythm'*)

Both in 2/4 and in 6/8 time you can have a slower alternation :

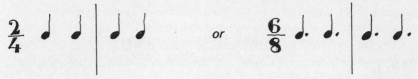

(which we can call 'walking rhythm')

This is a very good example of the way in which simple participation activities introduce basic musical ideas which will be required when children come to attempt more complex music-making. It also suggests some of the more developed activities that may arise from a simple starting-point. For instance, when a child knows the story, you can tell it again and let him make the sounds with the instruments or sound-making objects. If he has lots of chances to talk about things that make sounds he will often make suggestions for other sounds to go into the story – thus Danielle, aged four, decided that the workman ought to saw the top off the post because it would be splintered from all the banging ! – and may suggest an instrument to make the sound. Again, you may extend the story by incorporating a related song or rhyme. The song *Peter Hammers With One Hammer* (in *This Little Puffin*) goes well with my story, and children will quickly suggest their own words to sing – 'The workman hammers with a big hammer' or 'Floyd hears the sledgehammer', and so on. Taking the whole thing a stage further, you may have been inspired to tell such a story by seeing some local road works or a building site. Why not go and have a look with your child ? You can listen to the sounds, talk about them and so on.

So much that is musically more complex does arise out of doing very simple activities with children, and usually it is the children themselves who direct the development, which ensures that they progress at a pace with which they feel secure. Provided that you do plenty of different things there is no need to worry about 'stretching' the child. Nor is there any need to provide more complex equipment, or to give under-fives experience of conventional instruments. You don't need to take them to concerts or to play them 'good music'. As ought to be obvious, a child can get all the basic musical experience he needs without such things – after all, people have been becoming musical for thousands of years without them.

Part two Towards formal music-making

7

Enjoying other people's music making

So far we have concerned ourselves, rightly I think, with those musical experiences that are a very intimate part of the relationship between you and your child. For him these must be the centre of his early musical development. But you will be concerned also with the way they lead towards his enjoyment of other people's music-making; this is going to be the key to much of his later musical enjoyment.

But immediately you start thinking about this issue various vexed questions spring to mind. When should young children start to go to concerts? What is the place of mechanically reproduced music – on radio, TV, record and tape? How much should young children know about musical instruments, composers, orchestras, and so on? People have all sorts of answers to these questions. Frequently their answer is 'the earlier the better', and they try all sorts of methods, ranging from the continuous playing of a background tape of classical music to the staging of special concerts for 600 four-year-olds, to give children 'musical experiences'. But in fact these questions are not the basic ones. We need to dig a bit deeper, with questions like : What can mechanically reproduced music do that you cannot? Why do you want children to go to concerts, or to know about instruments and orchestras? There is one obvious answer : that through playing recorded music and going to concerts we make it possible for children to get great pleasure in the future. But we then need to ask ourselves how far the obvious answer is a mask for the real answer ; that we wish to indoctrinate them with our own cultural assumptions and ambitions. Could it be that the basic question at the back of our minds is 'How can we make sure children hear and like plenty of "good music" (i.e. the music we think they ought to know about)?'

You notice that I say 'our own cultural assumptions and ambitions', and not 'our own culture'. There is no need to inculcate our own culture – that happens automatically. The baby whose father plays him lute music, the girl whose Mum has Radio One on all day as a background to be worked and talked against but rarely listened to, the children whose Dad shouts at them to 'turn off that highbrow rubbish', will all pick up their parents' respective attitudes and cultural expectations. As Peter is fond of saying at the moment, 'No trouble !' But from guilt, or ambition, or concern, or a mixture, we want our children to have something more than this. The availability of a huge range of mechanically reproduced music, the ease of sticking on a record or tape, the survival of the 'ram it in often enough and the kids will pick it up (and thank you for it later)' theory of education, all encourage us to think in terms of playing 'good' music to children early. If it's good music, it must be good for them. *We* need to believe this.

Of course it's good for children to hear 'good' music. Of course! Of course! But what is 'good' music, and how is it good for them? Classical music? Good quality light music? Progressive pop? Traditional music of our own culture? Contemporary music? All these styles have their advocates, each assuming that children will benefit from more of 'their' music. Are all of them right? None right? How are we to know?

When thinking about young children we have a blessed escape route from this kind of puzzle. When in doubt, look at the child. What does he need? What will he enjoy? What problems may he have in coping with other people's music?

The first point to realize is that hearing mechanically reproduced music is not necessarily a *musical* experience for the listener, nor is going to a concert. Both *can* be a way for the listener to have a musical experience, but this depends entirely on the way he responds. It is important to stress this because even a child's enthusiastic response and enjoyment may not be caused by the music. This was first brought home to me when I took a small group of musically interested young children to a concert. When they came back they were full of the trip, but they talked about the ice-cream I bought them, about the tube ride, about the walk across Hungerford Bridge above the Thames with boats below and trains passing a few feet away — nothing about the concert. I didn't give up, though. I got Deborah (the most promising one) by herself and, after a few preliminaries about the concert, asked, 'What was the nicest thing you heard?' She smiled dreamily, savouring the moment, and then said, 'When the doors close in the tube, they sort of sneeze first, then they go, "Mmrumm — bump!"' I gave up!

Clearly, a child enjoying a musical occasion may be revelling in the music, but he may just be relishing sharing an activity with you and going somewhere formal and special (a child may similarly get great pleasure from going to a restaurant with you, even though he only picks at the food). Again, his interest may be in something quite different from what you expect — here is a Catherine Landreth story:

An aunt took her six-year-old nephew to a children's symphony concert in an opera house. The boy sat in rapt absorption throughout the first number, his head back, his gaze aloft. When the number ended and his aunt was congratulating herself on the musical pleasure she was giving, he asked matter of factly, 'How do they change the lights in the ceiling?'

Apparently he had been pondering the mechanics of changing light bulbs at a height of several storeys. For all his aunt knew, he had been barely conscious of the music. (*Pre-School Learning and Teaching*)

The point of these two stories is not that concerts, or playing recorded music, is bad for children. Deborah and the nephew both got an enormous amount out of their experiences. I am merely stressing that the musical element may be very limited in such situations.

A second point is that children's attention span at this age is immensely variable, and may be very short. This is especially likely where mechanically reproduced music is concerned and there is nothing to see in order to help their concentration. Mind you, this is true for adults as well as for children. Even as a teenager I used to listen to Promenade Concerts or Test Match commentaries on the radio with my eyes fixed on the loudspeaker grille — if I didn't, I soon found my attention had wandered and I had missed chunks. How much more will this be true of the distractable four- and five-year-olds?

Thirdly, the fact that mechanically reproduced music is all around us has created some problems of its own. Many adults and children are used to hearing music as a background, with people talking, making noises and listening only in bits. So they get into the habit of listening in this imperfect way, cutting out whole chunks of music. They may even get into the habit of talking as soon as they hear music. This was brought home to me first when I went to an infant school assembly. The headmistress and I were in the hall before any of the children ; then they started to come in. They came in naturally, in informal groups, and sat down wherever they liked, all in silence. I was very impressed by their self-control because there was no evidence of them having been violently disciplined into this. When we were all assembled, still in a beautiful silence, the headmistress put on an appropriate record. Within twenty seconds at least a quarter of the children were talking ! This is a major reason why the value of recorded music with young children is limited — after all, if sheer exposure to recorded music made children musical we wouldn't need musical education today ! In the same sort of way, when children with poor listening habits go to concerts they can't concentrate and tend to use the live music as background to their chat just as they do with the recorded music.

Fourthly, young children do not separate their experiences one from another. We have talked about this a number of times already. The significance of music for them is likely to lie as much in its context as in the music itself ; as Alice Yardley puts it :

Although children enjoy short spells of direct listening, much of what they hear is intimately bound up in other aspects of their daily experience.

When we play music to young children we must try to ensure that it is meaningful to them by talking about it and relating it to familiar experiences.

Using recorded music

If we understand these potential difficulties, we may be able to see some of the ways in which we can make use of recorded music and help the child to appreciate the music of others. Paradoxically, the first way doesn't involve recorded music at all. It is by being prepared to *listen* to the child when he talks, when he sings, when he plays instruments for you. In a real sense, having his own contributions and performances respected and accepted is the way he learns to respect and accept the performances of others. This process starts with him respecting your own singing to him. The next important thing is that you need to establish it as a convention that people are quiet when listening to music, or to someone's conversation, or when watching television. Far too many adults expect children to listen, but themselves don't observe the same conventions. Your child should be very familiar with remarks like :

'It's not polite to talk when Auntie Betty is talking. We can't hear properly what she's saying.'

'If you're not watching the programme, Darren, turn off the television. You can't watch and draw at the same time.'

'Wait a bit, Pauline, till the end of this song, then I will talk about your doll. I'm listening to the song.'

The last kind of remark is especially important, I think, because the child needs to realize your own respect for and enjoyment of music. This has nothing to do with the *style* of the music – Beethoven or the Bay City Rollers deserve the same attention. If your child sees that *you* respect and listen to music, he will do the same.

He also needs to see the value of self-control and self-restraint in a wide variety of situations. For instance, if your child realizes that sudden noises and movements frighten away the birds or wild animals he wants to watch, he will be better able to cope with listening to music. Similarly, a child who has had practice of simple listening through the kinds of games I described earlier in the book will have less difficulty with the complex and sophisticated skill of listening to recorded music. He has already learned to concentrate, to focus his attention, to sit still and quietly, saving up his responses until the piece is finished. Children do not find this easy ; instinctively they talk about what interests them and ask questions in the middle. However, provided the piece is short, the child with previous listening practice will have no trouble. He will also cope with another problem of listening to recorded music. When a record or tape is being played there are a lot of small sounds going on that are not part of the music. There are sounds from the house and from outside, sounds of other people, sounds from the working of the record-player or tape-recorder and possibly hiss or surface noise (our records and equipment are not always in perfect condition). Cutting out all these and concentrating on the music demands focusing skills and quite a fine discrimination between sounds. The fact that the process has become second nature to you doesn't guarantee that your child has mastered it.

Even if your child has these skills you still need to help him with his listening. To begin with, you will have to listen *with* him. You do find some children who will sit and listen on their own (usually to records they have already become fond of) but in general your child will need to share the activity with you. Even when my children were well past the age of five, when they would listen to several LP records on the trot while I was working at my desk, they would rapidly give up listening if I finished my work and left the room. Although this tie has some disadvantages, it does mean that you can do very important things. You can *name* the pieces played and talk about them. In doing so you can introduce technical language where appropriate. This kind of labelling is very necessary if children are to be able to refer to what they have heard and to talk about the pieces with other adults. It is true that children will sometimes give their own names to pieces of music — 'my dancing music', 'the fast running tune', 'smurgly music', 'music for the pony and two giraffes' are some typical titles I have heard from pre-school children— and no one would suggest that you should say 'No, it's not your dancing music, it's *Rondo Furioso*'. But there must be hundreds of times when children don't talk about music that has made an impression on them because they don't have an easy way to refer to it !

In this situation you can also show children your own enjoyment. As long as the music is not too complex or sophisticated, children will tend to like what you enjoy, and if you try to play as wide a variety of your favourites as you can, you will give them plenty to choose from. When they do find something they like, don't be afraid to play it as many times as they want, even if it seems a ridiculous number of repetitions. Young children tend to want to hear something over and over until they have absorbed the last ounce of enjoyment from it, just as in other kinds of play they will roll a ball down a slope again and again, or paint sheet after sheet of paper with red paint. It is very rarely the result of unadventurousness. One story will perhaps indicate what may be going on during such repetitions. When Peter was five I learned an English folk song called *The Two Butchers* and used to play the tune on the mandolin. One day Peter for the first time heard me singing the words, and asked to hear the song properly. I sang it all through (fourteen verses and no chorus). He asked for it again. I repeated it. He asked for it again ! I refused (!) but, as I had the original on tape, I put this on for him. He listened to it four times more, occasionally humming the tune or singing quietly a snatch of the words. This done, he walked away without a comment. Next afternoon Pauline and I were in the kitchen when we heard Peter say to Katherine, 'Come here, Kiffen, and I will sing you *The Two Butchers.*' We listened, and he sang straight through all fourteen verses with only three or four minor changes of words (such as 'the' for 'this'). A similar level of absorption must go on with children listening to instrumental music (though it is harder to get evidence of what they have taken in). I think it is revealing that most nursery children can identify (and often sing) the vast majority of television theme tunes. It is a good example of the effectiveness of repeated listening to labelled pieces of music that appear in meaningful contexts.

As your child begins to build up a collection of pieces of music he enjoys it is worth making a list of them for your own reference, and to remind him of things he used to like. Better still, if you have a tape recorder, is to make a tape or cassette of these pieces, so that he can ask to have his own tape played through. This has the great advantage that you can just record those *sections* of music or songs that your child likes, rather than fiddling about with LP records to find the right track. However, if you do record, you will need to make the recording through a connecting lead rather than by putting the tape recorder microphone in front of the radio or record-player loudspeaker. (If you are in doubt about how to do this, go to your local tape-recorder shop with the instruction booklets [or full names and model numbers] of your radio or record player and tape-recorder. They will tell you what kind of connecting lead you need.) Otherwise you will get a poor quality of reproduction, and that will make it difficult for your child to listen to his music.

Another important principle is that you should always try to introduce a piece of music you want your child to listen to. Talk about the plot of a song, the story of a piece of programme music, the instruments he may be able to hear (we'll come back to that later) or even some features of the music. I realize that this is open to abuse. No one wants a child to be subjected to a ten-minute lecture before each piece of listening. On the other hand he will listen with more awareness and interest if he has some specific things to listen for. It will also mean that he will be made aware of the kinds of things people listen for in music. The sort of remarks I have in mind are these:

'The cowboy sings about riding his horse at night, looking after all the sleeping cattle.'

'This piece of music is meant to make us think about a great storm at sea.'

'In this piece the tune is played on the trumpet with the other instruments accompanying; they play as well, but very softly.'

'Near the end the music gets very quiet, but in the last bar there's a great crash.'

Clearly, such remarks must be made suitable for your child. He may well extend what you say by asking questions or making his own comments.

All these suggestions about ways of using recorded music have been concerned with helping your child to see music in a context, not as something separate and abstract. But talking is not the only way of doing this. Indeed, the best way is if the stimulus for the choice of music comes from his interests or from something shared with you. If you can produce in such a situation a related piece of music, listening will be particularly meaningful.

'Do you remember we were talking about electric guitars yesterday? Here's a piece of music played by men with electric guitars. It's called *Apache*.'

'Do you remember that military band we saw playing in the park this morning — all those soldiers with their instruments? I have got some military band music here on this record. Would you like to listen to it?'

If your child has a particularly strong interest at a certain time, you can keep your ears open for any music that relates to it. Katherine, for instance, was (and still is) passionate about horses. Over a couple of years we came across such things as the cowboy song *I Ride an Old Paint*, *Skewbald*, *The Galtee Farmer* (an Irish folk song about selling a horse), the Don McLean song about a white mare *The More You Pay*, the Byrds' *Chestnut Mare*, the TV theme tunes from *White Horses*, *Follyfoot* and *Black Beauty*, the overture *William Tell* and many other pieces of 'galloping music'. All these she listened to with great interest and enjoyed hearing, though she liked some much more than others. Similarly, Danny was passionate about soldiers and so his parents were able to find and play a lot of music with a marching beat (including a funeral march), military band music and songs about soldiers like *Soldier, Soldier, Won't You Marry Me?* and *Johnny Has Gone for a Soldier*. This is not to suggest, of course, that your child's listening should be geared entirely to his preoccupations. You can, and should, try to introduce a wider range. But for heaven's sake don't get hung up about this. At this age and stage you are mainly concerned when you play recorded music to establish habits and attitudes. You want your child:

● to get used to listening to recorded music attentively

● to hear a variety of styles and types of music

● to learn that recorded music can have something special to offer him

● to realize that he prefers certain pieces to others — and that this is right and proper

● to enjoy his listening.

134

If you have any common sense you are not *trying* to give him an extensive cultural background. If a variety of music about horses develops the habits and attitudes you want, that is fine. There is plenty of time for him to extend his tastes later, but if you don't establish the habits and attitudes he may never listen with care and attention.

One further factor needs to be taken into account when we are thinking about the ability of young children to relate to recorded music. This is what I call the 'magic box' factor. We have already talked about how young children often do not establish clearly that sounds are always produced by a sound-making object of some kind and are not clear about the basic principles of sound production. At the same time they are surrounded by a range of 'magic boxes' producing sounds – public address systems, Muzak in supermarkets and railway stations, transistor radios, portable record-players, televisions and so on. It is no wonder that, although these things are so familiar, many children have a very imperfect understanding of them. Has anybody not heard a young child say, 'How do those people all get inside the television?'

This suggests to me that we ought to do a good deal to make clear what is happening with a recording. The obvious and simple activity is talking with the child about what is happening when you put on a tape or cassette or record, but there are several other things you can do. One is to allow the child to work the tape recorder or record-player himself. Young children are perfectly capable of working such equipment – unlike us, they are children of an electronic age, and will tend to have less difficulty with equipment than we do. This familiarizing can start very early. Peter as a toddler used to press the on/off button for me and handle record sleeves; soon he learned to work volume controls and if we had possessed a cassette player at that stage would certainly have been able to work it by the time he was three. Mind you, he was still unsure of the concept of recording and playing back. For instance, when nearly three he had a patch when he was very keen on being recorded singing with me. We would record ourselves singing into the microphone and Peter would watch the volume level dial, occasionally saying 'Not too loud, Daddy and Peter not too loud.' But the moment we stopped (although the recording was still being made), he would look anxiously at the recorder and say, 'Moosik coming on now? . . . Daddy, moosik *not* coming on now.' He couldn't understand, of course, that the sound had been recorded on the part of the tape which had passed through the heads, and that it would have to be run back before it could be replayed. It was another year before he seemed to have grasped this.

This also indicates that there is a need for children to be involved in the process of making recordings and listening to the results. For instance, with a cassette recorder it is simple to record the sounds of your child playing a number of his favourite sound-making objects, then play them back for him to identify. You can do the same on a walk, in a shopping centre or (less conspicuously) in a park, and play back the sounds for identification. An extension of this is for you to record by yourself some familiar sounds or the voices of people he knows, and play these back for him to listen to. As well as being good listening practice for him, it will also get him familiar with what a recording is – the reproduction of a real, happening – and this will make much easier his listening to recorded music.

Listening to live music

An important way of helping your child to enjoy other people's music-making is to let him see and hear live music-making. Ideally, this should come *before* listening to recorded music. In families or communities where making your own music is a normal part of life children have the fortunate experience of seeing their adults playing music together. For most children in an urban community, however, live music comes in the form of big public concerts, and these are quite inappropriate for most five-year-olds. But there are still some important preliminary experiences you can give your child.

Once again, the first of these is for him to have good experiences of making his own music, of playing (and playing at playing) instruments, and of being listened to. Given this, there are certain situations where a child may be able to see and hear live music-making outside the confines of the concert-hall. These will range widely : a busker outside Woolworths or a band in the park bandstand ; a young person sitting on the grass strumming a guitar, or a group of children playing a ring game in the playground ; a one-man-band advertising a supermarket opening or a military band in a parade. All these will catch and hold your child's total attention *for a short time*. Then he will want to comment, to ask questions or to respond with movement. Carter, aged five and a half, was fascinated by the one-man-band, and particularly by the business of doing different things with different parts of your body. He spent a long time trying to wriggle the fingers of his left hand, bang an imaginary drum with his right and kick a leg, all simultaneously. He tended to overbalance ! After a while the game turned into a 'falling-down robot' game, which went on for a good while longer.

If a young child is going to listen to live music, it must be for a short time, and then he must be able to respond in his own way. Even the shortest concert will be too long for most under-fives. But an invaluable bridge is for you to take any opportunity you can to get people to play to your child. These can be friends, relations, older children, people you know who play an instrument – as long as it's very informal. I find the most successful way is for the player to begin with the instrument packed away in its case ; to take it out (and put it together, if that is appropriate) ; to show how you hold it and make a sound ; to make the characteristic sounds and patterns of the instrument ; and then to play two or three tunes familiar to the child – nursery rhymes or TV theme tunes for example. The whole process probably won't take more than ten minutes, unless your child shows such enthusiasm or asks so many questions that it gets extended. In doing this several points about instruments, composers and professional musicians may well arise. Talk about them with your child if they seem natural and appropriate.

After some of these kinds of experience you may feel that your child is ready to go to a concert. You will almost certainly be right – you know better than anyone else. But if you do take your child, make sure you talk beforehand about the music that you will hear. It helps, if possible, to play some of the music on record beforehand so he can get used to it, but you have probably chosen the concert in the first place because its programme contains music he already knows and likes. When you actually get to the concert, be prepared to come out when you feel he has had enough. This may go against the grain, but unless you are prepared to spend the price of a ticket for a mere twenty minutes of the music, don't plan to go in the first place. You are likely to do much damage by forcing him to stay for the whole programme.

'Good' music for the under-fives

I hope you will have realized that in this chapter I am once again on my hobby horse : with very young children the memorableness of a musical experience is nearly always the product of a *personal* relationship and situation. Modern equipment and reproduction are so good we may be tempted to feel that they can present music better than we can. We may even go further and feel that the record replaces the adult, parent or teacher. Perhaps this was what lay behind the answer of a nursery teacher when her headmistress asked whether she had done any music that week – 'Oh no, Miss X, I haven't got a plug !'

A record or tape cannot replace you. All it can be is a tool, just like a piano or a guitar. Like them it is quite unnecessary in providing musical experience for young children. Like them it can be used to provide an enlarged and enjoyable musical experience, but only if you use it with the needs of your own child clearly in mind. And in assessing these needs the first thing you need to clear from your mind is any lingering traces of the attitude – 'If we constantly played children good music we'd get rid of this pop nonsense and make them all musical.' For young children 'good' music will be that music which you can make meaningful and enjoyable to them. We don't make five-year-olds study pictures by Rembrandt or listen to Shakespeare on the assumption that doing so will automatically make them cultured. Why then should we assume that playing Beethoven will be any more effective ?

8

Musical instruments –
what and when?

Very little of what I have talked about up to now has been the kind of activity we expect from music lessons. We have had little about formal singing, nothing about learning how to read and write music, little about rhythmic training and nothing about playing conventional musical instruments, even the ones like triangles, tambourines, drums, xylophones and cymbals that we expect young children to play. I have left out all these things because I believe they are not at all important in the early musical development of young children. But even when I have said that, you may still be surprised that I have mentioned nothing about instruments. If you ask people what they associate with children's music, you will find that most of them straightaway mention the percussion band, or learning to play the piano or recorder. Books on music with young children talk about the importance of providing instruments for children to experiment with ; they always give the impression that all you have to do to make children musical is to give them instruments.

There is a small element of truth in this. If you give children plenty of instruments and allow them complete freedom to experiment they will probably learn a great deal. They will also probably drive you barmy with the noise and leave you with a large bill for broken or damaged instruments ! I don't say this because I am cynical or disillusioned about children's behaviour. I say it because of two very important truths about musical instruments. Firstly, they are specialized (and often delicate) machines, invented and made to be used in precise ways – they are not raw material for experiment. For much too long this basic truth has been obscured. We have thought (rightly) that young children need early musical experiences and the chance to experiment with sound. As a result we have always thought (wrongly) that we need to provide musical instruments in the way we provide sand or water. But a xylophone is not like clay or building bricks. It is a subtle, carefully constructed machine – much more like a transistor radio or a book or a lawn mower. Secondly, children need to have some clear idea of appropriate behaviour when using instruments, just as they do with other specialized machines. Without a clear idea they can't understand why they shouldn't use the instruments just as they fancy – so they get into trouble for 'bad behaviour'.

I sometimes think we don't realize how much we expect in terms of appropriate behaviour from young children : we praise them for painting sheets of paper on an easel but are shocked if they paint sheets of paper in a book ; we praise Anita for wiping up spilled coffee with a floorcloth but are horrified when she wipes up spilled paint with a sheet from her doll's cot. I am not saying we shouldn't expect appropriate behaviour, but am merely pointing out how much the child has to know before he meets our expectations. This is shown very clearly with musical instruments set up for children's use. I learned the painful way that you cannot provide musical instruments as free play material and expect them to be treated 'properly'. I can remember Ainsworth, a very musically interested West Indian, experimenting with a £23 xylophone ; I found him hitting the bars with the sharp corner of a metal shelf bracket, pitting and denting them so badly that they all went out of tune and had to be replaced. I also remember Billy, a very inhibited Brixton boy, putting a stick through the top of a drum and bursting into tears. That wasn't a 'good experience' for him, in any sense of the term.

But, apart from the matter of damage, I think we should question how much musical learning a child gets from banging instruments at random. True, the instruments themselves are fascinating manipulative toys, and this is largely the way they are used by children who have not been introduced to using them appropriately and musically. I am not questioning the value of this play to the child, but I do suggest that it frequently gets in the way of his musical learning. Such learning only really happens when the child becomes *aware* of the characteristics or patterns of the sounds made by the instrument and strives to repeat or vary them. This will only happen significantly often with a child who is aware of patterns of sounds, who is used to making them with his body, who has had much experience of finding/making/experimenting with sound-making objects from the environment and of discussing them with adults, and who then comes to use conventional instruments as a natural extension of this process.

I hope I have already made my case that there is no need for children to be provided with conventional instruments in order for them to get basic musical experiences. It goes further than this. They won't get these basic experiences from conventional instruments, so we can't expect them to use such instruments with care and sensitivity until they have had a wide experience of making sounds from ordinary things. Until this stage has been worked through, the conventional instruments have very little advantage over found objects, except sometimes a slight improvement in tone quality, and then not always. Almost any metal shelf bracket or coat hook suspended from a loop of string will make a better sound than the conventional infant school triangle ! In any case, at this age it is not the instruments themselves that are important; it is what the children can do with and understand about them that counts, and we've seen how much easier it is to understand ordinary objects.

Making musical instruments

Clearly, what I have just said affects very much the question of making home-made musical instruments. People often say this is the best way of approaching music with young children. I don't believe it. I think that when you come to introduce conventional instruments it can be a good way in. However, it is not a starting point. A young child has to have had a lot of previous experience if the making is to be musically valuable.

It is worth pointing out firstly that a child who is given reasonable freedom to play with an interesting range of materials already makes a lot of musical instruments. (Just think of Katherine and her biscuit tin, Peter and his 'poison-gas spray', Danielle and her paper 'thunder' and so on.) Think too of the child's plastic washing-up bowl of favourite sound-making objects that I talked about in Chapter 4 'Understanding sounds'. That is a collection of home-made instruments made by choosing them, in exactly the same sense as Marcel Duchamp made a mass-produced urinal 'his' work just by signing it! After all, choosing an existing piece of wood that makes the sound you want is merely a simpler version of choosing (and shaping and joining) the pieces of wood to make the violin that makes the sound you want!)

Before the age of three or so the child is not likely to be very interested in making an instrument, even if you do it with him. He may be five before the idea of making an instrument will come to him spontaneously – though if his home is obsessed with products he may be conditioned earlier. Even at five he is not likely to have the long-term concentration to make anything very complex. He will want something that can be made quickly, that doesn't need to dry or be painted, and then can be used sooner than immediately!

All this limits very much the usefulness of making musical instruments with this age group. If it does happen, it probably arises best out of the kinds of games, experiment and talking that we discussed in Chapter 4. Sometimes your child will be particularly interested in a certain kind of sound that you have been playing with, perhaps a plastic pot shaker or a scraped shell. 'Let me have it!' he'll say. Simply for you to say, 'Yes, all right, it can be your own instrument. Let's write your name on the pot with this felt pen' (or 'Let's find a good stick to scrape the shell with') is a very important thing. It makes the instrument special. It becomes something to be used and looked after, or perhaps to be broken through misuse or over-enthusiastic playing. Even this can be musically valuable. To say 'Oh dear, Beverley, you've broken your shaker. Things like that aren't very strong and if you hit them with your spade they will often break. Never mind, we can make another if you want' helps Beverley to realize appropriate ways of treating musical instruments. The cost ? – nothing for a plastic pot instead of £1.30 for a commercial shaker.

Sometimes a child will say, 'Mum, I want a drum' or 'Can you make me a really big shaker ?' or 'The bottle-tops make a nice noise – can we make an instrument out of them ?' In such situations it can be very useful to know some simple techniques for making instruments, and you and the child can have a lot of fun making them. Of course, his question will itself often suggest a technique, or he may have an idea himself, but there are some good sources of further information. One of the best is Peter Williams's *Making Musical Instruments* (see Bibliography). This is a set of twenty separate cards, each describing a very simple musical instrument that can be made out of junk or ordinary materials. Also very good for ideas about simple instruments, but including plans for more complex projects, is *Musical Instruments Made to be Played* by Ronald Roberts (see Bibliography). There are also many other booklets and books, most of which have some good ideas, for you to bear in mind.

Providing musical instruments for children

At what point, then, is it sensible to introduce conventional instruments to young children ? My answer is : when they will provide something significant that the child wants or needs. For instance, a child who has had lots of experience of drumming on boxes and improvised drums will sometimes say, 'I want a *proper* drum.' If, from your knowledge of the child, this seems a real wish (and if you feel the family can stand it), I think you should buy a tambour or a good quality school drum. Again, a three- or four-year-old who loves music, sings lots of songs, plays with improvised rhythm instruments and has a good understanding of sounds, needs to have his musical development extended. It may well be a good idea to buy him some chime bars or a xylophone. As always it is the needs of the individual child that should determine what you do.

Providing such an instrument will not be cheap, but please don't think it is just as helpful for a child's musical development if you buy toy instruments for him. (I don't mean scaled-down instruments devised for use by children, but the kinds of plastic and cheap metal toys you get in toyshops.) To start with, they tend to break very easily, and that's disappointing. Obviously, they usually have a very poor tone, and though (as I have pointed out) children are not particularly concerned with beauty of tone, it is wrong to give them things that, for instance, claim to be trumpets and produce only a miserable squawk. The instruments are also confusing and misleading in many cases – for instance, many instruments sold as xylophones in toy shops have metal bars instead of wooden ones. But the biggest danger is not to the child but to you. Toy instruments are quite fun for make-believe play and they won't do any serious harm, but they may make you believe that by buying a red plastic toy guitar you have met your child's musical needs. That *will* be damaging. It is much better to buy a secondhand ukelele than a toy guitar, or three or four chime bars rather than a Pixiephone from Woolworths. Or this is a point where it may be worth the adult taking some time to make a simple homemade instrument like a chime bar or a rubber-headed drum or a one-string guitar, based on suggestions from the books mentioned above.

If you aim to buy instruments for this age group only when they will *extend* your child's musical experiences, you can see that many instruments that are conventionally provided for children are not worth buying. You get nothing from children's triangles or jingle bells that you can't get from a suspended coat hook or a tin with glass beads or nails in, unless you go to the expense of buying an orchestral triangle with sides at least 20 cm long or a large set of sleigh bells with the bells wired to a leather strap. A drum needs to be something like a 25 cm tunable tambour costing about £5, if it's to provide anything significantly better from a musical point of view than an upturned plastic bowl or a large coffee tin with a snap-on lid. No commercially produced shaker is worth buying for a child of this age ; no rhythm sticks or woodblocks are significantly better for him than the sticks and other objects he finds to bang together.

What improvised or found instruments can't usually provide is the experience of tuned notes, sounds related to each other in the conventional musical scales and intervals. It is for this reason that I believe it is better, in the majority of cases, to save up instrument money to spend on tune-playing instruments. A wide range of such instruments for children is available and most of them are very suitable. The points to be careful about when buying are :

● Go to a reputable music shop or write to a reputable manufacturer (see Appendix). Proper musical instruments are not cheap, though there are a host of cheap imitations or versions. Go somewhere reliable and take the shop's advice.

● If children under five are going to be able to pick out patterns of notes on an instrument, the bars need to be at least an inch wide so that the chance of hitting other bars is lessened. This fact eliminates many of the cheap 'Pixiephones' ; it eliminates the small soprano and alto glockenspiels (although some are instruments of very good quality) ; it eliminates some of the instruments sold as 'chime bars'.

● There is no need with this age group to buy the full chromatic forms of these instruments (those having all the sharps and flats – the piano 'black' notes as well as the 'white' notes). Ask for the *diatonic* xylophone or metallophone or glockenspiel if you are buying one. You will save money and it will be more suitable for your purpose.

● If you buy one of these tuned instruments you need at least four suitable beaters with which to play the instrument – two for the child to use and two spares (or for you to use in games with the child.) Check when you get the instrument how many beaters are provided, and if necessary buy extra ones. Hitting the instrument with other objects may well not produce a good sound, and could damage the bars.

● In my opinon the most suitable tuned instrument to buy for the child under five is the chime bar. It is robust and easy to play, produces a good sound and (its greatest advantage) each note can be bought separately, with its own beater. Since young children only need a small range of notes (as we shall see later) this saves a lot of money. What's more, you can start by buying two or three, and build up a bigger set gradually.

What then would be my list of instruments to buy over a period of time? I think it would be a very simple one:

Stage one   Three chime bars (I suggest the notes E, G and A).
Stage two   Add chime bars of the following notes – C, D and upper C. You then have this scale
C, D, E, G, A, C'
which makes possible a great deal of experiment and tune-making.

Stage three
Either   a Buy a tambour or triangle or recorder or ukelele *that the child wants to have and play*.
Or   b Buy some more chime bars – I suggest some of the following notes: low G, C sharp, F, F sharp, B flat, upper C sharp and upper D.
Or   c Buy a soprano diatonic xylophone or soprano diatonic metallophone.

But by stage three you are really equipping for quite complex musical activities. Few children in the 0–5 age group will need stage three instruments, provided that they are having plenty of simple music opportunities.

Introducing musical instruments to young children
When you have provided musical instruments you may well wonder whether you ought to do something with them. I think the only thing that you ought to show the children is the appropriate behaviour with them. This arises best if you unpack the instrument with the child and remain with him as he first has a go with it. In the conversation you can introduce the relevant information; that hitting a drum too hard, or with pointed objects, may split the head and spoil it; that chime bars need to be tapped with a beater, not clashed together like cymbals, as one nursery teacher I met thought was the correct method (!); that the beaters need to be allowed to bounce if the chime bar or xylophone is to sound properly.

We shouldn't forget, though, that a good deal of a child's sense of appropriate behaviour with instruments will come in less direct ways. To start with, any child who is lucky enough to have relations who play will pick up a great deal just from seeing them handle and play instruments. I quoted earlier the baby with the lute-playing father. When that boy is older he will already know a great deal – and not just about handling a lute ! This sort of experience is even more valuable if the child has chances to play with instruments in the company of involved adults. This can't start too early. John Holt describes Lisa, aged sixteen months, imitating his playing notes with one finger ; Marcus was sat on his father's lap at the piano from an early age, and at six months would play notes with great care, using his index fingers : Peter, surrounded by a variety of stringed instruments, learned very early to strum gently across the strings, and by two and a half would strum rhythmically on a ukelele in time to songs we sang together (though, of course, he couldn't change chords !) So if you, or any of your relations or friends (including their children), can play an instrument, even very badly, make sure that the child gets the chance to see and hear you play occasionally, to ask you questions, to notice how you empty spit out of a horn or rosin a violin bow or strum guitar strings with a plectrum. It all builds up his sense of what kinds of actions are involved in playing an instrument. If you don't know anybody who can do this with you, you may get chances to look and talk about playing instruments when you see a band on the park bandstand, or a street musician, or even when an instrument is demonstrated on *Play School*, though that's much less satisfactory !

Another way in which appropriate behaviour with musical instruments is developed is through a child learning the need for appropriate behaviour with other kinds of delicate and complex things. After all, the concept that you treat such things with care and respect is a very powerful and necessary generalization for a child to make, and a child who can handle a typewriter, a beautiful book or a pet hamster properly is likely to be able to handle a xylophone or a glockenspiel without damaging it.

Given this awareness of behaviour, the important thing to do is to let your child get on with his own exploration, talking with him if it seems appropriate.

Children experimenting with instruments
Children's experiment with new materials follows a standard pattern, and their experiment with instruments is no exception. It falls into two main stages.

At first the new materials make him curious and excited. He explores the materials in a very random way, finding out what they are like. There may be a lot of effort and some tension in the child. He may repeat the same pattern over and over and over, to your irritation ! There won't be

144

any nice end product coming out, no pretty tunes or regular rhythms.

Once through this stage, everything relaxes. He has got confidence and understanding of the materials, and he can start using them to enjoy himself and to express himself. He shows great pleasure in what he's doing and may well start producing little tunes or patterns for your appreciation. However, these products may be very idiosyncratic, very personal, very unlike what we, with our adult tastes, expect. For instance, he may 'celebrate' his mastery of the instrument by playing it continuously and repetitively; the only way you can tell the difference between this and the repetition of the first stage is by the relaxation shown. Another way of using the instruments at this stage may be in make-believe play or dramatic play. The instrument may be used as a 'prop', in the same way as Peter's 'poison-gas spray'; or very idiosyncratic meanings may be attached to particular notes or patterns. For instance, children will often take a single note and call it something. Angela, aged four and a half, called the G chime bar 'Penny' and the E chime bar 'Freddie' but didn't use 'Penny' and 'Freddie' in a story or talk about them as people, nor did she name any of the other bars. Robert had his angry tune (which was played entirely on the B flat chime bar, and perhaps got its name because the bar was black). Yet another thing that happens is that children may make up their own tunes, or find tunes they know on the instrument. Sometimes, as with their singing, they may claim to be playing a known tune, but the tune that comes out is nothing like it.

We see these stages whenever children explore instruments, and we cannot hurry them. The child must be given plenty of time to take in what he finds out about the instruments before we expect any product to come out. This period of exploring and absorbing is the most valuable to the child. Pressing him to speed up the process merely devalues what he's doing. However, it is important to stress that the movement from the first to the second stage may happen at different speeds for different parts of the experience, and this will depend very much upon the previous experience the child brings to the instruments. If he has had lots of the experiences we have talked about he may move to relaxed expression very quickly.

Let me describe a typical example : Christmas Day 1970. We had just bought a set of chime bars for Peter and Katherine. There were the following notes in a tray : low G; C; C♯; D; E; F; F♯; G; A; B; C'; C♯' and twelve beaters separately. Peter was just over five and his only experience of conventional percussion instruments was playing a triangle and a drum at school. Katherine was almost three, with playgroup experience. When they opened the bars there was great excitement. They both took two beaters and played the bars at random. Katherine played with her index fingers along the beater sticks and let the beaters fall 'dead' on the notes, and Peter did the same most of the time, especially at the end of phrases, where he let the beaters lie on the bars.

They discarded the bars to open their other presents, but Peter soon returned and wanted me to play with him. We divided the bars as follows :

Peter: Low G, C, E, G, A, C♯, F♯

David: D, F, B, C'

Peter demanded the C♯ and F♯ because they were black, though at first he didn't play them. He wanted us to make tunes in turn, which we did for a while. He wasn't interested in my tunes, though ; if I tried to point out something he said, very sharply, 'It's *my* turn now.' Suddenly he played :

C   E   G   G   A   A   G   E

He stopped dead. 'That sounds like . . .' and he sang the opening bars of *Johnny Todd* (the Z Cars theme tune).

He had rapidly discarded his 'dead' beater technique and played continuously with two beaters, sometimes alternating hands. Soon he began to experiment with the C♯ and F♯, and immediately said 'That sounds like space music'. He experimented a good deal with various combinations like, A, F♯, G, C♯, C, delivering a monologue about rockets and space, and occasionally playing two notes together. After a bit of this he took all my notes and so had the whole set. He started playing all the white notes up and down. When, by accident, he hit the C♯ he said, 'That's not in it – that sound doesn't fit'.

At this point Katherine returned and Peter grudgingly let her have the chime bars I'd had (D, F, B, C'). She started to play, and Peter immediately told her that she had to let the beaters bounce, so she did. She said she would play a tune, so she played from right to left along her four bars and repeated this many times. When Peter impatiently told her to play a different tune she agreed, and changed the places of her bars on the table. She then played from right to left along her new arrangement ! She changed the places several times, but always played from right to left. She was not concerned at all that anyone should listen to her, but went on with her 'tunes'. Peter, however, decided that he ought to be recorded, and played a number of tunes and patterns for posterity ! It was particularly noticeable that at times he stated that he was going to play 'beautifully' : he then played softly and with great care. After this both he and Katherine had had enough, and didn't play the chime bars again for several days.

In that one example you can see illustrated many of the points about children's experiment, and in particular some of the differences between the three-year-old and the five-year-old. Most noticeable is the older child's much greater interest in performance and in playing together with other people. This doesn't usually become a strong inclination with most children until about the age of six, so don't be surprised if your child doesn't want to. It is most likely to arise out of the social pressures of playgroup or school, and can safely be left until then.

You will have noticed too how crucial it is for a child to be *aware* of the patterns he is making if he is to be able to use them for expressive purposes. Children who need a great deal of time on the first stage of experiment seem to be those who find it hard to make sense of all the experiences they are having. It is therefore important for you to do things that help the 'making sense' process. Talking with the child whenever there is an opportunity remains the most important single technique.

Games with instruments

There are various kinds of games with instruments that you can do, but I have to utter one very strong warning. We have to be very careful not to restrict and inhibit children's experiment by making it seem that certain kinds of activity are valued and others not. This can be done directly, by remarks like, 'You don't want to make ugly sounds like that, do you, Fiona. Music is beautiful sounds, isn't it?' It can be done more subtly by structuring the kinds of experiment children do, by making very demanding suggestions, by playing the instruments ourselves 'to show you how to play it', by trying to get the children to play tunes they know, and so on. This is easily done, and with the best of motives. We adults have a strong tendency to view children as machines which will run even better on what Mark Cohen once called 'our generous adult fuel'. In fact, such fuel may well choke the engine!

Mostly this is because we may make the child feel insecure or tense or frustrated. If you think that's the prerogative of adolescents, let me again quote John Holt.

Many years later a friend told me a story about his daughter, not yet a year old. She had been given a little plastic whistle, which she loved to toot. It was her favourite toy. One day one of her parents picked up the whistle, and, seeing that it had holes in it like a recorder, began to play a little tune on it. They both amused themselves with it for a minute or two, then gave the whistle back to the baby. To their great surprise, she pushed it angrily aside. At the time her father told me the story, she had not blown it since. (*How Children Learn*)

We don't *know* why the baby did this, of course, but I think we can see several reasons why it might be. The child may have felt originally 'I'm the only one who can play this whistle', and then been shown that this wasn't true. She may have felt that her parents had now set a standard that she could not reach. All we know is that it obviously upset her and prevented her using the whistle again.

You may feel that my suggestions about inculcating appropriate behaviour with instruments can also be criticized because they inhibit experiment. There is an element of truth in this. The justification lies, to my way of thinking, in two factors:

● My 'restrictions' are specifically concerned with how to avoid damage. They teach children how to protect and use the instruments; they do not lay down what the children should play on the instruments. I feel the distinction is significant.

● As I have said, using instruments is not a basic stage of sound exploration but a sophisticated stage. I would not stop a toddler bashing a plastic pot shaker on the floor and breaking it because at that stage he would learn a great deal from doing so, especially when we spoke about it afterwards. I wouldn't give a commercially produced shaker to a child who was still at the breaking things stage; nor would I let a child beyond that stage break the shaker just because he felt like it or was careless.

I think, too, that we can avoid most of the dangers by not playing instrument games with children until their intial excitement in the new instrument has subsided (which may take more than a month) or until they ask us to play with them.

Having given my warning about the dangers of conditioning children's experiments, we can look at how you can play games with instruments. Most of these will be ones where the child is free to play in his own way, but some will focus his attention specifically on the patterns he can make or copy. You remember how you danced to music with your child in your arms, then did fingerplays, then later clapped or tapped or stamped to a piece of recorded music (as we described in Chapter 6, 'Patterns of rhythm'). One of the simplest instrument games is when you and your child both have an *untuned* instrument and play freely to the music. Once again, the child may play rhythmically and in time, but he may not, even though he has been rhythmically confident and accurate in his clapping or stamping. Playing an instrument in time is a much bigger step forward for a child than we sometimes think. He may need a good deal of time to try things out by joining in, to make mistakes, and to build up the rhythmic skill required. This kind of informal play gives such chances. You may find also that if you make simple rhythmic patterns yourself the child will listen and copy, especially if you have already played some of the copying games described later in this chapter.

Another possibility is the adding of instrumental patterns into songs — but let me utter one word of warning. The majority of children under five have not reached the stage where they understand the concept of accompaniment in our sense of the word. They will be interested in doing something at the same time as the song but not necessarily *with* the song. You need to be specially careful not to try to get across ideas of harmony, a concept which develops quite late. For instance, Peter, who had had extensive experience of people accompanying singing, used at two and three-quarters to strum a ukelele tuned to one chord all through a song, oblivious of chord changes. Over three years later, when his singing was at a very sophisticated level, he got hold of an autoharp (on which it is simple to play a chord by pressing down a button and strumming across the strings). He sang *Skip to my Lou* and accompanied himself on the autoharp, in strict rhythm, but only using one chord throughout. He was entirely satisfied with this performance and repeated it many times. It was only three months later that he first expressed an unease : 'David, this chord doesn't quite fit here. What do I do ?' When I told him that he would need the D_7 chord in some places instead of G he was able to go through the song and sort out the chords by trial and error. But till that point it hadn't occurred to him that the one chord wouldn't do.

This should suggest a couple of things to us. Firstly, this song accompaniment activity with the under-fives will need to be done only with untuned percussion instruments. Secondly, most of the playing will have to be quite loose and improvised. It is no good expecting a child to play a fixed rhythm throughout without a lot of further experiences which are not really appropriate with your child at home (we will look at one or two of them in Chapter 10 'Music in the playgroup and nursery class').

One of the best ways of using instruments is with a song that allows improvised playing. Such a song is *Tidey-Oh*, which I quoted in Chapter 5. Your child can have a shaker or bell or jingle bells and simply be free to jingle them in his own way in the chorus. The rhythmic impetus may pull him to play in rhythm, but it may not — and it doesn't matter. Another song where you can do this is *I'm a Dingle-Dangle Scarecrow*. Again, any shaking sound goes well here. Particularly good fun can be had with a couple of bracelets of wide elastic with small bells sewn on them (like those worn by Morris dancers) ; with these on his wrists and/or feet the child can 'dingle-dangle' and accompany the song at the same time. With *Train Is A-Coming* you can have shakers or sandpaper blocks or a scraping sound-maker like a shell to make train noises while you sing. Another kind of song that makes improvised accompaniment easy is one about horses or ponies. Here is one I like :

Old Texas

I'm going to leave —— old Tex-as now ——,They've got no

use ———— for the long - horn cow ————————.

They've ploughed and fenced my cattle range,
And the people there all talk so strange.

I'll take my horse, I'll take my rope,
And hit the trail upon a lope.

In rain or shine, in sleet or snow,
I'll ride that trail to Mexico.

Yes, day or night, in rain or hail,
I'll ride along that lonely trail.

I'll ride the range from sun to sun,
For a cowboy's work is never done.

He's up and gone at the break of day.
He drives the cows on their weary way.

I'm going to leave Old Texas now.
They've got no use for the longhorn cow.

You don't have to sing all the verses ; choose several that you like.

Little children like to pretend to ride, swaying backwards and forwards.
They also love making the sound of the horse's hooves. Coconut shells
are the obvious instrument for this, but any wood instrument, like sticks
or woodblocks or just a wooden box will make an adequate sound.
Perhaps the most easily available is a pair of yoghurt or cream plastic
pots. They are simpler to hold than coconut shells, they make an excellent
sound and they are replaceable if they get broken. I usually approach
accompanying this song by saying (after talking about the instrument, if
we haven't already done so) 'You can make the sounds of the horse and
I'll sing the song.' The response of different children varies considerably.
Sometimes they will only start to play when I get to the second or third
verse ; sometimes they start immediately I mention the idea but stop as
soon as I begin to sing, and only resume later in the song ; sometimes
they play in a very random way ; sometimes they play rhythmically, but
not fitting in with the rhythm of my singing ; sometimes they play very
much on the beat ; sometimes they will make quite sophisticated
suggestions, like 'I'm making the cowboy go further away at the end —
he's getting quieter and quieter and quieter.' All these responses are
valid and valuable. All of them are giving the child important
instrumental experience.

There are a lot of children's songs written about playing instruments ;
many of these allow the child to play an instrument in the song. Here's a

very simple one I use, based on the tune of *One Man Went to Mow* :

The Instrument Song

Bil—ly, you can play ———, play on your sha — ker;

Bil—ly you can play ———, play on your sha — ker.

La —la—la—la — la ———, la —la— la— la — la-la ———,

La-la—la-la — la ———, La la—la la—la

What instrument are you going to play now? Your drum? Right! Let's sing.

Billy, you can beat,
Beat on your drum.
Billy, you can beat,
Beat on your drum.

La-la-la-la la,   *instead of singing this to 'La' you*
La-la-la-la la-la.   *can hum it, or sing a sound like*
La-la-la-la la,   *the instrument —e.g. 'Boom-Boom'*
La-la-la-la la-la.   *for the drum*

This gives the child a chance to play a wide range of instruments, either in a very free way or quite strictly in rhythm. As with all the activities we have been looking at, it helps the child to become familiar with the instruments, to get used to playing patterns with them, to become aware of some of the difficulties and to begin to play instruments with other people. At the pre-school stage this is all that can be expected of him.

Many of the children's songs about playing instruments are more complex than *The Instrument Song* because they expect the child to play fixed patterns at fixed places. This is much more demanding. To cope with it a child needs to have had plentiful experience of playing patterns of body sounds at the appropriate places in fingerplays (like *I Can Knock*, p.114), songs (like *Five Little Men*, p. 117) and stories (like *The Little Indian Boy*, p. 121). Given such experience, you can, find patterns for the child to play from within a song or fingerplay that you're doing.

An example is *Five Fat Sausages* :

Five Fat Sausages
Five fat sausages
Frying in the pan :
Sizzle, sizzle, sizzle, sizzle,
One went BANG !

Four fat sausages
Frying in the pan :
Sizzle, sizzle, sizzle, sizzle,
One went BANG !

Three fat sausages . . .

    and so on.

It is very simple for the child to play the 'sizzle' on a shaker or scraper or tambourine – and if it is the latter instrument he can also play the 'BANG !'. Once again it doesn't matter at all if the playing is slightly out of time.

    Many fingerplays and nursery songs give this kind of opportunity. We have already seen in Chapter 4, 'Understanding sounds', how *I Hear Thunder* was used by children with improvised instruments ; obviously, conventional instruments could be used in the same way. Many songs too have some kind of simple pattern that can be played – take my version of *The Old Woman and the Little Pig* :

The Old Woman and the Little Pig

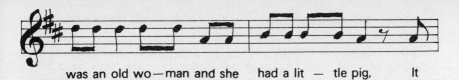

was an old wo—man and she   had a lit — tle pig,   It

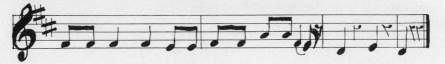

did—n't cost much 'cos it was—n't ve—ry big—, Oink, oink, oink!

Now this old woman kept the pig in the barn . . .
Prettiest thing she had on the farm . . .

This old woman fed the pig on clover . . .
It laid down and died all over . . .

The little old woman she sobbed and sighed . . .
And then she laid right down and died . . .

The little old man he died of grief . . .
Wasn't that a sad relief ? . . .

And that was the end of the one, two, three . . .
The man, the woman, and the little piggee . . .

There's apples and cheese up on the shelf . . .
If you want any more you can sing it yourself . . .

The obvious pattern to play in this song is 'Oink, oink, oink !' You can
either play it with an instrument that sounds a bit like a pig's snort (a big
shaker ? a scraped instrument ? sandpaper blocks ?) or you can just play
the rhythm on a drum or rhythm sticks. Either way it gives lots of fun and
lots of rhythmic and instrumental practice. Although the pattern is very
simple you have to concentrate and remember the pattern to get your
playing in the right places, so it is very valuable.

I have sung this song to lots of pre-school children, and never found
any of them in the slightest bit worried by the multiple deaths. I think that
if a child understands well enough to be bothered he understands well
enough that the song is nonsense ! However, if you don't like it you don't
have to use it – or you can use the pattern to make a different version.
Ruth Seeger, in *American Folk Songs for Children*, describes how she
improvised a version with 'three little pigs' who went to sleep, then were
woken and rolled out into the sun, then rolled back and went to sleep
again – all because a child lay down and rolled during the song. You can
always use a song in this way as the basis for your own invention.

You can often use the sorts of songs we talked about in Chapter 6 to combine with instruments – like *Clap Your Hands*. Any that provide simple, unstressful opportunities will be fine.

You can also use the instruments to play games that focus the child's attention on some of the basic musical concepts like fast/slow, loud/soft and, of course, high/low. The best of these games will tend to be informal and spontaneous. Perhaps you'll say things like :

'Can you make a very soft sound ? . . . Can you go on making sounds, getting louder until I wave to stop you ?'

'Make some very fast sounds on your instrument . . . Now make some very slow sounds . . . . Now some more fast sounds . . .'

Observing the child's reactions will tell you a lot about his understanding of any particular concept and will suggest what you should say or do to help his understanding.

There is an important point to make here. A child will not master a concept just by being told about it, or by playing a single game. As with all concepts, understanding will arise from a mass of experience of sounds – making them, listening to them and, in particular, talking about them with adults. One thing more. At this age and, indeed, until they are eight or nine, most children will find it very difficult to *define* a single sound or note, whether in terms of speed or loudness or pitch. They will need another note or sound to compare or contrast it with (or for the original note to be part of a sequence) before they are likely to get it right regularly. Thus, if you play a sound, a child may say that it was loud ; played the identical sound a little later, he may say with equal confidence that it was soft. It all really depends on what he was comparing it with mentally. You can see this process illustrated by an experiment I sometimes try, using a dull-sounding plastic egg-cup, a clinking china egg-cup and a ringing metal egg-cup. I play all the sounds to the child, and we look at the egg-cups and talk about them. Then I hide the egg-cups away in my cardboard box and play the plastic one, followed by the china one. The child will frequently say that I played the plastic one followed by the *metal* one (because the china one sounds more ringing than the plastic one). But if I say, 'Fine, tell me what I play now', and play the metal one followed by the china one, he says often that it's the metal one followed by the *plastic* one (because the china one sounds much duller than the metal one). Thus he has identified the china egg-cup as metal and then as plastic within a short space of time, entirely because of the contrast.

You can't possibly get over this problem with a couple of games. You have to give the child lots of experience of listening to sounds and talking about them over a period of years. Given this, however, some simple games may help to clarify his understanding of a particular concept. This is particularly important with the concept of pitch, which is a very tricky one to master. Much of the trouble arises because the terms 'high' and 'low', 'up' and 'down', have very definite connotations for the child in terms of familiar things like shelves, mountains, stairs, holes and so on, but there is nothing 'up' or 'down' in the sounds themselves. A 'high' sound is not really up in the air (we may feel it that way because of the associations we've built up) but we call it 'high' because it has a high number of vibrations per second. It would be just as easy (or just as difficult) for the child if we called sounds of high frequency 'right' and sounds of low frequency 'left' because that's where they are made on the piano keyboard.

Children have much difficulty sorting this out. I was in a nursery class one day and a musically very confident four-year-old called Dorothy came up to me and said, 'I can make a low sound on this triangle – listen.' She tapped the triangle on its bottom side, making the usual high ringing sound. I hesitated to question her definition of a low sound – after all, she might have been comparing the triangle sound with another very high-pitched sound. So I said, 'That's very clever, Dorothy. Can you make a high sound too?' She looked at me as though I was amiable but dim. 'Of course!' she said, and tapped the triangle on its top point (making exactly the same sound). Perhaps this doesn't surprise you from a four-year-old, but older children often have similar difficulties. Wendy Bird tells of the ten-year-old girl who, in a creative music session, was asked to produce a low sound. She thought for a moment, then, taking a piece of chalk from the blackboard, dropped it on the floor and said, in all seriousness, 'There! That's a low sound.'

What you must do is to help your child associate certain kinds of sounds with the words 'high' and 'low', and some simple activities are useful here. One is to tell a story about some kind of going up and down, and to illustrate it with sounds on an instrument. Particularly useful here is a xylophone, or glockenspiel, because you can turn it on its end and the child can see your beater going up the instrument for high notes and down for low notes. A piano or guitar or recorder or set of chime bars is not so clear in this respect, but you can well use one of them to illustrate the story. Here is one I improvised for Bob, a five-year-old who was fascinated by big dogs and a bit frightened of them.

Brutus and the cake
Bob's Mum had been out shopping and she came home with a cream and jam sponge for tea. It was the sort that Bob especially loved – yellowy cream and red jam in the middle and icing sugar on the top – and when she unpacked it Bob was very pleased. So was Brutus, Bob's big Alsatian dog. He stood up and wagged his tail and came to have a look. 'Don't, Brutus! Down!' said Bob. 'You can't have the cake!' Brutus wagged his tail and went on looking.
'Mum! Brutus is going to eat the cake,' cried Bob. 'Mum!' But his Mum

wasn't there — she'd gone upstairs, leaving the cake on the table.
'Mum ! Mum !' shouted Bob. He knew he wouldn't be able to stop
Brutus if the dog decided to take the cake. But his Mum couldn't hear him.
'I must go and fetch her,' thought Bob ; so he ran out of the kitchen ...
   (*tap with beater on the wooden body of the xylophone to make
   footsteps*)

and began to climb the stairs — up, up, up ...
   (*play 'up' the xylophone for four or five notes*)

But then he thought : 'Perhaps Brutus is eating the cake while I'm not
there.' So he ran down the stairs ...
   (*play 'down' the notes*)

and out into the kitchen ...
   (*footsteps*)

Brutus hadn't touched the cake, but he was standing by the table, still
wagging his tail. 'Stay, Brutus, stay,' said Bob, and quickly he ran out of
the kitchen ...
   (*footsteps*)

and up the stairs again — up, up, up ...
   (*play 'up' seven or eight notes*)

Then he stopped. 'I can hear him eating,' he thought ; 'I *know* he is.' So
he ran down the stairs, jumping down the last two or three in his
hurry ...
   (*play 'down' the notes, jumping to the bottom one*)

and ran back into the kitchen ...
   (*footsteps*)

Brutus had got one paw on the edge of the table ! 'No, no ! Bad dog,
Brutus !' shouted Bob. Brutus got down and moved away from the table,
but Bob could see that he hadn't given up. 'I *must* get Mum,' thought
Bob. He ran out of the kitchen ...
   (*footsteps*)

and up the stairs — up, up, up, up ...
   (*play 'up' all the notes to the top of the xylophone*)

right up to the very top. There was his Mum, coming out of the bathroom.
'Mum, Mum, come quick !' said Bob 'Brutus is trying to eat the cake !'
'Oh crikey !' said his Mum, and they both ran down the stairs ...
   (*play 'down' the xylophone*)

ran into the kitchen ...
   (*footsteps*)

and there was Brutus with both paws on the table, just about to lick the
cake with his long tongue. 'You bad dog !' shouted Bob's Mum, 'Get
down before I leather you !' Brutus got down quickly and slunk out of
the kitchen.

'You're a good boy, Bob,' said his Mum. 'Let's get tea ready and have some of the cake you've saved.' So they did.

When you've told that story I think it's a good idea to say something like, 'Did you hear how, in the story, when Bob went upstairs the notes got higher and higher (*do it*), and when he ran down they got lower and lower (*do it*)? The top of the stairs was a high note (*play it*) and the bottom of the stairs was a low note (*play it*). Would you like to have a go?' This can lead into a game where you say things like:

'Make the sound (tune?) go up a bit and then stop.'

'Make it come down again.'

'Make it go up and come down.'

'Can you make the sound stay in the same place?' (You may have to demonstrate playing a repeated note.)

'Can you make the sound stay in one place for a bit, then come down slowly, then go up again fast?'

Obviously, as always, you adapt the questions and the level of complication to the particular child. A variation of this can be played by hiding the xylophone away, perhaps in a big cardboard box, and then playing patterns. Perhaps you play up the xylophone, and the child has to say that the sound is going up; or you play the same note and the child has to identify that. At first you keep to simple patterns going up or down one note at a time:

But soon you can do rising or falling sequences that are more complicated:

When the child is used to these kinds of patterns you can try combining them, perhaps like these :

Remember a couple of things about this kind of game. Firstly, the examples I have given above are only examples. You do your own patterns, just as part of play with your child. Secondly, just as you play with your child, your child may want to play with you. It is excellent for his awareness and confidence to let him make the patterns for you to identify. It puts him in the position of power.

Another thing to do to help awareness of the instruments (remembering that your child must first have had plenty of chance to experiment with them in his own way) is to use them in variations of the Sound Game (p. 58). At the simplest level, you can ask your child to identify which of two instruments you are playing inside the cardboard box. Another version is to have one instrument like a tambourine and ask your child to say how you are making the sound he can hear (you might be tapping the skin, or the wood, or shaking or scratching or rubbing the skin, or tapping one of the jingles). You might even have a high note and a low note on chime bars or a xylophone. You could then play little patterns of two or three notes and ask your child to identify them. Patterns might be things like 'low, high', 'high, low', 'low, low', 'high, high, low', 'low, high, low' and so on, but I wouldn't make the patterns more than three notes long.

Another type of game with instruments involves copying or matching. Do you remember the kind of matching games that went on with sound-making instruments in Chapter 4, 'Understanding sounds' or the copying of different rhythmic patterns of body sounds that we described in Chapter 6, 'Patterns of rhythm' ? This activity can easily be extended into play with instruments. The simplest level is for both of you to have the same kind of untuned percussion instrument, and you say, 'I'm going to play on my instrument. You listen very hard and then see if you can play the same.' Then you play one loud sound ; or four quick sounds ; or two slow sounds ; or a long sustained sound (like a shake), and the child copies. Don't be worried about rhythm at this stage. The child may only approximate roughly to the rhythm, but will probably get the number and type of sounds right. This is fine. If your child is very confident with this, it is easy to go on to copying very simple rhythms, though this will only succeed if the child has had practice in copying body sounds (as in Chapter 6, 'Patterns of rhythm').

Once again you play a simple pattern for the child to copy; again you begin with very simple, regular patterns and move to slightly more complex ones. Here are some examples of the more complex patterns (but you must make up your own):

Please don't be worried by the look of these patterns written out on the page. Just think of yourself walking (2/4) or waltzing (3/4) or skipping (6/8). Imagine yourself doing the movement, and just clap or tap something to fit in. If it is simple enough for you to do, it is likely to be simple enough for your child to copy. Once again, your child will want to make rhythms for you to copy – take part in this game.

Copying a sound or a rhythm becomes a little more difficult if the two of you have different instruments, but this difficulty is a very productive one. For instance, supposing you have a shaker and your child has a drum. When you make a long shaking sound your child may say:

'I can't do that with my drum.'

'Why not?'

'Because I can't shake it.'

'That's true, but you could make a long sound by hitting your drum lots of times fast. Or you could scrape it with your fingernails. You try it.'

Through conversations of this kind the child learns many things. He clarifies his impression that different instruments make different kinds of sounds and so are good for different musical purposes. He learns that you can treat instruments in different ways to get different types of sound, and this in turn encourages him to experiment more widely with the instruments he has. He learns that you need different skills and techniques with different instruments, and so is encouraged to practise them. This last point is reinforced by the fact that certain rhythms and patterns are difficult for particular instruments. For instance, fast patterns are difficult for a child to play on sticks; crisp clear patterns, especially complex ones, are tricky on shaker or tambourine. In turn, this motivates and encourages practice on the instruments.

Copying games are also valuable on tuned instruments, but adding the element of pitch to the rhythmic copying does make things more complex. Because of this it is crucial not to use a piano, or xylophone with all the bars on, to start with. This introduces far too many distracting complications. I begin with two notes – two chime bars, or a xylophone – with all the notes except two removed. I then start by playing a simple rhythm (of the kind we played with untuned percussion) *on one of the notes only*. You must have both notes there so that the activity is not exactly the same as with an untuned instrument, but having chosen the right one to play on, the child avoids the complication of matching which of the two notes you used. Play a lot of patterns on one or other of the notes. When the child is used to this you can ask him to hide his eyes while you play. This involves an extra element of auditory memory, since he had to hear the pitch of the pattern and then find the right note to play it on.

Naturally you can go on to copying patterns using two notes, and then increase the number of notes if you feel it's appropriate. You can complicate matters by playing the game with a different instrument each; perhaps you make the two note pattern on piano or recorder or xylophone and your child copies it on the chime bars. But we are getting quite complex in our demands. Such complications will only be appropriate for a child who has a lot of musical confidence and experience.

It is important to stress, in conclusion, that all this work with instruments is in a real sense a *preliminary* to formal music-making. The under-fives are unlikely to be ready for playing in an ensemble with other people, or for learning notation, or for having formal lessons on the techniques of playing an instrument. But the kinds of experience we have been discussing will be an excellent preparation for such activities, whenever during the next four years they are introduced.

9

Learning formal musical skills

Are no elements of formal music-making and music education
appropriate for young children under five ? Is there any reason why you
shouldn't teach them to read music ? Why can't they begin lessons on
piano or some other instrument ?

We should take these questions seriously, of course. Perhaps the first
thing to do is to look at what we do with such children in other fields. We
don't usually teach other formal skills before five ; we don't expect
children to have to go into school before five ; even when they get to
school we don't put them into formal learning situations. Can we justify
such things with music ? The comparison should make us pause, but
does not necessarily convince us. As I said at the very beginning of the
book, most of us somehow believe that music is rather different from
anything else ! Let's look at the two main issues in more detail.

Learning to read music
An awful lot of people have an obsession about children learning to read
music. They call it 'musical literacy' and like to pretend/claim that it is
essential for any kind of musical activity. Because of this they are
prepared to drive children through a dreary slogging process, which has
probably destroyed more people's enjoyment of music than anything
else (except perhaps school hymn practices). Such an attitude is
ludicrous. The vast majority of the world's musicians produce their
beautiful and satisfying music without the need for conventional notation
and most use no notation at all. Neither children nor adults *need* it in
order to lead a musically satisfying existence, though it can be a useful
skill to have. Instead of assuming, therefore, that it must be taught to
young children, let's look for a moment at the advantages that it gives to
a musician. Perhaps then we can see whether it is worth teaching to a
young child :

● It enables you to read, and so
play, someone else's musical
creation, even when you have
no one to teach it to you.

but : young children are not
interested in anyone else's
musical creation except
through their own adults.

● It enables you to take part in a wide variety of ensembles with other musicians	**but :** young children are not usually ready for his kind of ensemble performance. If they are, it is at the very simple level where they can learn their parts by rote.
● It enables you to write down and so pass on your own compositions.	**but :** young children are not interested in products ; they will only want to communicate their doings *personally* to the people they are in contact with.
● It helps in the process of learning to play an instrument.	**but :** few under-fives are ready to learn an instrument in this kind of way, as we'll see later in this chapter.

None of these advantages, you see, are necessary or even useful in the kinds of music-making that under-fives do.

But, people often argue, these advantages will rapidly assume importance as the child gets a little older. Shouldn't we get him a bit ahead ? This appeals very strongly to parents, of course ; we all like the idea of our child being a bit ahead, of giving him advantages we didn't have. All right — perhaps it is a good idea. What is involved ?

People often talk about reading music as if it were a matter of mastering a few simple tricks. In fact, music notation is a formal symbolic language. Reading it is based on the understanding that sound can be symbolized or represented, either in movement or in written shapes and patterns, and that these movements or patterns can then be interpreted back into sound. Like all formal symbolic languages, conventional music notation is sophisticated and complex. In order to interpret it children need to have mastered the underlying concepts. In other words, they need to be ready.

Parents are well aware nowadays that in order for children to learn to read books they need to have reached a certain stage of 'readiness' and maturity. There are even 'reading readiness tests'. It is logical to assume that there is a stage of 'music reading readiness' also, since the process is similar to learning to read, even though it is less complex. If you are wondering whether your child should be learning to read music, why not ask yourself the following questions about him ?

Section A

1 Are you sure he is not seriously retarded in intelligence or development ?

2 Is he generally self-reliant and able to concentrate on something that is not immediately clear to him ?

3 Is he free from any hearing defect or limitation ?

4 Can he understand and carry out complex instructions you give him ?

5 Does he show interest in music and things musical, listen to and discriminate between sounds around him, join in with songs, and so on ?

6 Does he listen with concentration to a story song or a short piece of recorded music ?

7 Can he repeat/echo simple rhythms in three time and four time that you clap for him ?

8 Can he tell if two short rhythms or tunes are the same or different ?

9 Does he understand the use of the 'high/low' convention for describing the pitch of sound ?

10 Can he tell if a second note is higher than/lower than/the same as a first note ?

Section B
1 Is he used to moving to musical sounds, clapping the pulse of a piece of music, dancing in his own way to music ?

2 Has he had a chance to experiment with *tuned* percussion instruments to make up his own tunes and to realize that notes of the same pitch can be made on different instruments ?

3 Has he become aware of the usefulness of notation and experimented with his own methods of writing down sounds ?

Section C
Are there any musical activities provided for him which can be seen to demand music-reading *and which interest him* ?

Done that ? Now, unless you have answered 'Yes' to every question in Section A you should postpone any teaching of notation until the gaps in his experience are filled. 'Yes' answers to the questions in Section B are important but not as crucial ; *if* the music teacher is aware of deficiencies in any of these areas it should be possible to include them in the programme of teaching musical notation. If your answer to Section C is 'No', ask yourself whether you want your child to learn notation at this stage to benefit him or just to satisfy your own needs ! In either case it is not likely to be successful without the stimulus of a clear use for the newly acquired skill.

I don't think that these questions will necessarily exclude every under-five, but it will certainly exclude 98 per cent of them ! If your child is one of those excluded, don't be unhappy. Go ahead with doing lots of the kinds of activities we have been talking about. Louise Myers (*Teaching Children music in the Elementary School*) observes :

For the actual reading process to be successful it needs
to be preceeded by three years of *rich* musical experiences.

Our activities build up the background that makes it possible for the child
to cope easily with music reading. Indeed, I know three children who,
between the ages of six and eight, used a simple child's recorder tutor or
a chart of notes in an infant music corner to teach themselves music
reading – because they were ready, and interested in a musical activity
that encouraged the use of notation. Hundreds of children do this ; most
children would do it, given the chance and the encouragement, as is
strongly suggested by the experiences of the Schools Council Project on
Primary School Music.

Music lessons for the under-fives?

People's faith in the educational value of providing young children with
instruments, their belief in the importance of learning to read music, and
their feeling that they're too unmusical themselves to help their
children's musical development, all tend to encourage parents to start
their children with formal instrumental music lessons as early as possible.
'I want Julia to have a good musical education, but I just *can't* find a
decent piano teacher,' one mother said to me. Julia, it turned out, was
only just past her fourth birthday !

Unfortunately this faith in instrumental lessons is based on an almost
total misunderstanding of what they are concerned with. A piano or
violin or clarinet teacher is concerned with training a pupil in the *skills*
required to make certain patterns of sound from the instrument. These
skills are largely a matter of physical coordination and habit. The
experience of generations of musicians has shown the best ways of
achieving such skills, and there is only minimally the opportunity for the
pupil's own ideas or experiment. As with the transmission of any skill, it
is an intensely authoritarian, formal, structured and demanding process :
'You do it like this because *I* say so, because *my teacher* said so, because
Paganini said so, because if you do it my way now you will become able
to do many things later.' Of course, the more educationally aware the
teacher is, the more she will be able to relate this process to the pupil's
stage of development and his difficulties ; the more musically aware the
teacher is, the more she will be able to relate the process to his musical
awareness and education. With the very good teacher the business of
learning an instrument may also be a profound musical education. But in
the majority of cases it will do little more than provide the pupil with a
skill which he can use for his own musical expression, pleasure and
education – that is, if he survives the pressure !

Don't get me wrong ! It is a very important skill. I am not devaluing the
process of learning an instrument, which must be a major part of anyone's
total musical education. I am trying to define the process in order that we

may decide whether it is appropriate for the five-year-old. And if you do accept my definition you can see that there are a number of ways in which it may not be appropriate.

To begin with, the learning of most instruments depends on the child having reached a certain stage of physical development and coordination, in particular the independence and coordination of his two hands. Such a stage will not have been reached by some children before the age of five or six. Even if reached, unless the teacher is aware of young children's development (and few professional musicians are, naturally) there is the danger that she will press the child to do things that are really out of his scope. This links up very clearly with the fact that for many instruments children really need scaled-down versions on which to learn ; these also tend to be expensive and need to be changed at regular intervals as the child gets bigger. Unless these scaled-down instruments are provided the child will again be stretched beyond his true capabilities.

Secondly, the pre-school child is not likely to be geared to a structured approach that largely eliminates the element of play and experiment. '*Why* can't I bang it with my bow ?' 'Why can't I lean my arms on the piano ? – it makes such a lovely noise.' These are typical attitudes of young children to the restrictions of conventional music-making. I well remember Peter, aged six and a half, at the ILEA Carol Festival in the Royal Festival Hall, singing one of the audience participation carols somewhat out of time with everybody else. This was partly because he was reading at the same time a comic bought to occupy the waiting period beforehand ! When it was gently pointed out to him that Peter Fletcher was conducting in order to help everybody to keep together, he countered with great reasonableness, 'Ah, but I can sing much better when I look at my comic.' At this stage a child tends to be quite happy with his own way of doing things, and he develops skills largely as he feels *he* needs them, not because an adult says he ought to develop them. This is particularly true when the skill has no immediate application for him, but still demands painful concentration and self-discipline (like holding his left wrist in the proper position for playing the violin). There is no obvious reward, so to him there is no good reason for doing it. It is not usually until a child is between seven and nine that he begins to understand the possibility of preparing himself to receive a deferred gratification, that he becomes interested in developing skills (such as football techniques or realistic drawing) and that he becomes able to submit to the disciplines of a rigid learning process.

Even then the wish to develop skills depends on several factors. The material used, and the instrument, must be exciting in themselves, and the social situation must give great encouragement and support. It is rare even for seven-year-olds to succeed at instrumental lessons unless the parents or the school (or both) give a lot of positive help, and unless the teacher is able to make a good relationship with the pupil, giving him lots of security and encouragement.

Should you ever think of formal music lessons for a child of five or under ? I think I am now able to make a clearer statement of my views without being seriously misunderstood. To me, unless your child seems *exceptionally* musical and has had a wide basic experience of music, there can be no question – formal instrumental lessons will be a waste of time and money and may well damage his attitude to music. Of course, you may have a four-year-old genius on your hands ! If he is very advanced musically and is passionate to learn a particular instrument ; if you can find a warm and affectionate teacher who will take a very young child ; if as a parent you are prepared to be at every lesson and to take a positive part in every period of practice ; if both you and the teacher are prepared for considerable fluctuations in the child's length and level of concentration and an unpredictable rate of progress ; if you can satisfy all these conditions, then formal music lessons may be of value. If not, you might just as well wait. There are real advantages in starting violin, 'cello and piano reasonably early, say by the age of eight, and of course the recorder is an easy instrument which can be started at first school. Otherwise there is no major advantage in beginning formal instrumental lessons before the age of ten or eleven. On other instruments the gain in strength, coordination and concentration by the later stage more than compensate for the delay.

What then about the Suzuki method of learning the violin and other instruments ? This approach has received a great deal of publicity and has been hailed by some people as the answer to the problem of teaching music. Pictures of thousands of Japanese children playing the Bach Double Violin Concerto impress us greatly, especially as we are geared to think of playing an instrument early as proof of musical ability and a musical education. If we look closely at the Suzuki method, however, its relationship to what I have been saying becomes clear.

To begin with, a young child's mother has not only to be present but actually to learn the instrument with the child ; thus, learning the violin becomes a shared adult/child activity within a continuing, intimate relationship. For a long while children do not learn from written music, which would place impossible demands upon them, but by a combination of listening to the music played, live or on record, playing games and imitating. They have to have the appropriate size violin and bow (ranging from one-sixteenth size to full size) for their stage of physical development, and the stress laid upon making them secure and comfortable during the lesson even extends to the room, which is supposed to be carpeted, decorated and laid out in a pleasing, comforting and reassuring fashion. Practice is done with the mother, in very small chunks, with an emphasis on the crucial importance of enjoyment. You can see how very different this is from sending a small child off somewhere strange for a half-hour music lesson each week !

Looked at in this light the Suzuki method can be seen as an elaborate and complex equivalent of many of the kinds of games and shared activities described in this book. It is, of course, much more specifically geared to a conventional musical goal, but it works very much because it takes account of the nature of small children. It also works, I suspect, because the vast majority of children who learn come from the kind of involved, interested home background which will, quite incidentally, have built up many of the kinds of ability and confidence that we have been discussing. I think it is true to say that you could teach a young child many skills if you took this amount of trouble over it – and if you are prepared to take this amount of trouble for a musical young child then music lessons will probably be successful. The question is, are you prepared, and is it worth it ? I tend to think not, but I am convinced that you need to be pretty sure before you risk it with a child under seven. The price of failure will be a very substantial blow to your child's musical enjoyment and confidence.

Part three Musical activities in the playgroup and nursery

10

Music in the playgroup and nursery

A four-year-old child is a four-year-old child, whether at home or in playgroup or at school. What a profound statement with which to begin a chapter!

It is important, though, because it explains why I have left until now all mention of musical activity with larger groups of children. Whether at home or anywhere else, the under-fives are going to need the same kinds of things to help their musical development. So this chapter is not really about new activities or new principles – it is mostly about organization. The nature of a playgroup or a nursery class means that some musical activities need to be organized differently from the way you'd do them with your own child. Above all, several special problems arise when you have children together in a large group.

The first problem is that a mum at home usually has her one or two young children for most of the time every day; the playgroup leader has perhaps twenty-five or more children for a short time on some days during the week (and not every week during the year). Because of this you can't just wait for musical activity to arise spontaneously in a playgroup. The kind of entirely individual music that is so successful with a child at home can't be the sole basis for large group music. Again, a teacher who gives each of her children an appropriate amount of individual musical attention will have no time left for anything else! This does not mean that you have to abandon doing music with individual children, of course, but it does mean that you have to compromise.

The second problem arises from the first. The teacher doesn't know each child in the way that his mother does – and this is as true about his music as about everything else. So the teacher has to make a deliberate effort to find out about a child's musical level. This is made an even more urgent task by the third problem. A very large number of children come to school musically deprived and retarded. Some of the children in your group will have had few of the experiences we have seen to be so necessary. Many will have had a lot of experiences, but will not have been helped to coordinate them and become aware of them, so they will only be able to use them in a limited way. At the same time there will be some children in your group who are musically mature and interested.

You have to provide for them in the same room. Your group will have an age range of about two years and a developmental age range of perhaps four years. One five-year-old will not be able to tell from its sound whether a shaker contains glass beads, split peas or pins, although he has seen the fillings put in ; a rising three-year-old in the same group will do it confidently.

If you are a playgroup leader or nursery teacher these problems have practical consequences for you. In the first place, you will need to observe each individual child and get a clear idea of his musical level. This doesn't mean you have to have special musical knowledge. Nor does it mean elaborate testing or filling in detailed records – you don't have time for that ! It means observing and thinking about your children. A set of questions to ask yourself about a child may help you to clarify your impressions. Why not sit down and write yourself a set ? Or use the set given below.

Child's name:

Hearing:
Has the child any hearing defect ?

Listening skill:
Can the child sit still and listen to a sound ?
Can he identify sounds from familiar objects hidden away ?

Understanding sounds:
Does he play with sound-making objects ?
Can he talk about the sounds he makes and hears ?

Singing:
Does the child join in with fingerplays and songs
    with actions only ?
    with speech and actions ?
    with singing (not necessarily always in tune) ?
Can he echo different sounds or notes that you make to him ?
Can he sing recognizable tunes ?

Rhythmic sense:
Can he bounce or clap or move in time to any sort of rhythmic
    stimulus ?
Can he do in time a rhythmic action in a fingerplay or song ?
Can he copy a rhythm you clap ?

Enjoyment of music:
Does he *enjoy* the activities described above ?
Does he show an interest in other kinds of musical activity
(e.g. playing instruments, listening to recorded music, talking
spontaneously about instruments or musicians) ?

Your answers to these questions will not give you a precise level, but should help you to see where further experiences may be useful — or to see what aspects of the child's music you need to look at more closely !

Your own set of questions will be just as good as mine, of course. But, one thing I want to stress. You mustn't let the systematic nature of these questions condition your musical activity too much. If you find that certain children have gaps or weaknesses you shouldn't attack them with systematic exercises or drills. This leads very rapidly into performance demands and certainly will tend to put pressure on the child. Just do a wide range of simple activities — these will make it possible for the child to develop and mature through his natural enjoyment.

The second practical consequence is that you are going to have to *structure* musical experiences and activities more than a mum needs to. This is both because you need to provide at times for large group activities (for practical and for social reasons) and because you have to give musical opportunities for all the children (which, as we have seen, you can't always do on a one-to-one basis). The third consequence is that you will have to pitch such activities at a pretty basic level, so that *all* the children will be able to participate and benefit. In turn this means that you will have to be specially conscious of the musically able children and try to help them individually. This is an interesting reverse of what always tends to happen with children's music in school ! When this is based, as so often, on getting them to perform it is the more able children who are catered for and the less able who are ignored. This is a self-fulfilling situation, as the Plowden Report points out :

The advanced and well-controlled children may be given the most interesting and demanding tasks, and may claim more of the teacher's time. They thus advance even further. Meanwhile a clumsy child may sit neglected, falling further and further behind.

If we want all children to be musically confident we must avoid perpetuating such an approach ; but if we gear music to the less able we mustn't forget the talented.

From this point arises the fourth consequence. The structured basic activities must always be open-ended. They must always provide points of extension and departure, both for individuals and for you. You must be able to use music flexibly in response to children — you mustn't think of your games as some kind of syllabus or rigid curriculum. Remember John Holt on games (pp. 61–65) ? Whatever I may say about structuring never implies ignoring the needs of individual children.

In the rest of this chapter I am going to look in turn at what I consider the important areas of musical activity. My approaches have already been covered in earlier chapters, so here I shall discuss ways in which the larger group situation forces you to provide and organize musical experiences in slightly different ways.

Listening to and understanding sounds

In my experience this is the area where the greatest difficulties arise, in particular with the children whose listening skills are poorly established. One restless child in a group disrupts listening activity, as you know only too well ! Because of this you will probably need to start by doing a good number of structured, simple listening and attention-rewarding games as basic training for everybody.

I find it helpful to begin with a new group by doing a game like the Pot of Beads (p. 60) or the simple version of the Sound Game (p. 58) with everybody. Of course, you have to do these games quite formally. You have to choose your own sound-making objects rather than using ones that an individual brings, and there will be less opportunity of talking with individual children. Nevertheless, the children enjoy the games very much in this situation, and get a lot out of them. As you play you will notice those children who have difficulty in doing them, and which children, if any, cannot focus their attention at all. For instance, some children may just wander off ; and some will remain, but will not be able to concentrate on what you are doing. These are probably very immature children. With them you will have to be prepared to work individually, going back to the very close range contacts we described in the early chapters. When you want to catch such a child's attention you may have to touch the child's arm as well as speaking to him ; you may have to bend down to his eye level and put your arms round him as you speak ; you may have to hold him by the shoulders or even take his face between your hands as you speak his name. Pauline had to do this with Ben, a three-year-old in her nursery class, to get his attention ; his eyes would roll around wildly before eventually focusing on her face. I know – it's tempting to feel, 'These children are in school now – they should be *made* to listen.' Unfortunately it doesn't work like that. You can't make children listen ; and in most cases that is not the root of the problem anyway. A child like Ben has never been helped to feel that careful listening is worth it ! You have got to reward his attention if you are going to build up habits of listening. Indeed, you may well find it worth giving a child like Ben a Smartie or a Jellytot every time he responds to you without having to be touched or held. Individual work with children like him is worth it ten times over in terms of making possible activities with the group, let alone in terms of benefit to the child himself.

Other kinds of simple listening games are worth trying with the group. When you have them all sitting in a ring, or on the carpet, or lying in a space, try asking them to close their eyes and sit or lie quite still and silent. Simply observe how long it is before a child speaks or moves significantly – with young children they often sit up after a few seconds, just in order to see what's going on. As soon as anyone does, say something like, 'Open your eyes now. You did very well; you were beautifully still and quiet.' Then go straight on to something else. (You will, of course, have noted mentally which child broke the silence, because this may tell you something about his powers of control and concentration.) I usually play this game once a session until I find that the group can manage at least twenty seconds of stillness and silence. This length of concentration may not come for quite a long while – twenty seconds is a surprisingly long time for young children. If there is no improvement after five or six goes I encourage by saying something like, 'Today we're going to try to be still and quiet for a long time. Let's see how clever we can be.' If the group still cannot manage anything more than a few seconds I abandon the activity for a few months. But I *don't* short-circuit the process by telling the children in the middle of the supposed silence to be quiet.

The value of the activity, both for them and for you, lies in seeing what they can manage without undue pressure. If they can manage the twenty seconds I say something like, 'Let's play a game. You shut your eyes and be still and quiet, and I'll whisper someone's name. If you hear your name, you stand up.' We start the silence and after a few seconds only I whisper the name. We all look to see if the child has stood up; then I reintroduce the silence, and after a few seconds whisper another name; and so on. Children greatly enjoy this game, but it is very important that you should establish the still silence convention first and only whisper a name when the group is quite quiet. Otherwise the value is lost. You can, of course, make the game more complex and interesting by whispering different instructions, whether to all the children : 'Put your hands on your heads.' 'Wiggle your fingers.' or to individuals : 'Bayo, come here to me.' Don't be in too much of a hurry to move on to that stage, though – and don't spend too long on this game at any one session. Half a minute is quite enough.

Another kind of listening for the whole group can be to listen for a very familiar sound within the room. For instance, if one of the adults (or one of the children) is wearing a distinctive-sounding kind of footwear, like clogs or high heels, I say to the group, 'Listen to Marcia walking around the floor in her big heavy shoes. Can you hear the sound they make on the wooden floor ?' Or I say, 'Mrs Anstey is going out into the kitchen. Let's be very quiet and see if we can hear her close the kitchen door.' This is partly to make children aware of familiar patterns of sound, and partly to get them used to the disciplines of group listening. Another activity at playgroup comes during the time when the children have their apple and drink. I arrange for the pieces of apple to be on four or five plates, so that they can be given out very quickly. Before we start I say, 'When you get your apple, don't eat it straightaway – hold it for a minute. We're going to listen to the sound it makes when we bite it.' We all get our bits of apple, then I say, 'All ready ? Then bite !' We all bite, and the lovely crunchy sound makes many of the children smile or even giggle with pleasure. It is quite likely that many of them will never have listened carefully to that sound. You notice that these activities don't expect children to talk about the sounds – in any case, you can't with a mouthful of apple ! They aim to establish patterns of group listening, since without these little musical activity is possible. They also help the adult to identify the children who have most difficulty in listening. Any games that help with this are just as valuable – you don't have to do my games.

Naturally, many other kinds of listening can go on within the room, especially with smaller groups during play. During a course in 1974 Sue Temple described a conversation she had under the playgroup slide with some children, discussing whether you could tell from the sounds how each slider was sliding down – sitting ? lying ? backwards ? You might try talking with the group around the clay table about the sounds that are made when you play with clay. One little girl called Rachel noticed that when she banged her clay on the table the nest of plastic pastry cutters rattled, and it was not long before the children had created through talking and experimenting a rhythmic structure where they banged in turn and then shook their bodies to the rattling sound that followed. This is only one example of the sorts of listening and musical activity that can arise spontaneously from all sorts of things in playgroup.

Talking is crucial in developing listening skills, but so is the exploration of sound-making objects. Here too, having a large group means that you have to modify the way you go about things. In particular you have to increase your structuring. For practical reasons it is impossible to provide every child with his own washing-up bowl of sound-making objects (p. 66), or to allow everybody to bang their biscuit tin with a wooden spoon for long periods (p. 22). Experiment with sounds has to fit into a manageable pattern.

In view of this, and of your very wide range of maturity, the use of books and pictures as a stimulus to talking about and imitating sounds (p. 54) is a basic activity ; so too is the telling of stories including sounds (p. 55), especially as you can involve the group in the various ways of following up and extending such a story (p. 56). Structured games like paper-tearing are also very successful with the large group and provide many meaningful experiences. All these activities can be managed by the adult with a big group.

Another point to be taken into account when deciding how we arrange experiment with sounds is that there will be a particular need for the objects used to be very familiar ones. We saw in Chapters 4, 'Understanding sounds' and 8, 'Musical instruments' how children's understanding of sound is based on a strong awareness of the links between ordinary objects and the sounds they make. When a child is at home most of the things he picks up will be familiar ; this may not be true at playgroup or in the nursery class. Because of this, introducing sound-

175

making objects through games like the Sound Game or the Pot Game will be particularly important for him. Also very necessary, I believe, will be the introduction to the children of the small groups of sound-making objects linked in some way. This can be done for the large group quite easily, and will give all the children some familiarity with the objects.

All this is of great relevance to the question of how you provide opportunities for children to experiment with sounds. Such experiment, as we have seen, will be crucial for their learning and understanding, but an arbitrarily set-up music corner will not be of much use in this (we have already seen some of the problems children may have with conventional instruments, (p. 138). A sound table will be a little better because it will tend to have familiar objects on it, and the children will find these easier to understand, but if the table is just set up at the beginning of the term and left (as tends to happen) much of the value will be lost.

Even when a music corner or sound table doesn't run into the problems of noise and damage, you still see two great difficulties arise with young children, especially with the less mature or less able. When a conventional music corner is first set up you tend to have a great burst of enthusiasm from most of the children, but within a few days this has evaporated. Thereafter the music corner is used almost entirely by a small group of children ; they tend to be the musically more able and experienced. The less able use it rarely. In a sense, therefore, those children who need it most will get least out of it. Secondly, the quality of experiment by many of the children in the music corner tends to be very poor. A typical pattern, which I have observed from children of all ages between three and eleven, is for the child to wander up to the corner ; bang desultorily on a xylophone ; drop the beater ; pick up a shaker and shake it ; throw it down ; and wander away again. For many children this is their only contact with what the music corner can provide.

Why should this be ? Sound-making things are exciting and interesting. According to most people's ideas about children's learning this should be enough to stimulate rich experimenting ; but it doesn't always seem to do so. I think that the element of unfamiliarity is one reason. Some children don't seem to see what they can do with an instrument except clout it (hence ordinary objects are better for young children than conventional instruments). But there is more to it than this, I'm sure. Alice Yardley writes :

Attractive and imaginative materials can in themselves inspire some children, but many of our children need help from their teacher if they are to become thoroughly awakened to the qualities of the materials we offer them. *(Sense and Sensitivity)*

Why should they so often need such help ? I believe that the child's ability to be interested by materials, to see their potential, to explore them enjoyably and profitably and confidently, depends at root upon his learning during the very early weeks and months of life. If you make it possible for your child to explore at that stage he develops an attitude and a confidence which he will apply to all new situations. Do you remember the Bruno Bettelheim theory (p. 15)? Again, if at a slightly later stage you help him to talk and think about what he does, he will develop mental tools which he can use to clarify and make sense of his experiences. This is specially important because of another truth about children's play and experiment. It is not the act of playing itself that is stimulating and educational. Desmond Morris describing learning situations, writes:

A great deal of exaggerated effort may be put into the activities, but it is those actions that produce an unexpectedly increased feedback that are the most satisfying. *(The Naked Ape)*

We see this very clearly with a child's drawing. He enjoys the physical activity of moving a felt pen across the paper (perhaps in imitation of an adult?), but it is the moment when he *becomes aware* that it has produced a great, striking mark that really stimulates and extends his experiment. Again, the moment when, much later, he *recognizes* out of his scribble a pattern which looks like a face, is a moment of powerful learning.

You notice that this depends on the child becoming *aware* of the pattern. From this you will see how all the problems of listening to sounds and making sense of them may make it difficult for the child to get rewarding experiences from his experiment with sound-making objects. If he doesn't notice exciting and satisfying patterns of sound when he explores instruments, he will not go on with his experiment for very long. Because of this the conventional music corner or sound table is often of very little use to the very children who need its opportunities most.

For all these reasons I don't begin sound exploration by setting up a music corner, even though I know well the importance of experiment. I begin by playing games with sounds like the ones I have described. After I have played a game or told a story with sounds, the objects used go on to a sound table, and I tell the children that they are available for experimenting. When two or three lots of objects are on the table already, and I produce a new set, I remove one of the old sets that has been there longest. Thus I have on the table a constantly changing range of things that all the children are familiar with and which they have heard used. Enormous advantages arise from this approach:

● My sound table is much quieter than a table of conventional instruments because found objects tend to make quite small sounds. This is an important consideration for lots of reasons!

● When my objects are damaged, which happens occasionally, little has been lost, compared with the cost of damage to conventional instruments – but you can still use the fact of such damage to help the children understand the need for care and appropriate behaviour (see p. 140).

● A much larger proportion of the group uses the table, and because the range of objects changes regularly there is no tail-off of interest after a few days.

● The children do much more individual experimenting and discovery, not less ! This really was a great surprise to me. I originally adopted my approach to the sound table in order to limit the noise and damage ; I expected the greater structuring to inhibit children's experiment, but accepted this as a lesser evil than preventing all experiment. Lo and behold ! It didn't happen. I now realize that by putting children more closely in touch with the materials and making them aware of some of the kinds of things they can do with them I tend to free them to experiment more confidently.

Despite its success I don't leave it at that. I do some further structuring of experiment. One of the problems in the playgroup or nursery class is that it is very difficult to provide each child with enough stimulating and encouraging adult company to extend their understanding. Naturally, I give this whenever possible, but that can only be sometimes. Because of this I reckon to gather groups around the table and initiate various kinds of activities. I encourage comparison of sounds and generalization about them ; I set up specific experiments like the one to find out whether the shaker container makes a difference to the sound produced ; I get the older children to sort out the objects on the table in any way they choose, and then explain to the rest of us how they have done it ; I use a set of related objects like the ones that make scraping sounds to introduce to a group the making of a simple home-made instrument like sandpaper blocks (for all these see p. 67). In turn, all these activities lead to further talking and individual experiment by the children.

Please remember, though, that this approach arose first out of the needs and difficulties of children and teacher, not because someone told me that it was the right thing to do. It may be unnecessary or irrelevant for the group of children you have. In any case, I see it as a way of *beginning*, as the first stage of children's experiment. For instance, when children have got used to the pattern of experimenting, I introduce conventional instruments in the same way, through games or stories like *Brutus and the Cake* (p. 155). I also become much more willing to put out interesting things that I or one of the children has brought without having to introduce it first through a game. You must do what seems right for your group.

One final point about exploring sounds. With the range of age and maturity you usually have in your group you may well get the problem of having some children who want and need to do more complex activities and to use conventional instruments; yet you worry about putting out instruments because of the less mature children who cannot use them appropriately. Like so many problems of this kind (the interest level of stories you tell, for instance) there is no easy answer. I feel that, while the more able children will be able to experiment in their own way and at their own level with the simpler materials, the reverse is not true – so, if it comes to the crunch, the conventional instruments should go.

However, there are a couple of possible alternatives. You can get out the instruments only at chosen times as a group activity for particular children; you will need to have an adult in attendance to make sure that they are not interfered with and to encourage what they are doing. This is not ideal. Some people allow the younger children to use the instruments only when paired with an older child, but the potential dangers and disadvantages of this with under-fives should be clear. Alternatively, you can have both a sound table *and* a music corner. This is my approach if I have the space. Of course, you have to have some fairly strict rules about the music corner which the children understand, and you have to keep an eye on it. Also, to be fair, you have to be ready to provide alternatives for the immature child who wants to bash a xylophone or a drum. I usually substitute a sound-maker of the same type (p. 67); it is invaluable to have within reach a supply of small cardboard boxes, a simple xylophone base and some 'bars' to go on it (p. 69), a bag of sound-making objects and even some old discarded cymbals, triangles and so on. But, as with any area where you are forced to try and provide early experiences for older 'deprived' children, there are no easy answers.

Singing and joining in
Exactly the same is true in the field of joining in and singing. A very large number of children who come to playgroup or nursery school are musically backward. They arrive unable to use their voices and bodies in the ways that should be normal and natural. They don't sing with confidence; they don't make up songs and tunes; they have a poor rhythmic sense and little ability to join in with others. You are already faced with the need for remedial action. What should you do?

There is nothing new to say. I have talked at length about the process of encouraging and making possible singing development. You have got to help them to join in with very simple structures at their own level, but not to force or to 'teach' songs in any formal sense. What I may need to stress here is that even a five-year-old may still be functioning at an eighteen-month-old level in his singing – don't be put off by his size and apparent maturity. In a playgroup you may well see all the stages of singing development represented, from complete non-singers to budding 'Opportunity Knocks'! candidates. In turn this means that you must be ready to provide what individual children need, and you mustn't be conditioned by expectations about 'normal four-year-old development'.

For instance, you will frequently need to hold a particular child close, to croon to him, to rock him, to baby him, to do individually some of the patting and jogging games (see pp. 7, 31, 107), to hold his hands and clap them together in time. In case you feel this is odd with five-year-olds, let me assure you that this level of contact can be needed by juniors in school. I remember occasions with my class of eight to ten-year-olds in Brixton. On one particular afternoon I remember us snuggled in the book corner; I was singing *Stewball*, a slow, rocking story-song. I had a child's head on each thigh, and I glanced up to see a row of six large children, eyes closed, thumbs in mouths, rocking gently in time. If children have missed out on the intimate singing experiences with their relatives, they will not get very far musically unless they get them from someone else in some way. (This accounts for many of the features of teenyboppers' musical enthusiasms; much of this kind of pop is infantile singing experience in a socially acceptable form!) It is possible to provide this intimate experience at playgroup more easily than in a junior school. In any case, at a practical level, children who can't concentrate in a group singing time may well manage, and even join in, if they are on someone's lap.

As well as providing this kind of intimate singing it's crucial that you should recognize and encourage the early stages of singing development, especially the use of vocal sound in play situations and the making-up of songs. *The* unforgiveable sin is for the adult to reject something like *The Lavatory Song* (p .76). Such encouragement will involve you in joining in spontaneously in play situations (p. 42), in improvising little patterns or questions for children to echo or answer (p. 96), in adapting songs to fit the names and the situations of the children (p. 45), and in the encouragement of singing as play rather than performance.

It will also lead you into singing *to* children as much as you possibly can. I have stressed this throughout; when you think how much of such experience some of your group will have missed, and how little time you have with them, you can understand why I underline this need here. As well as building up their musical experience and training them in listening to a musical performance, it provides a simple, meaningful ritual and cements the feeling of a close relationship between you and the group. And don't forget — it doesn't matter if you don't sing very well.

These points do involve one organizational matter. Clearly, much of the activity concerned with stimulating a child's singing development is best done individually or in a very small group — some of the children will not need such help in any case. Does this mean that there is no place for a formal 'music time'? I believe there is. I think young children should get used to the particular satisfactions and disciplines of social music-making, and to have a regular session, even at a fixed time each day, does no harm. However, participation should be voluntary (no one should be made to sing) ; it should be very short (not more than seven or eight minutes at the outside) ; and it should contain only the very simple participation rhymes and songs, or the simple listening games. More complex or demanding activities should be done with smaller groups.

Rhythm, pitch and the use of instruments

The earlier chapters, especially 'Patterns of rhythm' and 'Musical instruments' should give you lots of ideas, but you will have to think carefully about organization. Some of the activities, like rhythmic actions with fingerplays or songs (pp. 86–91), or a story like *Brutus and the Cake* (p. 155), will clearly be for all the children and can be done in a large group situation. Other activities, like the echoing of a tune you sing (p.96), the copying of rhythms on an instrument (pp. 158–160), or the copying of a two-note tune (p. 160), are much more demanding, and you will only be able to do them with individuals or small groups of children who have had the relevant preliminary experiences. In general, I find that such more developed activities arise naturally when you join some children at the music corner, but occasionally you may wish to take aside a selected group for such work.

There is one type of activity very important in a child's musical development which is *easier* to do with a large group than with a parent and child at home. We mentioned it in connection with song accompaniment. It is the business of learning to hold your own independent part while other people are playing or singing something different. This is basic to most kinds of music-making, so it is useful to give children some experience of it as early as possible. However, since under-fives usually need the help of two adults at the start in order to cope, playgroup or nursery is a good place to try it.

The basis of the skill is a clear awareness of sounds from different sources going on alternately or at the same time. Once again we come back to the root of so much – the talking about sounds around us. A child who has identified and understood a washing machine running while his Mum chops up food on a board, or has talked about his Mum's footsteps and his own sounding different but going along the road together, has got a head start with hearing two parts going on together. It also helps if he has played games like *Peek-a-Boo* (p. 10) or the *Leather-Feathers* game (p. 95) or any copying games (p. 96, 158–160).

I usually introduce the holding of independent parts by splitting the group of children into two. I take one group, a parent or helper takes the other, and each group has a word or phrase to say. Sometimes I choose these arbitrarily ; sometimes they arise spontaneously. For instance, I was having a brief joining-in session in a playgroup and there was a disagreement about what song we should sing next ! So I got all the children who wanted *Peek-a-Boo* to sit with Mrs Rubens and those who wanted *Five Little Men* to sit with me. The two groups turned their backs on each other and started to say their own favourite very quietly. There was no attempt to fit the two rhythms together, but Mrs Rubens and I tried to keep our groups saying their pattern in time with us, *and quietly*. This is an important point. It is not difficult to keep your own part going if you drown out the other part, or if you stick your fingers in your ears, but it is precisely the skill of hearing the other part yet keeping yours going that we wish to develop. For this reason choosing your own words or patterns may be better than using a disagreement as a basis ! The children are more likely to shout if anything hangs on it.

When they can do this you might try getting them to say at the same time two very short rhymes *that they already know well*. Again, the two groups must each be with an adult ; again, they must speak quietly ; again, the two rhymes will not necessarily 'fit'. This is important to stress – it won't sound 'musical' but don't be bothered. The children are learning some significant things from it. I did it in a nursery class using these two rhymes :

Rain, rain, go away !
Come again another day.

Blow, blow, winter wind !
Blow through my hair.

When we stopped, Petronia said, 'That sounded just like a storm – the wind and rain were fighting.' It's exactly this kind of awareness that we want to build up.

You use the spoken word because young children are more skilful and accurate and confident with it than with rhythmic movement. The next stage is to get them used to saying things in the same rhythm, but in two groups. I do this by a simple copying game. We are in two groups, each with an adult, but this time we face each other. We all talk about something (anything ?). Let's say, toys. We pick out one, *Action Man*. We all say it, over and over :

Then I say, 'My group will say it two times – like this' :

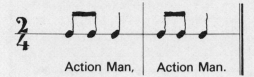

Action Man, | Action Man.

'Now Anna's group can say it two times – you do it' :

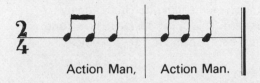

Action Man, | Action Man.

'Let's try it like this ; my group will say it two times, then Anna's group will say it two times.' We try alternating between the groups in this kind of pattern, over and over again :

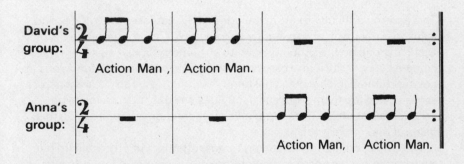

David's group: Action Man , Action Man.

Anna's group: Action Man, Action Man.

Perhaps the next day we talk about another toy – maybe a 'Tea Set'. We say this over and over ; then we alternate saying it, as above ; then perhaps we add it to the pattern we have already tried, and get a piece of music like this :

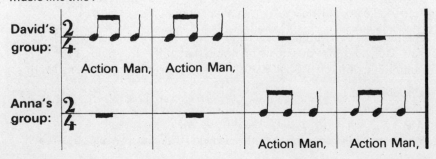

David's group: Action Man, Action Man,

Anna's group: Action Man, Action Man,

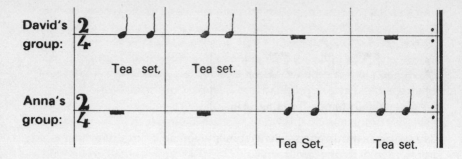

You can also include in this game an element of pitch imitation by chanting the words to a pitch pattern. This doesn't have to be a 'tune' in the conventional sense ; it can just be a rise and fall of your voice :

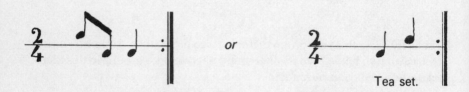

This adds no difficulty to the game but greatly increases the interest and value. Another way of varying it would be to let Anna's group go first and David's group do the echoing. As with all games you can make it more complex very easily – you can use three or four toys' names, and you can get the children to clap or tap or stamp the rhythms or the different names as well as saying them – but such activities will only be possible with very confident under-fives. Normally it is more than adequate to do this game at the simple levels.

The kind of confidence in saying things together which is built up by such games makes possible the holding of very simple independent parts in rhythm. I begin this by chanting a word in rhythm with the whole group. The word is either one that has come up in discussion ; or I get it by asking about something like what they had for breakfast. So we might chant :

Corn-flakes, corn-flakes, corn-flakes corn-flakes . . .

Perhaps we do it getting louder and louder – or softer and softer. Then I say, 'Do you think you can go on doing that with Mrs Taylor, even if I say something different ? Shall we try ?' So they start, and I come in, like this :

Children and ⎱ Corn-flakes, corn-flakes, corn-flakes, corn-flakes . . .
Mrs Taylor: ⎰
Me :   Tea   , tea   , tea   . . .

When they are confident with this, I divide them into two groups (each with an adult, of course) and each group says one of the words. By this stage, and given the adult's lead, they should be able to say the words in rhythm and with each other, though, as always with the age group, the performance skill will vary from individual to individual. Again, this can be extended by asking the children to play their word with a body sound – perhaps Mrs Taylor's group says and claps 'Cornflakes', while my group says and stamps 'Tea'.

When a group can do this kind of activity they may even be able to use their skill to make a very simple accompaniment. For instance, in any simple song or rhyme about walking or marching one small group with their adult can chant 'Left ! Right ! Left ! Right !' while the rest speak the rhyme with their adult. You might get this :

Group 1 : Mar-ching in our well-ing-tons,   Tramp, tramp, tramp,
Group 2 : Left !   Right ! Left !   Right ! Left !   Right ! Left ! Right !

Group 1 : Mar-ching in our well-ing-tons we won't get   damp.
Group 2 : Left !   Right ! Left !   Right ! Left !   Right ! Left ! Right !

The marching children could well stamp their feet or slap their thighs in time with their speech pattern.

But let me re-emphasize my basic point. Such activities *may* be relevant and valuable for your group, but only if they have had a lot of previous experience. Many playgroups and nursery classes where a great deal of excellent and appropriate music-making is going on will never reach this stage with large groups. You must always look at what your children need and can do, rather than think what musical activities ought to be being done.

Enjoying the music-making of others

The factors making it difficult to use mechanically reproduced music with your own young child apply even more strongly to a large group of children with their enormously wide age range, maturity range and interest range. In a playgroup or nursery you know relatively little about each child's musical background, his experience of listening to music and his particular musical interests. To stick on a record and demand that every child listens for a fixed time is little more than an exercise in crowd control or lion-taming ! Any musical value is likely to be dissipated by cries of 'Sshssssh !' and 'Umesh ! Sit down and listen !' On the other hand, to stick on a record and *not* demand that children listen is likely to achieve very little, and may well encourage the unfortunate habit, already common enough, of using all recorded music as a background noise. As for the suggestion of having radio or records on all the time, it is likely to have a pernicious effect and to make children's perception of patterns of sound even more difficult (p. 53).

On the whole, therefore, I don't find recorded music very helpful in a playgroup or nursery class, and I think you should have very good reasons before you use it. There are, however, several situations where I do use it. The first is to record some short, simple pieces of music that I enjoy on my portable cassette recorder. Then I go and sit in a corner of the playgroup and turn it on quite quietly. This usually draws one or two children who look and say (or think) 'What are you doing?' 'I'm listening to some music I like. Here's a tune called *Saddle the Pony*; would you like to listen to it with me?' Lo and behold! I have a listening group – and we listen, and talk about the music, for as long as individual interest lasts. Some children drift away; others come. It's very flexible. In some situations there is no interest, so I give up! If there is a great deal of interest I may leave the cassette recorder and cassette for the children to play themselves. In case you're saying, 'But they're under-fives . . . the man's mad!', I'd point out that most under-fives are as skilled at using a cassette player as my Mum – and more confident. My only precaution is to doctor the cassette so that they can't rub off the recording; your tape recorder shop will show you how. (After making the recording you break out the little flanges of plastic on the top edge, furthest away from the playing edge.)

The second use of recorded music sometimes grows out of the first; sometimes it is separate. As mentioned earlier, I use recorded music as a stimulus for free dance, movement, clapping or playing instruments. This may be with the whole group, but is usually with a smaller number. There is only one rule – *don't* tell the children what kinds of things they ought to be doing to the music.

The third use is when I feel I can play a piece of recorded music to illustrate something the group has seen or heard or been talking about. A perfect example came with Pauline's nursery class. She had read them *Patrick,* by Quentin Blake (Puffin), a story about a boy who buys a magic fiddle and does wonderful things with it. They loved the story but clearly had little idea of what a fiddle was. Pauline showed them the pictures but couldn't convey to them the sound. That night she recorded on to a cassette some traditional Irish dance tunes (*The Fairy Jig, The Fairy Reel, The King of the Fairies*) played by an unaccompanied Irish fiddler, and next day she played them to the children. They listened with unusual attention, and then said, 'Can we dance?' In fact, they listened twice through, a remarkably long time for a whole group of nursery children. But you would *never* have got such listening from them if the music hadn't been made specially relevant and interesting by being put into a context.

Apart from these three situations I don't find recorded music of any use at the playgroup or nursery stage. Nor do I try to take children of this age to concerts. I do make a great effort to let them see other kinds of live music-making, in particular by inviting people to come and play to them. I also give them plenty of experiences of being listened to intently when they speak or chant or sing or make sounds. I think that is more valuable than any number of records or concerts.

Music and movement?

I can sense cries of 'Haven't you forgotten music and movement? Surely you can use records there?' No, I haven't forgotten! In my view the use of records there is very limited, for many of the reasons we've already discussed, and for a whole set more to do with the relationship between music and movement. I am not a movement specialist, but I am very sure of my ground where it's concerned with music.

Throughout this book there has been a great deal of movement in connection with patterns of sound. Clearly movement is fundamental in the way young children become aware of the patterns of sound (see p. 16) and practise musical skills. Through the kinds of activities I have been describing the child does a great deal of movement with music — there is no need for any more as part of *musical* development. The music and movement time in a playgroup or nursery school has very little to offer under-fives. I think it is another example of adults presuming that something must be good for young children because it is good for older children (and perhaps because it is what we expect to have to do). It also fits very neatly into organizational patterns. The playgroup equipment has to be cleared away, or the nursery class is timetabled for a session in the Hall; what could be better than a nice music and movement time when all the children can move to music?

If we follow the basic principle of looking first at children, we see lots of things that are wrong with it. To begin with, a fixed session with all the children runs into the problems of the enormous maturity range we have talked about. A number of the children, especially the inhibited, don't really want to come, perhaps frightened by the speed and confusion of these sessions. The space is usually a big one, much too big for many of the children; some rush wildly about, others are overawed by its size. Many children under five just have not reached the conceptual level where they understand the idea of a hall being a volume of space into which different shapes or bodies can fit in different ways, and so they cannot understand the idea of using all the corners or spreading out and finding a space each. As Margaret Shephard says:

No good either to tell this age group 'spread out and find a space'. Space means absolutely nothing to them unless they are in a rocket heading for the Moon. They simply settle like a swarm of bees on your other foot. (*My Kind of Playgroup Music*)

Nor does the pre-school child necessarily understand the wide variety of shapes and patterns his body can make (after all, he may well not even know the names of many parts of his body). He certainly has only a limited repertoire of body movements which he has fully mastered and can use consciously.

This is crucially important because moving to music is a complex and sophisticated process of matching. You can see this clearly if you teach adults or older children an unfamiliar movement pattern and then ask them to do it in time to music. Unless they are very experienced in movement or dance either the movement will break down as they try to keep in rhythm, or they will do the movement accurately but quite out of time. After all, why do you usually first practise a new dance step to a spoken count, often very slowly, and only try putting it to music when you have fully assimilated it ? It's because you can only use to music those movement patterns with which you're at home, that you don't have to think about too much. It is no wonder, therefore, that when you play music to a large group of young children, most of them fall back on one of the small number of movements with which they are quite at home : they march or run or sometimes skip. Moreover, because of their lack of awareness of space, they all tend to follow the wall, so creating the clockwise 'letting out the bathwater' effect so characteristic of music and movement sessions with young children. (I have always wanted to ask an Australian or New Zealand nursery teacher whether they go anti-clockwise Down Under !)

This sort of activity, it seems to me, neither teaches the child much about his own movement nor practises new skills, since he only uses skills he has already mastered. It lets off steam, of course – a valid use – but doesn't have much to do with either music or movement as I envisage them. The kinds of rhythmic participation activities I have talked about a lot are much more useful in developing rhythmic skills and awareness. As for the specific awareness of his body and its movements, the child needs much more *individual* exploration and talking with the adult than is provided by charging around a large space with music playing. Again, the essence of many music and movement sessions is that they depend heavily on verbal instructions and stimuli, and we have already seen very clearly the limitations in listening skills (especially across a large hall), in vocabulary to do with sound and movement and in the ability to respond to the adult except at close range that many under-fives will have.

Some adults would say that they are not thinking of this kind of precise matching when doing music and movement, they are looking for a much more child-centred exploration and expression. They see music as stimulating expressive movement with children. But this doesn't work either with a large group of under-fives. Children express themselves spontaneously through movement (we see it often in their dramatic and imaginative play) but this comes from within themselves, at their own time and speed. They *may* be inspired or influenced by hearing music, but it is always an individual response. Leila Berg describes a classic example :

Lea, at four, cut some clown shapes and ghost shapes out of white paper (she had been to the circus). She spread them carefully on the dark floor, and now there were dark clown shapes and white clown shapes and dark ghost shapes and white ghost shapes. Her father picked up one of the numerous instruments he plays and wanted Lea to sing a song he had written. Lea refused. Instead – for though put out he went on playing – she began to dance, and as she danced, from time to time without pausing in her movement she bent down and picked up a ghost or a clown, and holding in both hands at arm's length turned round in a circle, then laid it down again and continued gravely dancing. Her movement was completely natural, unforced from without or within, for quite serenely she had refused manipulation.

A year later I saw a leaf floating gently down a wide stream in Norfolk. Every now and then it turned round in a circle, then continued downstream. The same movement.

Yet if you were to say to a child 'Be a leaf floating downstream' you would be stupid. The child is far ahead of your adult artificiality.

(*Look at Kids*)

A whole group of children will not all be ready to respond in this way. Any attempt to get them to do so will be a 'manipulation', an imposition. What is more, expressing yourself to/with music is again a more sophisticated process than we may think. To do this you have to have a considerable awareness of the qualities of your different movements. You then have to look at the stimulus critically and assess which of its qualities can be expressed *through* your movements. This is very demanding for under-fives. They will sometimes manage something of this kind that is very simple. For instance, the movements of tree branches blowing in the wind are very like some of the movements of a child's arms, so he may be able to express through movement his awareness of a windblown tree. But music is always a much less precise stimulus, so the relationship is much more complex. Of course, you can teach a child movements to do to a piece of music – but then it is questionable whether he is expressing himself!

You can see from this that sticking on a record and saying 'Move as you *feel*!' is useless. If you do this with under-fives some stand around helplessly; others charge around using their confident movements. Nor is a verbal stimulus much help. You often hear things like, 'When you hear the pretty music flap your wings like fairies' – but how do fairies flap? It's an impossible demand. The great danger is that the adult, for the best of motives, begins to flap and swoop and glide herself. The children, delighted to have some sort of guidance, follow, imitating their Joyce Grenfell-type mentor. We find ourself once again involved in the business of showing children what we expect them to do. When the adult refrains from moving herself you tend to have one or two of the more confident children (little girls who are having ballet lessons ?) showing the way, and the other children imitating them, with the same limitations.

What amazes me is that we don't work in this kind of way with this size of group in any other activity with under-fives, because we recognize how unsuitable it is. Basically you are asking inappropriate things of the pre-school child if you do music and movement in a formal session. Most children are at least six before they can do the necessary matching and have the necessary awarenesses. Forget it with the under-fives.

But it would not be fair to leave you just with that negative statement. Under-fives are on their way to being six, after all. What do you do about music and movement ? First, I think you do a great deal of the rhythmic participation activities with movement that I have described ; much of the preliminary experience of matching movement to sound will be greatly helped by this. Secondly, I think you should try to develop a good deal of movement awareness *on its own* by talking and playing with the children and watching what they do – this will give you a lot of clues to the kinds of experiences they need. Thirdly, I think you can move gradually towards the use of music with movement. Let me give you just one example of what I have found to be a reasonable approach. I work with a small group (twelve or less) of interested children and I start with familiar objects which we talk about. For instance, I sometimes bring in a large plastic ball. Perhaps we talk about Bobby Moore and Colin Bell ; perhaps we take turns in bouncing it ; perhaps we talk about birthdays and birthday presents. Then I will say something like, 'Wait a moment – let's watch what happens when I drop it and no-one touches it.' We watch the ball bounce lower and lower, then roll to stillness, and we talk about this. After two or three tries I will say : 'Can you bounce like the ball when I drop it ? Let's try.' I drop the ball again and the children respond in their own ways. You notice that although there is a very positive and concrete stimulus, there is no attempt to lay down the kinds of movements with which the children must respond. Some children reflect very sensitively with their bodies the ball's behaviour, others just throw themselves to the floor in a heap, but *all of them* feel completely confident about responding, in contrast to their uncertainty in many conventional music and movement situations. We do this, with lots of talking, as many times as seems enjoyable ; still there is no attempt to impose a 'correct' response, merely to focus attention on the stimulus.

Another day I start with the ball-bouncing and rolling movements, but after a bit I say : 'Suppose you pretend to be a magic ball, a special ball, and when I bounce you *don't* stop bouncing – you go on bouncing all over the place.' We try this a couple of times. You usually find that because of their age and stage they tend to bounce at a roughly similar speed. If so, I may take a drum or cardboard box, or even use my hands, to beat out a rhythm *taken from their movements and their speed.* I watch carefully to see if there is any sign of them fitting in with me and the rhythm. If there is, we perhaps talk about it and do the bouncing again with the rhythm. Only then, if they can do that, do I think of saying at a later movement session, 'Do you remember our magic ball bouncing ? Well, I've got a piece of bouncy music recorded on my tape recorder. I'll play it and you do the bouncing' (and I play, say, the section from *The Sorcerer's Apprentice* by Dukas where the broom comes alive). It seems to me that this will be the first point where the *group* of children will have the necessary awareness and skill to respond to a simple music *and* movement demand. But you notice that I will only make the demand when I have done a lot of talking, a lot of confidence building and a lot of practice.

Conclusion

Perhaps that's not a bad example to finish with. It sums up a lot of things about music with the under-fives. If you are ready to play and talk with them ; if you look very closely at what each child can do and needs ; if you refrain from doing conventional, expected music activities until you are sure the children are ready for them ; then what you do, whatever it is, will be right for those children. No one can tell you what to do with your own group. They can only help you to think more closely and more perceptively about children. And I am no exception.

Forget about 'music' — concentrate on children.

Bibliography

SONG BOOKS AND MUSICAL ACTIVITIES
There are now a good number of useful song books for the under-fives, but very few about musical activities with this age group – few, that is, that I can recommend with confidence. Here are some that adults have enjoyed using with small children. I have marked with an asterisk * my own 'best buys'.

Fingerplays, rhymes and songs
Carrick, Malcolm (1973) *All Sorts of Everything*, Heinemann
Chesterman, Linda (1935) *Music for the Nursery School*, Harrap
Chroman, Eleanor, ed. (1970) *Songs Children Sing*, Oak Publishing
Fletcher, M. I. and Denison, M. C. (1954) *The High Road of Song*, Warne
Ginglend, D. R. and Stiles, W. E. (1965) * *Music Activities for Retarded Children*, Abingdon Press (This can be obtained in the U.K. through William Dawson and Sons Ltd, 10 Macklin Street, London WC2)
Harrap, Beatrice, ed. (1975) *Apusskidu, Songs for Children,* A. and C. Black
Matterson, Elizabeth, ed. (1973) * *This Little Puffin*, Penguin Books (Puffin)
Montgomerie, Norah, ed. (1966) * *This Little Pig Went to Market,* Bodley Head
Poston, Elizabeth, ed. (1972) *The Baby's Song Book*, Bodley Head
Poston, Elizabeth, ed. (1961) *The Children's Song Book,* Bodley Head
Raza, Cynthia (1975) *The Lollipop Man,* Stainer & Bell
Raza, Cynthia (1975) *Mungo Mouse and Other Songs and Stories*, Stainer & Bell
Sansom, Ruth, ed. (1964) *Rhythm Rhymes*, A. and C. Black
Seeger, Ruth, ed. (1948) * *American Folk Songs for Children*, Doubleday. (This can be obtained in the U.K. through Belwin Mills Ltd, 230 Purley Way, Croydon CR9 40D.)
Tillman, June and Braley, Bernard (1974) *New Horizons*, Stainer & Bell
Whyton, Walley, ed. (1964) * *100 Children's Songs*, Music Sales Ltd

Talking about sounds
Ogle, Lucille, Thoburn, Tina and Wilkin, Eloise (1972) * *I Hear – sounds in a child's world*, Collins

Roberts, Ronald (1965) *Musical Instruments Made to be Played,* Mills &
    Boon
Showers, Paul (1961) *The Listening Walk,* Mills & Boon
Southworth, Mary (1973) *How to Make Musical Sounds*, Studio Vista
Spier, Peter (1973) *Crash! Bang! Boom!*, World's Work
Spier, Peter (1972) *Gobble, Growl and Grunt*, World's Work
Williams, Peter (1971) *Lively Craft Cards*, set 2 : *Making Musical
    Instruments*, Mills & Boon

Musical approaches for young children
Aronoff, Frances Webber (1969) *Music and Young Children*, Holt,
    Reinhart & Winston. This is an American book and like many American
    educational publications is full of jargon, but it is worth study by
    anyone seriously interested in the subject, particularly for the links
    between music and movement.
Bailey, Eunice (1958) *Discovering Music with Young Children*,
    Methuen. Although this is nearly twenty years old it remains one of the
    few stimulating books on the subject.
Gilbert, Jean (1975) *Musical Activities with Young Children*, Ward Lock
    Educational
Pape, Mary (1970) *Growing Up with Music: musical experiences in the
    Infant School*, Oxford University Press. This is interesting because it
    shows some of the directions that children may take in their infant
    school music. It also has some good ideas that can be used with
    younger children.

GENERAL REFERENCES
Bentley, Arnold (1966) *Musical Ability in Children and its Measurement*,
    Harrap
Berg, Leila (1972) *Look at Kids*, Penguin Books
Britton, James (1970) *Language and Learning*, Allen Lane ; (1972)
    Penguin Books
Chukovsky, K. (1966) *From Two to Five*, trans. M. Morton, Univ. of
    California Press
Holt, John (1968) *How Children Learn*, Pitman ; (1970) Penguin
Jameson, Kenneth (1968) *Pre-school and Infant Art*, Studio Vista
Landreth, Catherine (1972) *Pre-school Learning and Teaching,* Harper
    & Row
Millar, George, quoted in Britton, *Language and Learning*
Morris, Desmond (1967) *The Naked Ape*, Cape ; (1969) Corgi
Myers, Louise (1953) *Teaching Children Music in the Elementary
    School,* Prentice-Hall
Plowden Report (1967) Central Advisory Council for Education,
    Children and Their Primary Schools, H.M.S.O.

Postgate, Oliver and Firmin, Peter (1969) *The Flying Machine: a Saga of Noggin the Nog,* Kaye & Ward

Shephard, M. (1973) *My Kind of Playgroup Music*, Pre-school Playgroups Association Publications

Schools Council (1968) *Enquiry One: Young School Leavers*, H.M.S.O.

Watson, Doc (1971) *The Songs of Doc Watson*, Oak Publications

White, Burton (1973) *Experience and Environment: major influences on the development of the young child,* Prentice-Hall

Wilkinson, Andrew (1971) *The Foundations of Language: talking and reading in young children*, Oxford University Press

Yardley, Alice (1970) *Sense and Sensitivity*, Evans

Appendix

Firms supplying children's musical instruments

Here are the names and addresses of several firms which supply tuned and untuned instruments suitable for children's use. They will be delighted to send you catalogues and price lists.

Schott & Co. Ltd, 48 Great Marlborough Street, London W1V 4BN (01-437-1246/8).   Suppliers of Studio 49 Orff Instruments

Parson's Percussion Instruments, E. J. Arnold and Son Ltd, Butterley Street, Leeds LS10 1AX (0532-442944)

The Premier Drum Co. Ltd, 87 Regent Street, London W1R 7HF (01-734-3372).   Suppliers of New Era educational percussion

Boosey and Hawkes Group, Deansbrook Road, Edgeware, Middlesex HA8 9BB (01-952-7711)

M. Hohner Ltd, 39 Coldharbour Lane, London SE5 (01-733-4411)

ACKNOWLEDGEMENTS

We are grateful to the following for permission to reproduce copyright material :

Abingdon Press for an extract from the song 'Little Fish' in *Music Activities For Retarded Children* by David R. Ginglend and Winifred E. Stiles. © Abingdon Press 1963 ; Belwin Mills Music Ltd. for an extract from the song 'Wide Awake' reprinted from the collection *Wide Awake* by kind permission of Mills Music Limited, 250 Purley Way, Coydon CR9 4QD ; Faber Music Ltd. for an extract from the song 'I Can Knock' by Elizabeth Barnard reprinted from *Nursery School Music Activities* by permission of Faber Music Ltd. on behalf of J. Curwen & Sons Ltd. ; Inner London Education Authority Music Centre for an extract from the song 'Clap Your Hands' by Wendy Bird in *Sing A Song: Autumn* 1975.

Index

General index

197

SHARING SOUNDS, by David Evans
Longman Early Childhood Education Series

Binding: paper
Pagination: 128 pp.
Size: 8½ X 5½

ISBN: 0-582-25008-0
Price: abt. $4.50
to be published June 1978

A book about children and how to help them become sensitive to all kinds of
sounds, to enjoy music and have confidence in making their own kinds of music.
Aimed primarily at parents, demonstrates how parents can help make their
children aware of rhythms and sounds by singing, humming and talking to them.
Also deals with musical experience in playgroups or nursery schools, with
emphasis on building confidence in children.